OVERSEAS EXPERTS ON CHINA'S POVERTY ALLEVIATION

海外专家谈中国扶贫

（荷）斯蒂芬·彼得曼等　著

图书编委会　译

光明日报出版社

目录 / Contents

序

研究中国扶贫脱贫的外国专家

马丁·阿尔布劳

面对新冠肺炎疫情的袭击，中国的反应速度之迅速、抗疫程度之彻底，令世界震惊不已。这一切的发生仅仅不过一年。很快，世界就得向中国学习另外一个经验，即中国战胜了长久以来面临的一个根深蒂固的挑战——脱贫。

根据世界银行制定的衡量标准，中国将于 2020 年年底全面消除贫困人口。1978 年改革开放伊始，贫困人口高达 7 亿。不到半个世纪，中国通过实施一系列脱贫攻坚政策，最终实现了"全面小康社会"。

2016 年我就写到，当代中国是"世界有史以来人类最强大的群体组织"。这句话背后包含了关于共识、动员、愿望和能力等诸多因素。除这些因素外，我们还可以参照中国过去的成就来看待中国。如果我们这样看，肯定会将中国扶贫的胜利誉为新的世界奇迹，与举世闻名的古长城或埃及金字塔一样值得称道。

本书是世界其他地区的专家对中国表示的合理致敬。他们能从自身文化的视角来理解中国取得的成就及其背景和范围。这些专家来自不同大陆——亚洲、非洲、拉丁美洲和欧洲，汇集了各自不同的专业学识和与中国接触的经历，为世界其他亟须了解中国扶贫方案的地区提供能够适用于当地的经验教训。

本书中的专家报告和思考是密切关注中国历史文化具体特征的产物，充分解释了中国社会主义制度为何适应当今的现实情况。穆罕默德·哈利勒来自摩洛哥，他从 1978 年在北京学医时就开始接触中国的改革开放。从那时起，他就注意到外国人观察中国时往往忽略的东西，即务实作

Foreign experts on China's poverty alleviation and out of poverty

Martin Albrow

The world is just astonished at the speed and thoroughness of China's response to Covid-19. That has all happened within a calendar year. Soon the world will learn another lesson from China, which is success when faced with a much more protracted and deep-seated challenge, the poverty alleviation.

By the end of 2020, according to the measurement standards set by the World Bank, China will have eliminated poverty. In 1978, when the country began its reform and opening-up there were 700 million people living in poverty. In less than half a century, an every intensifying succession of measures culminate in this moment of triumph, in the achievement of a 'moderately prosperous society in all respects'.

Back in 2016 I wrote that contemporary China is "the most powerful collective human agency the world has ever seen". Many assumptions lie behind the statement, about consensus, mobilization, aspiration and as well as about capability. Beyond those factors we might look into it by taking past achievements into consideration. If we do, then China's conquest of poverty can be compared with the most celebrated, with the Great Wall or with the Pyramids of ancient Egypt, as a new wonder of the world.

This book is an appropriate tribute from the rest of the world, from foreign experts who can appreciate the context and scope of China's achievement and can see it from the perspective of their own cultures. They come from different continents, Asia, Africa, Latin America and Europe, bringing together their own diverse personal expertise and engagement with China to provide what the rest of the world so greatly needs, and an understanding of its poverty alleviation programmes with any lessons which may be applicable elsewhere.

The reports and reflections of the experts in this book are the outcome of close attention given to the specific features of Chinese history and culture that go a long way to explain the appropriateness of its socialist system for today's conditions.

风——"实事求是"和因地制宜。这些都是习主席早期在福建省的工作经验中重要的方面，也成为他 2013 年宣布的扶贫目标的基础。

西方对待中国的方式基于对中国的种种设想，但那些设想和上文提到的这些要点相去甚远。杰弗里·萨克斯在 2005 年发表其备受推崇的著作《贫穷的终结：我们时代的经济可能》时预测，在 20 世纪的贫穷大国中，中国将会是第一个在 21 世纪脱贫的国家。目前来看，他的预测没错。不过他接着预测未来中国将朝着西式制度改革的方向发展，但这并未发生。因此，杰弗里·萨克斯在其 2020 年出版的《全球化时代》一书中提出，中国实现消除极端贫困的目标"用任何标准来看都是一大经济奇迹"[1]。但他没有提到具有中国特色的社会主义！

不过，如果开明的调查人员直接观察中国乡村的扶贫情况，就会对当地人民为实现全国脱贫的集体目标且能因地制宜展开的扶贫工作感到钦佩。诺伯特·梅迪纳在访问西安市鄠邑区东韩村时发现：随着社会主义新农村的建设，农业、小型制造业和旅游业相结合，增加了人民的收入。他在西安一个回民区也注意到了同样的成就。

尤里·塔夫罗夫斯基曾在一个章节中写到中国扶贫成就给世界其他地区带来了理论上的启示。本书引用了他的一个重要观点。有趣的是，他告诉我们，当他向俄罗斯观众讲述中国脱贫成就时，俄罗斯观众的反应跟上面引用的萨克斯的评论是一样的——这肯定是个奇迹。要知道他们可是相信西方经济的智慧！不过接着他揭露了这个"奇迹"的秘密。

塔夫罗夫斯基指出，共产党是能够解决市场与政府矛盾的组织。改革开放时期的扶贫运动将孔子对"小康社会"的设想变为"全社会共同富裕"，后来，习近平进一步将其发展为全面的小康社会和中国梦。塔夫罗夫斯基写道："中国共产党在战略上，第一次优先考虑的是人类社会，而非意识形态或是经济体制。"

共产党关注整个社会的战略也得到了韩国金胜一的支持，他认为这一战略给中国带来了其他地方无法复制的独特国家组织体系和制度优势，尤其是中国主要官员中的"精英"队伍都在致力于实施扶贫战略。

Mohammed Khalil from Morocco has been a participant in China's period of reform and opening up since its beginning in 1978 when he began his medical studies in Beijing and he has observed what foreign observers often miss, the pragmatic approach, 'truth from facts', and attention to local conditions. All of these factors were key aspects of President Xi's early experience in Fujian Province and underpinned the targeted poverty alleviation programme he announced in 2013.

These emphases are quite far away from the assumptions that often underlie Western approaches to China. When Jeffrey Sachs published his acclaimed *The End of Poverty: How We Can Make It Happen in Our Lifetime* in 2005, he predicted that China would be the first among the big poor countries of the Twentieth Century to end poverty in the Twenty-first Century. So far, so good. But then he linked its future to Western style institutional reforms. They didn't happen. So, in his book published this year, *The Ages of Globalization*, he mentions China's achievement of no extreme poverty as "an economic miracle by any standard."[1] No mention of socialism with Chinese characteristics!

But direct observation of poverty alleviation at the village level will impress the open-minded investigators with the extraordinary commitment of local people to collectivist goals that have been set for the whole China and adapted to local conditions. Norbert Medina found in his visit to Donghan village in Hu County of Xi'an that about the development of the *New Socialist Countryside*, with agriculture, small manufacturing and tourism combined to raise incomes. He also found the same success in a Muslim quarter of Xi'an.

The book contains an important statement of the theoretical implications of the Chinese achievement for the rest of the world in Yuri Tavrovsky's chapter. Interestingly when he lectures Russian audiences on the success of China's poverty recief, he tells us that their reaction is the same as in Sachs, comment quoted above – it must be a miracle. So much have they been persuaded of Western economic wisdom! But then he goes on to disclose the secret of the "miracle".

Tavrovsky points to the Communist Party as the agency that resolves the contradictions between market and government. Poverty alleviation in the reform and opening-up era changed Confucius' "a society of small prosperity" to "a society of moderate prosperity." In turn that was replaced with Xi's comprehensive well-off society and the Chinese Dream. Tavrovsky writes: "For the first time in the CPC strategy neither ideology nor economy but human society was given priority."

研究中国扶贫脱贫
的外国专家
Foreign experts on China's poverty
alleviation and out of poverty

但与此同时，金胜一指出，迄今为止中国政策成功超越我们的不同之处在于，中国政策的成功恰恰带来了"相对贫困"这一问题，即收入分配的顶层和底层之间日益扩大的差距要求我们必须关注社会的价值观。对此，他提出了一个有益的建议：关注韩国在 20 世纪 70 年代发起的强调生活精神要素的新乡村运动。

新乡村运动是韩国政府领导的强调合作和价值观建设的乡村发展项目，旨在增强公民意识和爱国主义精神。金胜一承认，诸如孟子很早就提出的道德价值观，已经纳入中国的社会主义核心价值观，但他也暗示中国对这些价值观缺乏足够的重视。值得思考的是，他的提议实际上在多大程度上能够直接解决中等繁荣带来的日益加剧的不平等问题。

金胜一的建议确实直接将我们引入另一篇论文的作者——安东篱所做的复杂讨论。他讨论了涵盖个人层面所经历的文化贫困和社会贫困之间的关联。不平等、排斥、社交失格、孤立、脆弱性都是为了在社会关系特定配置的背景下获得体验而提出的概念。与西方要求悉心关爱的个人主义相比，所有这些概念在亚洲文化中都有着迥异的原因与结果。亲属义务的概念在亚洲文化中极其普遍，而且得到有力的践行。

哈萨克斯坦研究员阿丽亚·阿尼皮娜和阿尔达克·哈力吾拉概述了中国务实做法带来的各种政策举措，这些举措也惠及其他国家。正如她所写道："70 多年来，中国向 170 个国家和国际组织转账人民币 4000 亿元、派遣 60 多万人道主义人员、修建了 5000 项人道主义设施，以帮助当地消除贫困。在中国的努力下，发展中国家培养了 1200 万名专业人才。对中国所肩负的对其人民及作为一个负责任世界大国的使命而言，这些数字意义深远。"

国际数据意义重大，但最终，我们每个人都在用独特的方式体验世界。因此，通过探索农村翻天覆地的发展变化以增加我们对这些数字意义的独特见解是完全恰当的。

自 2017 年起，荷兰设计顾问斯蒂芬·彼得曼就一直是世界著名建筑师雷姆·库哈斯（大约从他设计中央电视台在北京的总部大楼开始）

The Party's strategy that attaches importance to the whole society is also endorsed by Kim Seung Il of South Korea who thinks it gives China a unique national organizational system and institutional advantage that cannot be copied elsewhere. In particular an "elite" team of leading officials is dedicated to implementing the poverty alleviation strategy.

But at the same time Kim points to distinctions that take us beyond the success of China's policies to date by suggesting that their very success brings the problems of "relative poverty", the growing gap between the top and bottom, and income distribution which call for attention to the values of the society. He proposes that in this respect focus can usefully be put on the Korean Saemaeul Undong, or the New Village Movement, which South Korea launched in the 1970s and which emphasizd the spiritual elements in life.

Saemaeul Undong was a government-led programme on village development emphasizing co-operation and values, raising both civic awareness and patriotism. Kim acknowledges that ethical values, such as those Mencius advanced long ago, have been incorporated into China's socialist values but implies that sufficient emphasis is lacking. What is intriguing is how far his proposal actually can directly address the problem of growing inequality that moderate prosperity has brought.

What Kim proposes does lead us directly into a sophisticated discussion by the author of the next chapter, Antonia Finnane of the range of concepts that have been proposed to cover the cultural and social correlates of poverty that are experienced at a personal level.

Inequality, exclusion, social disqualification, disaffiliation, vulnerability are all concepts that are advanced to gain experience in the context of specific configurations of social relations. All of these have very different causes and consequences in Asian cultures where kin obligations are so extensive and strongly upheld compared with Western possessive individualism.

Kazakh researchers Aliya Anipina and Ardak Kaliolla provide an overview of the sheer diversity of policy inititatives that China's pragmatic approach has generated which has also extended to benefit other countries. As they write: "Over 70 years, China has transferred 400 billion yuan to 170 countries and international organizations to eradicate poverty, sent more than 600,000 people as humanitarian personnel and built about 5,000 humanitarian facilities. Thanks to China's efforts, 12 million specialists have been trained in developing countries. These figures speak for

的重要合作伙伴，他们与北京中央美术学院视觉艺术高精尖创新中心的同事共同研究一个关于中国未来农村的项目。该项目是纽约所罗门古根海姆博物馆开幕的展览——"乡村·未来"的一个主要展出主题，该展览于2020年2月20日举办。

这一经历使彼得曼思考乡村在全球化发展中所起的作用。他预计中国在2020年年底会宣布全国脱贫，于是走访了中国三个不同的乡村，去探索这些村子为创造自己的未来已经实现的各种可能。

在毛泽东时代，山西省的大寨村因为农民领袖陈永贵和一群在荒凉之地上开垦出新农田的村民而闻名于世。但后来这些农田难以维护，而现在关于陈永贵的传说也仅限于一个旅游村里一尊比真人更大的雕像。河南省的刘庄依然是个模范村，中国领导认为这是一个融农业和基础设施建设成果为一体的典范村镇，值得参观。贵州省的雨补鲁是个很小的寨子，这个寨子保存了传统的工艺品，因此也许能满足城市居民日益强烈的希望到"真正"的乡下去放松身心的愿望。彼得曼说，这个寨子"很接近这种神话般的念想"。

一切尚无定论，未来之路仍需前行。对本书做出的结论，这真是一个非常有趣且完全合适的注解。中国迈入小康社会后，又将何去何从，仍有待中国人民去决定和塑造。

2020年11月于英国伦敦

China's mission in its own people and as a responsible world power."

Global figures speak volumes, and yet, in the end, each one of us experiences the world in a unique way. Therefore it is entirely appropriate that the culmination of the volume is of the special insight gained through exploring how the countryside is changing beyond recognition.

Since 2017 Dutch design consultant Stephan Petermann has been a key collaborator with the world famous architect Rem Koolhaas (possibly since he designed the CCTV headquarters building in Beijing) and with colleagues at the Beijing Central Academy of Fine Arts Visual Arts Innovation Center in a research project about the future of the Chinese countryside that figures in the *Countryside, the Future*, an exhibition at the Solomon R. Guggenheim Museum in New York which opened on February 20, 2020.

This experience has led Petermann to speculate on the role of the countryside in this global stage of development. Anticipating the national declaration of the poverty eradication by the end of 2020 he travelled to three very different Chinese villages to explore the possibilities they had for making their own future.

Dazhai village in Shanxi was famous in Mao's time for a farmer-leader Chen Yonggui and a group of villagers who reclaimed new agricultural lands from a bleak terrain. But the land turned out to be too difficult to maintain and the legend of Chen is now only kept by a larger than life statue in a village oriented to tourism. Liuzhuang in Henan on the other hand remains as a model village, an example of agricultural and infrastructure development that Chinese leaders make a point of visiting. Yubulu in Guizhou is a tiny village, which has target for rejuvenation that preserves old crafts but also, and perhaps consequently, caters for urbanites' growing desires for relaxing experiences in the "real" countryside. It "comes close to this mythic idea", says Petermann.

There are no conclusions, the future course is not determined, and that really is a diverting and entirely appropriate note on which this book concludes. After setting foot in the moderately prosperous society the Chinese future remains open for its people to shape.

London, UK
November, 2020

研究中国扶贫脱贫
的外国专家
Foreign experts on China's poverty
alleviation and out of poverty

IX

斯蒂芬·彼得曼

Stephan Petermann

百闻不如一见

To See Once, Is Better than to Hear a Hundred Times

斯蒂芬·彼得曼拥有荷兰乌得勒支大学（University of Utrecht）建筑史和建筑保护理论硕士学位（2001—2007），并在艾恩德霍芬技术大学（2001—2005）学习了建筑。从 2006 年起，他成为雷姆·库哈斯的长期合作伙伴，协助他进行研究、策略制定、编辑和策划。从 2010 年到 2019 年，他在 OMA 的专家小组 AMO 担任协理。自 2019 年以来，他担任中央美术学院视觉艺术高精尖创新中心的访问专家。2019 年，彼得曼在阿姆斯特丹成立了研究和创意设计咨询公司 MANN，为各类型客户就房地产开发、食品和农业以及数字技术的战略、概念和内容开发提供咨询服务。2020 年 2 月，他作为主要组织方，呈现了一场"未来"展览："中国乡村：乡村的新纪元"。该展览由纽约所罗门·R.古根海姆博物馆与北京 CAFA 视觉艺术创新中心合作完成，展览主要内容是探讨中国农村的未来发展。

Stephan Petermann holds a Master's degree in the History of Architecture and the Theory of Architecture Preservation of the University of Utrecht (2001−2007) and studied Architecture at the Technical University of Eindhoven, the Netherlands (2001−2005). Since 2006, he is a long-term partner of Rem Koolhaas assisting him with research, strategy, editing and planning. He was an associate at OMA's think tank AMO from 2010 to 2019. Since 2019 he has been a visiting expert at the Central Academy of Fine Arts' Visual Arts Innovation Center in Beijing. In 2019 he founded MANN, a research and creative design consultancy in Amsterdam working with a variety of clients on strategy, concept and content development in real estate development, food and agriculture and digital technology. In February 2020, he presented the "Future" exhibition *Chinese Villages*: *A New Era of the Countryside* as its major organizer. The exhibition, co-sponsored by Rem Koolhaas/AMO at the Solomon R. Guggenheim Museum in New York and the CAFA Visual Arts Innovation Center in Beijing, looks into the future of the Chinese countryside. He also contributes to various magazines and blogs.

对于中国在扶贫事业中取得的成就，有些国家会存在疑虑。这项工作极其庞杂，超乎人们想象，涉及农业改革、文化建设、经济刺激和大规模基础设施投资，其工作内容、时间跨度以及覆盖人口规模在人类历史上绝无仅有。中国的扶贫成就如此伟大，再加上人们对于中国发布的信息普遍缺乏信任，或许可以解释为什么这一事实被国际社会所忽视。人类登月的壮举无人不知，地球上发生的这一类似的、具有历史意义的成就却没有得到广泛理解。另外，国际管理调查研究及峰会经常渲染中国崛起，《经济学人》等杂志多次将中国置于封面，商界领袖纷纷称中国为世界未来最大的变革者。他们大肆渲染中国试图超越其他国家所做的努力，其评估却缺乏必要的现实基础。他们缺乏技巧和好奇心去近距离地观察、感受、聆听中国及中国农村生活：中国人是在怎样发愤图强，拥有怎样的雄心壮志，在工作中发挥了怎样的聪明才智。遗憾的是，这种裂痕随着新冠肺炎疫情的暴发而加剧，并且本来相对稳定的中间派态度也在逐渐转变。通过对中国生活更加直观的了解，我们希望推动更广泛的国际研讨与合作，以积极应对这些挑战。

本文标题是 1977 年荷兰王储贝娅特丽克丝公主首次访华向中国人民第一次发表讲话时引用的一句话。在当前国际社会撕裂的现状下，这句话似乎更加真实。修复遭受破坏的国际文化和社会组织迫在眉睫，这一点无可争辩。我曾访问过中国的许多村庄，并与当地人进行过短暂而真诚的交流，本文记录了其中三个村庄的故事，来帮助我们更深刻地了解中国农村。根据我的观察，中国乡村焕然一新、充满活力，人们生活幸福快乐、勤奋好学，给我留下了深刻印象。我们了解了中国精心制定的政策、地方参与的复杂性以及政策实施的实际困难。提供帮扶的组织有时能够取得成功，有时却会遇到更多难题。我们很难对形势做出正确判断，从而无法找到应对各种可能性的解决方案。中国在 2020 年全面消除贫困，这也引发了对未来行动的思考和猜测：扶贫攻坚工作现已初步完成，我们该如何进一步巩固扶贫成果并取得更大发展。全面建成小康社会后，中国面对的是更高的目标和发展空间。

There is a certain anxiety in the rest of the world about China's achievements in poverty alleviation. Most importantly the scale of work is simply too large to be comprehended: The colossal program—ranging from agricultural reform, cultural and economic stimulus initiatives, to massive infrastructural investments and involving immense work, time, and population—cannot be compared in world history. This fact, combined with a generally deep-rooted distrust about information from China, might explain how the great achievements are relatively unnoticed internationally. Everybody knows about the landing on the moon, but a similar unprecedented achievement that has been made on earth somehow lacks popular comprehension. On the other hand, international management surveys and summits continuously highlight the importance of China's rise. Magazines like *The Economist* have featured it on dozens of its cover stories, and business leaders all call China the largest game changer for the future of the world. They hyped up China's attempts to surpass other countries' efforts, but their assessment lacked the necessary realistic basis. They lack skill and curiosity to open themselves up to, to come closer to, to see, to feel and to hear what life is like in China and its countryside: How the Chinese people are working hard to become strong, what kind of ambitions they have, and what kind of ingenuity they have applied to their work. Due to the COVID-19 crisis, the rift is unfortunately widening, and the relatively stable attitude of the middle-of-the-roaders is increasingly shifting. With a more intuitive understanding of life in China, we hope to promote more extensive international research and cooperation to actively respond to these challenges.

The title of this article is a sentence quoted by Dutch Princess Beatrix in her first address to the Chinese people upon her first visit to China in 1977. In light of the current situation where the international community is torn apart, these words seem more true. The urgency of healing the damaged cultural and societal international organizations is undeniable. This article explores three villages amongst many others I have had the pleasure of visiting to help better understand rural China. There I met with the locals, and spent a short but precious time with them. Above all, I try to record what I experienced: the enjoyment, learning spirit, and newness that left me a lasting impression. I came to know the well-planned policies, the complexities of local involvement, and the difficulty of turning words into deeds. The organizations of support sometimes met with success, sometimes encountered more challenges. It is an effort to go beyond judgment and explore what possibilities they offer. The formal

百闻不如一见
To see once, is better than to hear a hundred times

2017 年以来，我和雷姆·库哈斯（Rem Koolhaas）以及中央美术学院视觉艺术高精尖创新中心的同事共同参与了一个研究项目，探讨中国农村的未来发展。这项研究是在 2020 年 2 月 20 日开幕的古根海姆博物馆"乡村·未来"展览的一部分，旨在探索全球化时代农村的角色。

在对中国农村的初步研究中，我们迫切需要了解中国广大的农村地区以及中国人的雄心壮志。我们和学生共同制作地图，帮助人们真切感受中国农村的变化。这场展览旨在借助地图集帮助观众了解中国，比较美国和中国的发展状况，特别是基础设施方面的鲜明对比：在美国，铁路客运量持续下降，高速公路建设几乎停滞；而在中国，交通网络四通八达，发展态势令人惊叹。我们还发现，两国在气候变化、能源转型、电子商务和旅游业发展方面存在很大的相似性。简述之后，我们将聚焦中国农村——我们观察到的变化极具代表性，并且能体现更真实的景象。

大寨（1977—2019）：初印象

1977 年 5 月 1 日，荷兰王储贝娅特丽克丝公主和丈夫克劳斯亲王前往山西大寨参访。随行的还有导游、记者和摄影师，他们负责记录这次行程。荷兰国家电视台每天通过电视新闻进行报道，大多数荷兰民众由此对现代中国产生了初印象。记者弗里茨·博姆（Frits Bom）对中国充满好奇，似乎自己来到了一个新的星球，他的报道令人激动，而王室夫妇在参访中遇到的人们都做了充分准备，个个精力充沛。这是荷兰王室成员首次访问中国，大寨是他们游览北京和长城后的第一站。对于尊贵游客来说，大寨是他们的必去之地，这里展示了中国农业发展的成就。大寨的故事家喻户晓：一群村民在村干部陈永贵的带领下艰苦奋斗，硬

elimination of poverty in China this year also calls for new thinking and speculation about the next steps: now that the initial relief has been finished, how can we go on with further consolidation and progress? The success in this phase of creating a moderately prosperous society leaves more to desire for and to develop.

Since 2017, Rem Koolhaas and I have engaged with our colleagues at the CAFA Visual Arts Innovation Center in a research project about the future of the Chinese countryside. The research is part of *Countryside*, *the Future*, an exhibition at the Solomon R. Guggenheim, which opened on February 20, 2020, and which tries to explore the role of rural areas in the era of globalization.

In our initial research on the Chinese countryside, we saw an urgent need to make sense of China's vast rural areas and the ambitions of its people in general. We created maps with our students to document the change and to give a whole picture of its scale. The result of the exhibition is an atlas intended to familiarize viewers with the change of China and shows a stark contrast between the United States and China where the development of infrastructure is concerned: the decline of passenger railway and a relative standstill of highway grid construction in the U.S., versus the staggering development of China's connectivity. We also show the great similarity between the two nations regarding climate change, energy transition, e-commerce, and tourism development. Following the overview, we zoom in on the villages, which are representative of the changes we have observed and can reveal more intimate detail from the ground up.

First glimpes: Dahzai 1977−2019

On May 1ˢᵗ, 1977, the Dutch crown Princess Beatrix and her husband Prince Claus visited Dazhai Village in Shanxi. They arrived with a group of guides, journalists and photographers documenting the royals in their travels. In daily reports of the National TV news, they offered for most Dutch the first glimpse of modern China. The journalist Frits Bom reported with a dramatic undertone about China as if he landed on a different planet, while the royal couple came across the people fully prepared and energetic during their trip. It was the first time the members of the Dutch royal family visited the People's Republic of China, and Dazhai was the third stop after their visit to Beijing and the Great Wall. For distinguished visitors,

5

是使用有限的劳动工具在条件艰苦的喀斯特地貌上开垦出了耕地，而这里也成为"文化大革命"期间的一个中心舞台。报道称，大寨村民，也包括儿童，为贝娅特丽克丝公主演唱了一些著名歌曲，她听得入了迷。虎头山上，克劳斯亲王一边俯视着人造梯田的壮丽景致，一边接受采访。

在被问及对大寨的印象时，克劳斯亲王称新开垦的农田让他记忆深刻。记者又问他这种模式能否推广到其他发展中国家，他回答说："这里取得的成就令人瞩目。劳动人民当家作主，自上而下的管控较少。如果能调动底层人们的劳动积极性，那么这些做法就能够推广到世界其他地方……没有人再忍饥挨饿，就说明这种农业体系行之有效。"他说他很赞赏中国共产党将权力下放给社会基层的做法。在中国之行的最后一次采访中，博姆询问他们这次参访的亮点有哪些，克劳斯亲王说大寨农业给他留下了深刻的印象。他称自己通过实地考察发现那里很少使用化肥。当被问及荷兰能够从中国学到什么时，他说荷兰社会受消费文化的驱动越来越强，喜欢使用一次性物品，是一种不好的现象；相比之下，中国人非常节俭，注重物品的回收再利用。早些时候播出的节目《中国旅游》（1972 年制作）为荷兰人展示了中国及其乡村风光。节目内容是一群来自大城市的学生前往杭州附近的西湖公社和湖南的韶山村游玩，这些地方不仅风景如画，而且生机勃勃，让电视机前的荷兰观众备感新奇。记者采访了一位年轻的荷兰学生托马斯，他曾在当地一些家庭生活过一段时间。托马斯说，农村居民的热情和勤劳给他留下了深刻印象。他说能够学习真是幸福，并坦言劳动十分辛苦，村民们凌晨四点半就下地干活，但他起得晚，七点才赶到地里。那里的农民非常热情，给他留下了特别深刻的印象，他很乐意住在村里。

Dazhai has become a must-go spot and the showcase of the progress China has made in agricultural development. The story of Dazhai is famous: under the leadership of a village leader named Chen Yonggui, a group of villagers worked arduously with extremely limited farming equipment to reclaim arable land on the harsh karst topography and became one of the central stages during the Cultural Revolution. In the report, we saw Princess Beatrix charmed by the locals, including the children of Dazhai, singing famous songs for her. Her husband was standing on top of the Tiger Head Mountain to overlook the man-made terraced landscape.

When asked about his view on Dazhai, Prince Claus said he was deeply impressed by the new farmland. When the journalists asked him if he thought this model could be used for other developing nations, he answered, "The achievements here are impressive. Working people are the masters of the land, and there is less top-down control. If the labor enthusiasm of the people at the basic level can be mobilized, then these practices can be extended to other parts of the world ... and no one will go hungry anymore, which shows that this agricultural system is effective." He said he appreciated the the Communist Party of China decentralization of power to the grassroots of the society. In the last interview during the trip to China, Bom asked him about the highlights of their visit. Prince Claus said that Dazhai's agriculture left a deep impression on him. He said that through field investigation, he found that fertilizers were rarely used there.

When asked what the Netherlands could learn from China, he explained how the Chinese people still had a keen sense of utilizing everything they could find and recycling in contrast to Dutch society's malpractice of using disposable items due to its growing consumption-driven culture. A program *Tourism in China* produced in 1972 and broadcasting earlier had given the Dutch people a simple glimpse of the immensity of China and its countryside. The public TV report documented a group of students from big cities touring the Westlake Commune near Hangzhou and Shaoshan Village in Hunan Province. These places are both picturesque and lively, giving the Dutch audience in front of the TV a sense of novelty. The reporter interviewed Thomas, a young Dutch student who had stayed with several host families for some time. Thomas said that he was deeply impressed by the enthusiasm and hard work of rural residents. Thomas explained how great it was to study at college because, frankly, work was hard. He admitted that compared to the villagers, he had made a late start by only arriving at 7 in the morning while the villagers had

2019 年年初，我在朋友及中央美术学院视觉艺术高精尖创新中心客座专家 Karl-Otto Ellefsen 的陪同下来到大寨。尽管我之前已准备好素材和资料，但他坚持让我来看一看。他很好奇，想知道到底能从大寨学到什么，以及原来的村庄留下了什么。他的一位朋友和国际社会主义有关系，曾在荷兰公主参访前后游览过大寨，成为首批到过这里的挪威人。那天虽然天气晴朗，却冷得要命，我们走下出租车，走到村口，首先看到的是一面巨幅国旗，四周风景秀丽，国旗基座四周装饰着描绘村民种田的彩绘雕像，栩栩如生。再往前走，便会看到"大寨"两个大字，与以前海报中看到的毫无差别。这片景观之外是村中心和宽阔的公共广场，一条道路通往阶梯式窑洞。我在这里看到了非常壮观的村庄设计范例，它们设计独特，建造精湛，庭院接连成片，甚是宏伟。

我们很快就发现大寨已发生了巨大变化。层层梯田几乎不见踪影，这里已改造成一个新的自然公园，到处郁郁葱葱。在这次旅行中，我们游览了其中一座山峰，参观了几个贵宾来访纪念亭。我们参观的博物馆资料全面、设计精巧，但里面过于阴冷，于是我们便匆匆离开这里来到名人堂。这里悬挂着荷兰公主以及卡尔·奥托（Karl Otto）朋友的小型画像。在名人堂外边，20 世纪 60 年代的一些遗迹依稀可见：团结沟渡槽依然横跨在那儿，似乎还在发挥着引水的功能，与渡槽相连的是一条新铺的普通石板路。导游告诉我们，村民将自己的窑洞置换成了平房，窑洞会在夏季提供给游客居住。新开垦的耕地很难维持生计，于是村里将目光转向了旅游业。这里的一切显得很安静，新经济可能并不如所期待的那样。大寨肩上的历史责任就像巨大的陈永贵半身雕像一样沉重：它仍在寻找一尊身躯来承载历史，续写辉煌。

started work at 4:30. He was specially impressed with how welcoming the farmers are. He was willing to live there.

We made it to Dazhai in early 2019. I was with my friends and Karl-Otto Ellefsen, a visiting expert at the CAFA Hi-tech Innovation Center for Visual Art. Although I had found the footage and documentation before, he insisted that I come for a visit. He was curious to see what they could learn from Dahzai, and what was left of the original village. He had a friend who had connections with the International Socialists Organization and was one of the first Norwegians to go to Dazhai around the same time as the Princess. It was a sunny and freezing day as we got out of the taxi that brought us there. Before entering the village, we were greeted by an enormous national flag. The surrounding scenery was beautiful, and the flag base was decorated with painted statues depicting life-like scenes of villagers' farming. Behind this, the large characters of "大寨" (Dazhai) were visible, just like those we had seen in the historical posters. Beyond this landscape lay the village center and the vast public square. A road led to the multi-storied cave dwellings, one of the most spectacular examples of village design I have seen, with well-crafted architectural structures of interconnected courtyards with unique design and magnificent appearance.

We soon discovered that great changes had taken place in Dazhai. Layers of terraced fields were almost gone. The place had been transformed into a new natural park with lush greenery everywhere. During this trip, we visited one of the peaks and a few memorial pavilions in memory of the visits by dignitaries. The museum we visited was comprehensive in its displays and well-designed, but it was a bit chilly inside, so we hurriedly left for the Hall of Fame, where there were small-sized portraits of the Dutch Princess and Karl Otto's friend. Back to the outside, some remnants of the 1960s were still visible: the Unity Overpass Aquaduct was still there and functioning. Connecting to it was a new slab-paved road. According to our guide, the villagers now lived in bungalow houses, making their cave dwellings available for the accommodation of tourists in the summer. The newly reclaimed land could not produce enough cereal crops to support the residents. Therefore, they had turned their attention to the economy of tourism. Since everything seemed quiet here, the new economy might not be as prosperous as everybody had hoped. Dazhai's historical responsibility is as heavy as the gigantic bust of Chen Yonggui: it is still looking for a body to carry on the tradition and continue to write another chapter of glory.

百闻不如一见

To see once, is better than to hear a hundred times

刘庄

　　大寨的故事让我想起了早前的河南刘庄之旅，我们在那里亲身体验了类似的变革。刘庄还受到了国家宣传部门的关注，并作为国家示范村在国际社会进行宣传。刘庄位于黄河岸边，这里经常洪水泛滥，村里也由此沉积了一层厚厚的河泥。20世纪初，这里极其贫困，人民饱受疾病和饥饿的折磨。经过几年改革及对现代基础设施和农业的大胆投资，刘庄逐渐摆脱了绝对贫困，解决了温饱问题，由此成为全国闻名的示范村。从那以后，几乎每位中国领导人都会来这里参观考察。

　　2019年4月，我们也有幸来到刘庄参观游览。穿过一扇大门便走进了村庄，我们发现这里非常安静，与其他喧闹的中国城镇截然不同。这里这么安静并不是街道上没有人，而是人们都用电动车和电动三轮车代步，来去无声；时不时还有儿童骑着自行车经过。村民说起话来也是轻声细语，看上去十分惬意。这里的生活看起来很简单。村子的中央是一座大型展览馆，大致是以弗兰克·劳埃德·赖特（Frank Lloyd Wright）的古根海姆博物馆为原型，由来自北京的设计师设计。该馆主要用于展示刘庄的发展历程，以及带领这座村庄走上繁荣发展之路的领头雁：史来贺。步入展览馆，圆形大厅中央是史来贺大理石坐像雕塑，两倍于真人大小，栩栩如生，脸上笑容可掬，脚上穿着一双便鞋，周围环绕着一弯盘旋斜道。

　　在展览馆，我们遇到了村党委副书记刘女士。多年来，刘女士几乎接待过所有到访的中国共产党高层领导。1991年江泽民视察刘庄时，她精神饱满地进行了接待工作，当时江泽民即将出任中国国家主席。"他不停地与史来贺握手，还不时拍他的肩膀。"展览馆里的照片显示，中国前国家主席胡锦涛也与史来贺同志进行过认真交谈，还在交谈过程中做笔记。现任中国国家主席习近平曾于2006年视察刘庄，坐在一个大沙发上与村民拉家常。江泽民对刘庄情有独钟不无原因。他是邓小平拉开改革序幕后的第一位领导人，必须尝试将市场力量与社会主义相结合，而刘庄非常巧妙地完成了这一壮举。自20世纪70年代起，依照家庭联产

Liuzhuang

The story of Dazhai echoes an earlier trip to Liuzhuang Village in Henan, which presents at first hand a similar transformation. Liuzhuang also got attention from the country's publicity departments and was presented as a model village of the nation in the international community. The village is situated on the banks of the Yellow River, which, with its frequent flooding, left a hefty layer of river clay in the village. In the early 20th century, the village was extremely poor, people there suffering from disease and hunger. But the village was able to rid itself of absolute poverty to solve the problem of food and clothing in a few years during the reforms by cleverly investing in modern infrastructure and agriculture and was heralded as one of the model villages in the nation. Ever since, almost every Chinese political leader has visited and inspected the village.

We were fortunate enough to also visit the village in April 2019. After entering the village through a large gate in the street, we noticed how quiet Liuzhuang was, which was totally different from other Chinese villages. It was quiet, not because there were no people but because they rode e-bikes or e-tricycles without making a sound. Now and again, a child passed by on a bike. The villagers spoke in a soft way, seemingly both concentrated and relaxed. Life looked simple. Central to the village was a large impressive museum roughly modeled after Frank Lloyd Wright's Guggenheim. It was designed by designers in Beijing. The museum is dedicated to the village and, more evidently, its historical leader who was responsible for its prosperity: Shi Laihe. As we entered the museum, we saw his statue sitting in front of us in the center of the rotunda: a double life-sized marble figure with a charismatic grin on his face, wearing slippers. The spiraling ramp revolved around him.

At the museum, we met the Vice-party Secretary of the village Ms. Liu. She received nearly all the high-level Party figures visiting the village over the years. She was in high spirits when Jiang Zemin visited the village in 1991, shortly before he became President of China. "He couldn't stop shaking his [Shi Laihe's] hands. He kept on patting him on his shoulder." Photos in the museum showed that China's former President Hu Jintao also had serious conversations with Shi Laihe. The current Chinese President Xi Jinping visited Liuhzhuang in 2006 and could be seen chatting with locals sitting on a large sofa. That Jiang Zemin was so pleased with Liuzhuang can be explained. He was the first leader who, after reforms

百闻不如一见

To see once, is better than to hear a hundred times

承包责任制，中国的经济建设责任从集体转移到了家庭。刘庄没有这么做，仍坚持走集体经济之路，但同时决定利用集体经济为市场服务。就这样，全村很快富有起来，这正是中国政府的目标。

今天，刘庄可谓是村强民富：所有居民只要在村办工厂上班，便能获得丰厚的薪水，吃穿不愁，享受到富足的生活以及医疗和教育服务。它可能是世界上仍在运转的、历史最悠久的人民公社。在刘庄，唯一的店铺是一台小型自动售货机。这并不奇怪，村里免费发放村民所需的一切生活物资，要商店还有何用？而且自行开店也是违反村规的。在这里，你看不到广告。另外，你会发现这些村民居住的房子面积非常大。中国人均居住面积约为 39 平方米，但刘庄的人均居住面积是这个数字的两至三倍。

刘庄所获得的成功，中国其他村庄难以望其项背，其中的原因不得而知。刘庄在政界的地位可能是其中一个因素，但通过展览馆记载的丰功伟绩你还会得出这样一个结论：史来贺很有才华和远见。早在 20 世纪 60 年代初，他就意识到农业机械化无法产生足够的利润，也不能让村庄发展壮大，因此，引入了汽车喇叭和冰激凌工业生产线。10 年后他又指出工业生产也不足以养活这个村庄，于是又转向了药品，时至今日，这一产业仍是该村最大的收入来源。无论是在毛泽东时代还是在新中国的其他发展时期，他始终坚持党的路线，说话办事恰如其分，同时又没有放弃自己村庄的发展愿景。2003 年史来贺逝世后，他的儿子继任村党支部书记。村庄的第一次发展挫折早已出现苗头。虽然 2006 年建成的这些房子看上去仍很气派，但 1999 年落成的公共中心早已是破败不堪。中国的药品生产竞争日趋激烈，村办工厂的经济状况已不如以前，村里的工人也出现了短缺。尽管留在村里的村民比中国大多数村庄的村民都要多，但大多数年轻女性还是选择了离开。

in Deng Xiaoping's era, had to experiment with the combination of market forces with socialism. Liuzhuang Village had achieved this great accomplishment quite cleverly. From the 1970s onwards, the responsibility of the Chinese economy was shifted from work units back to families under the household contract responsibility system. Liuzhuang had decided that the village remained a collective economy, but it would use the collective economy to work for the market. The entire village became wealthy soon – exactly the aim of the Chinese government.

To this day, the economy of Liuzhuang Village is strong and its villagers were wealthy: all inhabitants have access to favorable living conditions, generous salaries, ample food, healthcare, and education on the condition of working in the village plants. It's probably the oldest functioning people's commune in the world. The only store in the village is a small vending machine. It makes sense: why would you need a store if everything is provided? It's against village regulations to start your own store. There is no advertising. On closer inspection, the houses of the villagers appear to be very large. The average residential area per inhabitant in China is around 39 m^2, while it is easily double or even triple that amount in Liuzhuang.

It remains hard to explain why Liuzhuang was so successful while other villages cannot be compared with them. Liuzhuang's position in governmental circles might have helped, but the monumental achievements documented in the museum may lead you to conclude that Shi Laihe was just very talented and farsighted. He realized in the early 1960s that mechanized agriculture would not be profitable enough for the village to grow and moved to industrial production of car horns and ice cream. He also noted a decade later that industrial production would not be profitable enough and shifted to pharmaceuticals, which remains the largest source of income for the village. Within the political climate under and after Mao Zedong he managed to stick to the party line, using the right words at the right moments without giving up his vision on his village. In 2003, Shi Laihe died. His son took his place after his death. The first setbacks of the village had started earlier. While the houses completed in 2006 look in good shape, a community center built in 1999 had long been dilapidated. Competition in the production of medicine in China has been accelerated, and the economic condition of the factory is not what it used to be. There is a shortage of workers in the village. Although there were more inhabitants in the village than in other villages in China, most of the young women have made a choice to leave.

展览馆最后展示的是村庄的未来蓝图，既有摩天大楼，又像度假胜地；它前面有一本书，却是空白页。刘女士说："村里有人认为旅游业才是刘庄未来的出路。现在，人们参观展览馆之后会在酒店吃午餐，然后就会离开。"我们询问了在这里发展数字经济的可能性。参访刘庄之前，我们参加了一场阿里巴巴有关打造淘宝村的大会。大会宣称数字经济代表中国城乡发展的未来。刘女士掏出了自己的智能手机，说她自己也会在淘宝上购物，但对于村庄的发展则有些茫然。

刘庄的生活在很大程度上已超过中国政府所设定的到 2020 年全面建成小康社会的国家目标，或许更接近"中国梦"。很显然，这个村庄早已实现了这一目标。但附近的村镇似乎更加繁荣、富裕，那里建起了豪华酒店，豪车和奢侈品店随处可见。我们在公园里碰到一位年轻的父亲，他在中国电信上班，带着一岁的女儿住在刘庄，是为数不多的在外工作的村民之一。他之所以能领取村里的生活补贴，是因为由于工作关系他能帮助村庄以更优惠的价格接入电话和互联网。他对自己的生活感到满意，但认为未来存在一些不确定性。我们问他有何顾虑，他说："村里因循守旧，缺少基本的创新，比如不允许村民开设淘宝店。"我们问他其中的原因，他说："以前，村党支部书记解释过刘庄的民主决策制度，有些类似于瑞士的公投制度，并会通过较小的附属委员会将权力分散到社区。但是，解决这个问题并不容易。一方面是老一代人，他们曾经为村庄的发展呕心沥血，现在仍掌握着村庄的领导权；另一方面是不安分的年青一代，他们始终在追逐着自己的梦想，两代人之间似乎存在一道鸿沟。也许这反映了一个更大的问题，这个问题已引起了全国人民的广泛讨论。"

与大寨一样，刘庄也需要进行根本性变革，这是我们希望看到的。当发展模式过时，该如何实现经济转型？如何才能真正把握住未来的发展浪潮？旅游业是终极模式吗？史来贺如果在世会怎么做？面对越来越严重的世界财富不均问题，刘庄可被视为最大的社会平等体验中心，这

The future blueprint of the village presented at the end of the museum's exhibition was a large collage with parts that resemble holiday resorts and skyscrapers. In front of it was a solid white book with only blank pages. Ms. Liu explained, "Some people in the village think tourism is the future for Liuzhuang. Now people visit the museum, they have lunch at the hotel, and then they leave." We asked about the possibilities of the digital economy. Before coming to Liuzhuang, we had attended a conference sponsored by Alibaba about Taobao Villages, which boasted the Chinese digital economy as the undoubted future of the nation, both in urban and rural areas. Ms. Liu showed her smartphone and explained she also shops on Taobao. But for the village, she doesn't know where they would start.

Life in Liuzhuang largely surpasses the national goals that the government has set for becoming a moderately prosperous society by 2020 and perhaps comes close to the Chinese Dream. The village has achieved all of the goals clearly and already for some time. But the nearby villages and towns are wealthier with new luxury hotels, cars, and shops. We bumped into a young father in the village park, an employee of China Telecom. Living in the village with his one-year-old daughter, he is one of the few villagers who work outside. He still receives the village's subsidies because he had helped the village get a good deal for the phone and Internet connections. He was content with his life there but was not sure about the future. We asked him the reason. "The village is still following the beaten path without innovations. For example, it doesn't allow the villagers to open Taobao shops." We ask what keeps him from addressing this issue. Earlier the party secretary explained the democratic setup of the village decision-making with a Swiss-like referendum system and smaller subcommittees spreading power over the community. But addressing this issue is not easy. There seems to be a gap between an older generation still leading the village, rightly proud of all that has been achieved through immense hardship and dedication, and a younger generation somewhat restlessly looking for their own future. Perhaps this reflects a serious question broadly debated among Chinese people across the country.

Like Dazhai, Liuzhuang also needs a fundamental change that we expect to take place: how to shift the economy when the previous model is outdated – how to actually work on the next stage of development? Is tourism the final model? What would Shi Laihe do if he were here? In the face of challenges concerning the rise of wealth inequality in the world, Liuzhuang could be seen as the largest experience

可能是其未来理想的发展模式。

雨补鲁 / 板万

也许由于承载的历史过于厚重，下一步该如何发展仍是大寨和刘庄需要考虑的问题。另一边，贵州的雨补鲁村也在革新时遇到了难题。2014 年，地处中国西南的贵州省专门委托中央美术学院建筑学院院长吕品晶对该省的两个小村庄进行设计改造，这是中国乡村振兴计划的一部分。作为一名建筑师，吕品晶对农村情有独钟，主要研究民间工艺及非物质文化遗产的保护。吕品晶所设计的雨补鲁村面积不大，只有 200 多户居民。这里是中国西南丘陵地区的一个世外桃源。长期以来，这个地区一直是中国扶贫工程的帮扶对象。每一年，这项工程都会拆除和重建数百个像雨补鲁这样的村庄。对于这种看似生硬的做法我们一直备感困惑，但只有当亲眼看到农村的艰苦条件和当地人的艰难生活时，你才能明白规划者希望实现的目标，才会了解他们的良苦用心。雨补鲁并未遭到破坏，而是在实践一项振兴计划。这项计划旨在打造"真实"的乡村生活，帮助城市居民放松身心，继而解决农村所面临的经济、社会和文化问题。雨补鲁距离实现这一理想非常接近了。

离开兴义机场，我们驶上了一条崭新而平坦的高速公路，仿佛置身荷兰。我们脚下是壮丽的丘陵景观，高架桥在一座座村庄间穿行。路过几个大型燃煤电厂后，我们驶入了一座造型别致的寨门，寨门里面是一条石板路（而不是柏油路），感觉就像来到了一座天堂花园。周围绿树成荫，可以看到各种动物，令人心旷神怡（现在的位置正好看不见燃煤电厂）。吕品晶的设计改造十分精致。从他展示的村庄旧照来看，这里以前都是十分普通的混凝土平房。经过几十年的改革开放，这种混凝土建筑在中国农村的大部分地区随处可见。吕品晶在平房上增加了斜顶设计，为游客提供了新旅游体验。现在，有的外墙装饰着天然石材，还有的使用传统木质工艺将乡村气息渲染得更为浓重。第一天晚上，我们一边用餐，一边欣赏着声势壮观的苗族鼓舞，震撼的灯效和动听的乐曲是

center for an equal society, which might be its ideal future model.

Yubulu / Banwan

Perhaps due to the historical traditions they carry on, the questions about what to do next exist in Dazhai and Liuzhuang. The village of Yubulu in Guizhou has its own complexities in the process of innovation. In 2014, the government of Guizhou in Southwest China commissioned the dean of CAFA's Architecture Department Lv Pinjing to redevelop two small hamlets as part of a project to rejuvenate the countryside. Lv's passion as an architect lies in the countryside, with her focusing on the preservation of vernacular crafts and intangible heritage. Yubulu, one of the hamlets Pinjing has worked on, is a tiny village with 200 inhabitants away from the turmoil of the world located in China's southwest. The area has long been the recipient of China's poverty alleviation program. Each year the program tears down and rebuilds hundreds of villages like Yubulu. We have been puzzled about this seemingly crude practice. Only when we are presented with the severe conditions and local dilemmas in the countryside can we see what the planners were trying to achieve and start to comprehend the difficult decisions they must make. Yubulu was not destroyed; it was preserved with an experimental plan for rejuvenation. The plan is to face economic, social, and cultural challenges by catering to urbanites' growing desires for relaxing experiences in the 'real' countryside. And Yubulu comes close to this mythic ideal.

Departing Xingyi Airport, we drove on a brand new, remarkably flat highway, as if we were still driving through the Netherlands. But under our feet was a magnificent hilly landscape. And some of the overpasses floated a hundred meters above existing villages. We passed several large coal power plants before passing through an impressive gate where the road was paved in stone rather than tarmac. It felt like driving into a paradise garden. The surroundings are stunningly green, full of animals (the coal plant now just out of view). The renovations designed by Pinjing look subtle. In the 'before' pictures shared by Pinjing, the village had generic concrete flat-roofed houses. As a result of decades of opening up, the majority of the residential houses in China's countryside were constructed of concrete. Pinjing's project added gable roofs to the flat structures, generating in some cases new experience for tourists. Some facades are now decorated with natural stone,

对古老传统的一种现代诠释。雨补鲁周边的村民非常幸福。一位老农现在种植的是无公害南瓜，并以高价卖给游客，赚的钱比以前更多了。一位年轻人开了一家小火锅餐厅，平时就在兴义与雨补鲁村之间来回跑。他说，这种生活更加自由，他现在自己当老板，而且收入比以前的工厂收入更高。

就在我们参访之前，雨补鲁村民刚刚在一个公共假期期间接待了很多游客。中央美术学院的学生正在搭建一处书籍和设计作品商铺。其中一位学生参与了房屋设计，当天晚些时候很多村民来请教如何改造农舍以便接待游客。旅游经济在很大程度上是靠爱彼迎之类的平台来推动，这些平台激发了人们对乡村休闲的兴趣。政府振兴计划包括为农民提供培训，教授他们如何提供旅游服务和满足客人要求，这也许比强硬干预效果更好。村民们在曾经的稻田种植了更值钱的中草药。由第五工作室打造的陆地艺术品"天坑"是游客们的必到之处，这里还有一个有名的游客打卡地是一位著名演员到过的一家当地旅馆。游客只需短暂步行即可到达一个大型自然保护区，那里有壮观的瀑布以及几个新建的塔楼和步道。再往前走，便会发现山坡上铺满了太阳能电池板，这也是政府扶贫计划的一部分；电池板之间为小型动植物提供了生长和栖息空间。

到达板万（吕品晶设计改造的第二个小村庄）后，一场手机"互拍"大戏突然爆发：村民举着智能手机拍摄我们，我们也对着他们拍摄。板万居住着约 800 位苗族村民，苗族是中国 56 个民族之一。来板万之前，有人告诉我要注意这里的酒文化，45 分钟后五杯米酒下肚，我便明白了这句善意的提醒。我上了一次公厕——悬崖边上的一间带顶窝棚，地面开了孔洞——旁边蹲着一位村民，正在玩手机游戏。吕品晶在板万的主要设计是一所古香古色的木结构学校，并重建了一些土坯房，其中包括餐馆和从事布料生产的传统作坊。这些建筑看上去一片生机，但在学校利用方面存在问题。学校竣工后不久，当地政府就决定合并学校进行

and some more authentic reconstructed structures use traditional woodcraft to become more vividly rural. In the first evening, we were treated to a festive dinner with a spectacular drum performance by a group of Miao dancers, accompanied by bombastic looking light effects and dramatic overtures – a modern interpretation of older traditions packaged for new tourists. The farmers around Yubulu were happy. An older resident planted his pumpkins without chemicals now and sold them at a premium price to the tourists. He made more money than before. A young guy recently opened a small hotpot restaurant. He split his time between living in Xingyi and the village. He talked about the freedom his new life has brought. As his own boss, he was making as much or more money compared to what he had earned from a factory.

Before our visit, a public holiday brought a lot of tourists to the village. CAFA students were setting up a village shop selling books and design items. One of the students worked on the design of the houses, and later in the day, we met more locals to talk about upgrading their houses too, so they could receive tourists as well. The tourist economy is largely stimulated by platforms like Airbnb that increase interest in spending time in the countryside. More effective perhaps than the physical interventions, the government's plans include courses for the farmers on meeting the needs of the guests and providing touristic services. In the fields where there were rice paddies, more expensive traditional Chinese medicine plants are grown now. A piece of land art in the shape of a sinkhole, made by the Fifth Studio, is a must-visit site. Next to it is a famous local guesthouse visited by a famous actor. Just a quick hike away is a large nature reserve with dramatic waterfalls and several newly built lookout points and trails. A bit further on, a section of a mountain has been covered by solar panels – also part of a governmental anti-poverty plan. The panels are placed with spaces in between, allowing for co-existing space for smaller flora and fauna.

Upon arrival in the hamlet of Banwan, the second village Pinjing worked on, a smartphone filming exchange erupted in which locals filmed us, and we filmed them. Banwan is home to 800 villagers who are the Miao people, one of the 56 ethnic groups in China. Before traveling to the village, someone had given me a heads-up about the drinking culture here. I got the point after 45 minutes when I had gulped five cups of local *Baiju*. I went to release myself in a public toilet – a covered platform hanging over a cliff with holes in the floor – where next to me was squatting a villager who was playing a game on the phone. Lv Pinjing's key projects

集中教学，因此，这所学校可能因此会被闲置，至少不会得到充分利用。尽管村民和吕品晶强烈反对，但最终，学童们只能离开村庄，住进寄宿学校。傍晚时分，我们观看了一场地方戏剧，我们先前认识的年轻歌手莫西子诗随后也表演了节目。这位歌手通过《中国好歌曲》走红，酷爱把玩中国传统乐器。中国政府决心保护少数民族文化，而吕品晶也致力于保护中国传统文化，但对于板万村所发生的一切，我们最终无法做出定论。就传统文化的保护与发展而言，我们可能会遇到很多错综复杂的情况，也能够学到很多有趣的东西或对它们进行讨论。

展望未来

现在看来，荷兰公主和亲王访问中国那段时间前后对于荷兰非常关键。荷兰在战后初期实现了经济繁荣，包括阿姆斯特丹在内的一些城市成功组织了大规模的贫民窟清理行动，从根本上改变了城市面貌；荷兰逐步推进农田建设，公路和铁路基础设施更加完善。荷兰为产业工人建造了新的城镇（有些像公社），并初步建成了国家度假胜地。20 世纪 70 年代早期是一个关键的转折点，一方面，战后的乐观情绪逐渐消退，浮躁不安的年轻人失去了目标，产业萎缩导致大量裁员和经济动荡。另一方面，新自由主义经济已经出现，并将在未来几十年占主导地位。从那以后，改革与经济再增长就变得困难重重。此外，荷兰与其他许多国家一样，也面临着气候变化、能源短缺等严峻挑战，而且贫富差距日益扩大。中国可能正处在与荷兰 70 年代类似的关键时刻，只不过是在另一个时代而已。

in Banwan are a large new school built with a classical timber frame, and the reconstruction of rammed earth houses, which include new spaces for a restaurant and workshops for traditional cloth production. It looks as if they are flourishing, but there's a problem with the school. Just after completion, the local government decided on the collective teaching, so it seems that the school will not be used, at least not to full capacity. The kids will leave the village and go into boarding schools, despite the strong opposition of the villagers and Pinjing. In the evening we were treated to a theater performance by the locals, followed by a clever young singer we met earlier called Moxi Zishi. He has become famous because of his appearance on *Sing My Song* and has a passion for playing traditional Chinese musical instruments. The Chinese government is determined to protect the culture of ethnic groups, and Lv Pinjing is also committed to protecting traditional Chinese culture. However, we could not make decisions on Banwan's future. There are so many dilemmas about preservation and modernity that intertwine, and so many interesting directions to learn from or extrapolate.

The future

The years around the visit of the Princess and Prince can, in hindsight, be considered a pivotal moment for the Netherlands. The early postwar era had brought prosperity to the Netherlands. Its cities, including the city of Amsterdam, had successfully organized massive campaigns to clear up slums, fundamentally changing the way the cities look. Dutch farmland was rationalized in various stages while highway and rail infrastructure had been further improved. New towns, just like communes, were being built for industrial workers, and national holiday resorts were initially established. The early 1970s was a critical turning point. On the one hand, post-war optimism gradually subsided. Impetuous young people lost their goals, and the shrinking industrial sector led to massive layoffs and economic turmoil. On the other, the neo-liberal economy had emerged and would dominate the next decades. From that moment, reform and re-finding economic growth became difficult. Like other countries, the Netherlands also faced severe challenges in climate change, energy shortage, and deepening divisions between the haves and have-nots. China might be at a similar pivotal moment as the Netherlands in the 1970s, only that in a very different era.

百闻不如一见

To see once, is better than to hear a hundred times

以上村庄的故事是不同政策层面的一种真实写照，体现了它们在现实生活中的困难和所取得的成绩。中国取得了许多值得大书特书的伟大成就，希望更多其他国家人民了解、学习和参与中国的发展进程。我在1972年那套旅游节目中了解了韶山，但从未去过这个地方。在上文提到的村庄，我确实感受到了一种在其他地方未曾感受到的活力与创造力。我参观过其他一些生活富裕、算得上达到"小康"水平的地方，但那里还有很多工作尚未完成——这甚至可能不是它的最终目标。从我参观过的许多村庄可以看出，最初大获成功的制度现在也需要适应新环境，这条道路可能不仅充满坎坷，而且需要截然不同的发展理念。

与住在北京的乡村歌手莫西子诗的交流让我感触最深。他对收藏古旧乐器很感兴趣，经常走街串巷去淘宝，并希望将来能创办一家博物馆展览这些乐器。与陈旧老套的说教者和保守的保护主义者不同，他的思想很开明——这不是因为他不想保护即将失去的东西，而是他认为我们有必要、有需要也有能力推陈出新。他的兴趣来自洞察到的机遇，而不是善意的义务。我们在北京遇到极飞科技的年轻员工，他们向我谈起无人机进村计划时；当寿光的一对农民夫妇热情地接待我们，并通过快手与网友分享时；当阿里巴巴研究小组潜心探索城乡人口流动模式获得更多相关资料时——我都观察到了这种活力。正是这种不断创新的力量让中国在世界舞台上脱颖而出。

对于未来，我调查过遇到的每个村民。他们大多数人认为，未来是一种线上与线下、城市与农村的混合体，未来是变化的，还需要我们更加深入地理解和接受。我们需要弄清如何防止帮扶社区再次分崩离析；如何提高素质和能力，适应快速变化的环境；如何创新遗产保护方法，更好地保护传统文化；新一代如何体验乡村生活，建立网络品牌，探寻新的生活方式。下一步，我们要掌握不同的技能，其中包括采用更好的

The stories of the above villages are a true portrayal of the different policies implemented at different levels, reflecting their dilemmas and achievements in real life. China has made many great achievements worthy of being written in volumes. I hope that more people from other countries will understand, learn, and participate in China's development process. I have never been to Shaoshan, though I had learned about it from that TV program about tourism of 1972. I did feel a kind of vitality and inventiveness I have not seen that much elsewhere. I have visited some other places where life is affluent and can be regarded as "moderately prosperous," but there is still a lot of work to be done there. It may not even be its ultimate goal. From the many villages I have visited, I can see that the initially successful system now also needs to adapt to the new environment. This road may not only be full of bumps but also require a completely different development concept.

A conversation with Moxi Zixi, the Beijing-based countryside singer, resonates with me the most. He is quite interested in preserving old musical instruments and often travels through alleys and streets to collect them, hopefully one day in the future being able to open a museum to put them on display. Unlike old-fashioned preachers and conservative preservationists, he is open-minded. Not because he doesn't want to protect what is about to be lost, but he has an urge of necessity, a drive, and a desire to build the new out of the old. His interest is coming from seeing the opportunity, not from a well-intentioned obligation. It was the kind of energy I also saw in the young guys of XAG we met in Beijing when they were explaining their countryside drone development. I have found the same vitality from the farmer couple in Shouguang who enjoyed our visit and shared it on Kwai with their friends and in the Alibaba research group engaging in an energetic study of patterns in urban-countryside movements to get more insight into rural-urban migration. This energy of creating the new is the reason why China stands out at the moment.

I have asked everyone I met in the countryside about the future. For most, the future is a hybrid of things online and offline and urban and rural – a future of fluidity that needs to be embraced and better understood. A more daring path lies ahead of figuring out how to prevent the supported communities from falling apart again, how to improve quality and ability to adapt to the rapidly changing environment, how to innovate heritage protection methods to better protect the traditional culture and keep traditions relevant, and how a new generation experiments with life in the countryside, setting up online brands and finding new forms of living. The next

工具和保持良好的心态，这需要使用新的宣传手段。未来企业领导者必须提升自身能力，这需要为心思敏锐的新一代重新设计替代性产品——他们善于辨别真假，而且在乎这一点。

欧洲人对新冠肺炎疫情感到震惊，他们开始了深刻的自我反省，决心要改变生活方式。当我通过微信询问中国朋友是否也有这些感触时，大多数人提出一些建设性意见，或理性地回复一些链接，建议我学习一些实用的个人防护技巧。也许对中国人来说这只不过是生活中的一道坎儿，仅此而已。我从中看到的是对共同目标的一种信念，这种信念使人感到温暖，迸发着共同探索与追寻的激情。这两种力量结合在一起，使得深度交流更有益、更有必要和更具意义。

step will require a different skill comprised of finer tools and mentalities. It needs new sounds and images. The next generation of corporate leaders will be required to up grade their game. This requires redesigning alternative products for a new generation of keen minds – they are good at distinguishing true from false, and they care about it.

Europeans have been shocked by the COVID-19 attack, sending them in soul searching missions, with newspapers full of wishful ambitions to change the lifestyle. When I asked my Chinese friends on WeChat about whether they experienced the same impact, most came back to me with constructive and kind links of practical tips for dealing with the pandemic crisis. Perhaps for the Chinese, it's more like a bump in the road, nothing more, nothing less. What I see from this is a belief in a common goal. This belief makes people feel warm and bursts with a passion for joint exploration and pursuit. The combination of these two forces makes in-depth communication more beneficial, necessary, and meaningful.

尤里·塔夫罗夫斯基
Yury Tavrovsky

圆梦小康

A Moderately Prosperous Society—A Dream Fulfilled

尤里·塔夫罗夫斯基出生于1949年，成长过程中曾在苏联的不同地区生活——第聂伯罗彼得罗夫斯克（乌克兰）、堪察加彼得巴甫洛夫斯克以及列宁格勒，而他的父亲则在上述地区服过兵役。1971年，塔夫罗夫斯基从列宁格勒国立大学东方学系中文专业毕业。在大学期间，他曾翻译了以下中国古典文学作品——《道德经》《中庸》《大学》，并为其撰写注释。关于中国早期佛教历史的毕业论文是以他翻译的《佛说四十二章经》为基础而完成的。毕业前，他曾在新加坡南洋大学汉语培训中心进修了一年。

Yury Tavrovsky was born in 1949 and was raised in different parts of Soviet Union where his father served in the military – Dnepropetrovsk (Ukraine), Petropavlovsk-Kamchatsky, Leningrad. In 1971 Tavrovsky graduated from Leningrad State University, Chinese Language Department of the Oriental Faculty. At the University he was translating and writing commentaries to Chinese Classics – "Daode Jing", "The Doctrine of the Mean", "Great Learning". Graduation paper on history of early Buddhism in China was based on his translation of "Sutra in 42 Chapters". Before graduation he was engaged in advanced studies for one year at the Chinese Language Center, Nanyang University in Singapore.

摆脱贫困是无数中国人千百年来的梦想，对于这一梦想，中国古代名著早有描述。翻开孔子辑录的经典之作《诗经》，我们便能品味到古人对丰衣足食和幸福生活的向往。"小康"（小富）正是这位圣贤提出的一种理念，后由其弟子加以完善和充实。此外，中国历史上的伟大诗人杜甫也曾写道："朱门酒肉臭，路有冻死骨。"

富足生活不只是哲学家和诗人的梦想，也是黄巾军、赤眉军、太平军、义和团等农民起义军提出的口号。到了清末，在梁启超、康有为著作的推动下，消灭贫穷与耻辱的伟大思想开始盛行。在这种思想的激励下，孙中山及其革命追随者推翻了腐败无能的封建统治，"民生"成了孙中山所倡导的"三民主义"中的一项内容。20 世纪 80 年代，中国共产党在历经数十年的艰苦奋斗之后，最终开辟了一条改善民生的道路，踏上了实现"小康"的伟大征程。

1983 年春，我第一次目睹了中国贫困地区的真实状况。当时，我正在中国东北黑龙江省的一个小村庄，为俄罗斯电视台拍摄纪录片。我们获准采访一户农家。这家人在村里显然并不是最穷的，但与当时的苏联农村相比已是窘迫至极。他们穿的衣服破烂不堪，住的木房子又旧又破，室内陈设简陋、寒气逼人，为我们准备的午饭没有荤腥。即使如此，主人把我们领到当地政府分给他家的一块高粱地，看得出来，他对此十分满意。他的两个儿子正在地里劳作，使用的农具非常原始。家里的其他人大多数是女性，正在主屋旁边昏暗的畜棚里缝制皮手套。"现在我们是为自己努力劳动，生活很快就会好起来的。"一位 50 多岁但看起来有 70 多岁的农民说，这是"改革开放"初期的景象。邓小平将"小康"一词写入党的文件，带领中国百姓过上体面生活。我希望黑龙江的那位农民已实现"小康"，现正在享受着美好生活。

2016 年秋，我沿着甘肃的古代商道采风，一边创作《丝路新语》。甘肃是中国西北乃至全国最为穷苦的地方之一，那里气候干旱、耕地稀少、水资源短缺、交通不便，而且人们的文化水平较低。习近平主席提出到 2021 年全面建成"小康"社会，甘肃自然成了扶贫攻坚的前沿阵地。

To live without poverty was a dream of uncountable generations of Chinese for a few thousand years. We can see manifestations of these dreams in books of ancient philosophers. In the classic *Book of Songs* collected and edited by Confucius, one can find hopes for happy life without hunger and starvation. The great sage himself coined the "moderate prosperity" idea and left it to his disciples to develop. Du Fu, possibly the best Chinese poet in history, wrote: "Aroma of wine and meat spreads from the purple gates while roads are covered with skeletons of the poor frozen to death."

Life without poverty was not only a dream for philosophers and poets. Peasant armies such as the Yellow Turbans, Red Brows, Taiping Army, Boxers wrote their demand for justice on their banners... The great idea of putting an end to poverty and humiliation of the nation became extremely popular at the end of the Qing Dynasty thanks to the works written by Liang Qichao and Kang Youwei. They inspired Sun Yat-sen and his revolutionary comrades to overthrow the corrupt and inefficient imperial rule. People's welfare became one of the three pillars of Sun Yat-sen's teachings. It took the Communist Party several decades of struggle, defeats, and victories to open the way for bettering people's livelihood and realizing the great dream of *"moderately prosperous society"* in the 1980s.

It was the spring of 1983 when I first saw the real situation of poverty in PRC. In a small village in Heilongjiang Province in Northeastern China, I was shooting a documentary for Russian TV. We were allowed to visit a peasant family, apparently not the most impoverished in the village. But it was much poorer than Soviet villages of that time. The old wooden house was cold and poorly furnished. Family members wore multi-layered, worn-out clothes. There was no meat in the lunch we shared. At the same time, the host showed us a *sorg hum* field allotted recently to him by the local government. His two sons were working there using some primitive equipment. Other family members, mostly women, were sewing leather gloves in a semi-dark barn close to the main house. "We'll be fine soon because now we are toiling with our own hands for our own benefit," told me a 50-year-old peasant who looked as if he was in his seventies. Those were the early days of the reform and opening-up policy's implementation. Deng Xiaoping had recently put the words " 小康 " in the Party documents and helped millions of his compatriots start a decent life. I hope that man from Heilongjiang has reached *"moderate prosperity"* and now enjoys a good life.

Another memory goes back to the autumn of 2016. I was writing a book *New Silk Road* and traveling along the ancient trade route in Gansu province then. It is

中午时分，我们来到了武威市附近的"阳光新村"。这座村庄属于易地扶贫项目，5000多人已从贫困山村搬迁至此三年，但一切看起来仍然很新。小巧的白色房屋整齐划一，沿着两条街道排列开来，道旁新近栽植了常春藤树，土地干旱，呈棕色。起初没人晒太阳，但我们很快就遇到了一些村民，他们大多是妇女和老年人，其中还有一位年轻的基层党员干部为我们讲解。

一位18岁左右的女孩邀请我们去她家喝些水，我们跟她来到了一堵砖墙后面的一座小房，里面有三间小屋。这位女孩叫王占霞，马上要去河北的一所大学免费就读，那天正在屋里做准备；妈妈和哥哥正在玉米地里忙碌着。在这里，每个居民都分配到了1.75亩（1亩≈666.67平方米）土地，可耕种30年，而且免除了租金或税费。村里的房屋供居民免费居住，但他们需要承担水电费，即便如此，他们也很乐意，毕竟以前居住的山沟既不通电，也没有自来水。"阳光新村"和另外九个类似的易地扶贫项目共居住着40000人，18亿元的建设费用全部由甘肃省承担。

one of the poorest places of Northwestern China and the entire country. Arid climate, scarce agricultural land, and lack of water add to the underdeveloped road network and low education level. It is a small wonder that Gansu became the forefront of poverty alleviation after Xi Jinping has proposed that the country would have completed the building of the moderately prosperous society by 2021.

We entered Sunshine New Village near the city of Wuwei around noon. It was built for the people relocated from the impoverished mountainous villages. Everything looked new, although the village with a population of 5,000 was already three years old. Small look-alike white houses lined two streets with ivy trees recently planted in the dry brown soil. At first, no people were enjoying the warm sun. But very soon, some villagers joined me and a young local Party cadre gave explanations. They were mostly women and old folks.

A girl about 18 years old offered us some drinking water at her house. There were three tiny rooms in a small house behind a brick wall. The girl named Wang Zhanxia was home preparing to leave for a university in Hebei Province to study free of tuition. Her mother and elder brother were busy in their cornfield. Each person was allocated 1.75 *mu* (equaling to 0.0667 hectare) of land without any rent or tax for

过去五年来，我每年都要到中国各地调研贫困问题。对于这个话题，党委书记、市长、教授、工厂老板、出租车司机和农民的看法各不相同。在浙江和福建等富裕省份，有人告诉我几年前已经解决了这一问题；在陕西、山东、黑龙江和四川，我既看到了易地扶贫带给百姓的实惠，但有时也能听到地方官员贪污腐败的传闻；甚至在两三年前，还有人怀疑中国政府是否能彻底消除贫困。

　　坦白地说，2012 年，我对新任中国领导人习近平做出的到 2021 年要消除绝对贫困、全面建成小康社会的承诺持谨慎态度。我非常清楚，中国在 1978 年实行改革开放前大部分人都很贫困，到了 2012 年仍有 9900 万人没有摆脱贫困。好好考虑一下这个数字！相当于俄罗斯人口的三分之二！在不到 10 年的时间里似乎不可能带领这么多人实现"小康"。

　　鉴于此，当时很难相信习近平及其建设"小康"社会的"中国梦"。七年后的 2019 年 11 月，在上海举办第二届中国国际进口博览会期间，我在一个展馆看到电子公告牌赫然写着："距离完全摆脱贫困还有：421 天 8 小时 34 分 7 秒。"当然，这个数字不断变化，很多游客在驻足拍照。

30 years. The house was given for free. New owners have to pay for electricity and running water but did it with great enthusiasm because they did not have either in their mountain village. The Gansu Province Government paid RMB 1.8 billion (USD 279.71 million) to construct the Sunshine New Village and nine more similar poverty alleviation centers with 40,000 dwellers in them. Visiting different parts of China several times annually for the past five years, I've always asked questions about poverty. Party secretaries and mayors, professors and factory owners, taxi drivers, and peasants gave quite different answers. In the rich provinces like Zhejiang or Fujian, I was told that the problem had been solved several years before. In Shaanxi, Shandong, Heilongjiang, and Sichuan, I heard stories about beneficial relocations and sometimes about corrupt local officials trying to get money from the government property. Even 2-3 years ago, some people shared doubts whether poverty will leave China for good.

Frankly, back in 2012, I was also somewhat cautious reading the then-new Chinese leader Xi Jinping's promises to eradicate absolute poverty in the country and build what is called a "comprehensive moderately prosperous society" by 2021. Of course, I knew that before the reform and opening-up policy started in 1978, most Chinese were very impoverished. And by 2012, there were still 99 million poor people left. Just think about it! Almost 100 million people! Two-thirds of my big country's population! To make so many people "moderately prosperous" in less than ten years looked practically impossible.

Yes, it was hard to believe Xi Jinping and his Chinese Dream about "moderate prosperity" back then. But I was not at all surprised when seven years later, in November 2019, in one of the Second Shanghai International Import Fair pavilions, I

梁家河：习近平扶贫情结的起源地

上海是我最近中国之行的最后一站。我在 2018 年创作的《习近平：新纪元》将要推出新版，因此想寻找和补充一些新的感悟和资料。在 10 天的行程里，我遍访了习主席工作生活过的一些重要的地方。首先，我访问了陕西省的梁家河村。 1969 年"文化大革命"期间， 15 岁的习近平来到梁家河插队学习，"接受贫下中农再教育"。来自北京的 11 个男孩和 4 个女孩在村子安顿了下来，住进了窑洞。几百年来，当地人都是依山挖洞，建成民宅；即使在 20 世纪末也没能通电通水。传统的炕炉不只用来烹煮简单的饭菜，同时也能为床铺供暖。习近平的床铺由一块草席和两块厚床单组成，这些床单同时也被用作毛毯。草席中间有很多虫子，这些城市来的孩子一点也不习惯，劳作一天后要喷点药才能睡会儿。这些来自北京的年轻人需要与农民一起下玉米田干活、修建水坝、平整道路和开垦农田。

习近平在梁家河的 7 年知青岁月对他的品格和道德心的形成产生了决定性的影响。那时他年纪尚小，却得不到父母的帮助、安慰和建议；面对困难，他并没有气馁，而是继续与命运抗争着。他甚至还尝试着改善自己和当地百姓的生活。年轻的习近平建成了第一口沼气池，为村里供热、供电；他执意建起了一个小铁匠铺来打制农具，这样就不用掏钱购买。他赢得了同龄人和当地村民的尊重，后来甚至当选为村党支部书记。 22 岁时，他已证明自己是一位天生的领导者，并被选派到清华大学读书。

现在，梁家河村依然是梁家河村，但已不再贫穷。同样的黄土高坡，同样的玉米地，同样的溪流，同样饱经风霜而黝黑的脸庞，同样消瘦的身躯，同样简单的穿着打扮。其中一些老旧窑洞现在成了展馆。通过扶贫项目的实施，村里的 1600 多人已住进了由当地政府建造的气派的四层楼房中。陕西目前的贫困线标准为 3200 元， 2019 年 11 月的贫困发生率为 0.06%，而这一数字在 4 年前高达 13.6%。除了依靠政府

saw an electronic scoreboard stating: "Time to completely alleviate poverty left: 421 days, 8 hours, 34 minutes and 7 seconds." Of course, the figures were continually changing, and there were many visitors taking photos.

Liangjiahe, the birthplace of Xi Jinping's no-poverty dream

Shanghai was the last leg of my latest journey in China. I wanted to get fresh impressions and additional information for a new edition of my book *Xi Jinping*, *The New Epoch*, published in 2018. A 10-day trip took me to the major places of the president's life. Naturally, it started in Liangjiahe Village in Shaanxi Province. Fifteen-year-old Xi Jinping was sent there in 1969 during the Cultural Revolution to "receive education from poor and semi-poor peasants." Eleven boys and four girls from Beijing were settled among the villagers to live in their caves. For many centuries, local people dwelt in the caves dug into slopes of soft loess soil. Even in the end of the twentieth century there was no electricity or running water. Simple food was cooked on the traditional *kang* stoves providing also some warmth for beds. Xi Jinping's place on the *kang* consisted of a straw mat, two thick sheets used also as blankets. There were bugs in the mats and unaccustomed city children used herbicides to get some sleep after a day in the fields. The youngsters from Beijing were working alongside adult peasants in the corn fields, repairing dams, building roads and new fields.

Seven years spent in Liangjiahe were decisive for Xi Jinping's personality and conscience as a teenager who did not have his parents around him to help or reassure and advise him. Yet, he was not crushed by insurmountable difficulties and went on with his destiny. He even tried to improve life for himself and the people around him. Young Xi has built the first biogas station producing heat and electricity for the village. He insisted on constructing a small smithy to make agricultural implements instead of buying them. He earned respect from his fellow youngsters and the local people and was later even elected secretary of the Village Party branch. At 22, he proved to be a born leader and managed to enter Tsinghua University in Beijing.

Present-day Liangjiahe Village is the same Liangjiahe Village minus poverty. Same loess hills, same cornfields, and the same creek. Same people with weather-beaten faces, of the same slender stature, and dressed in the same simple attires. There are even some old caves now used mostly as exhibition halls. 1600 people live now in four-storied modern buildings provided by the local government in the poverty alleviation program framework.

援助，梁家河村村民也在努力赚钱。他们种植和售卖的苹果在国内品质一流，农闲时还会在不同景点担任向导。他们制作的纪念品很具地方特色：传统的布鞋，可爱的布玩具，甚至还有类似于习近平 40 年前使用的农具。

旅游业：扶贫脱困的抓手

全国各地的游客纷至沓来，在梁家河村感受习近平的奋斗精神，参观"中国梦"的起源地。国内旅游已成为中国的一项主要产业，2018 年，国内旅游收入占国内生产总值的 11.04%，创造工作机会约 8000 万个。此外，旅游也成为扶贫攻坚的一项有效措施。习近平是 20 世纪 80 年代初最早使用这种措施的地方领导人之一。 1982 年，他被派往河北省正定县担任县委书记。正定县历史悠久，但非常贫穷。习近平上任之后便提出降低农业税，帮助农民脱贫。他以当地草药为依托建起了化妆品厂，为困难群众创造了许多工作岗位。

习近平总书记另一个有名的大动作是创建了"中国好莱坞"。他努力说服上级部门，争取资金建设影视拍摄基地。正定县距北京仅 280 公里，这里老房林立，古墙连藤，风景如画，并且有各种特别的庙宇佛塔。170 余部历史影视剧在"中国好莱坞"拍摄，每年吸引的游客多达 150 万。

Shaanxi's poverty threshold is now RMB 3,200, and the poverty level in November 2019 was 0.06% compared with 13.6% only four years before. Local people in Liangjiahe village do not rely solely on government aid and do their best to earn more. They grow and sell apples considered to be the best in China. They work as guides on several sites. They make local souvenirs: traditional cloth shoes, beautiful cloth toys, and even agricultural implements like those used by young Xi Jinping 40 years ago.

Tourism as a tool of poverty alleviation

Tens of thousands of tourists come to Liangjiahe Village from all over China to feel Xi Jinping's spirit and see the birthplace of his "Chinese Dream." Domestic tourism became a primary industry in China, creating 11.04% of the national GDP and around 80 million jobs in 2018. It also became one of the most efficient methods of poverty alleviation. Xi Jinping was among the first local leaders to apply it back in the early 1980s. He was transferred to Zhengding County of Hebei Province in 1982 to be Party secretary. Zhengding was very ancient and very poor. The new leader started to fight poverty by lowering the agricultural tax. He proceeded with building a cosmetics factory using local herbs and giving dozens of jobs to the poor.

His most famous invention was later called "Chinese Hollywood." Xi persuaded his Hebei superiors to finance a permanent setting for developing the film industry. Zhengding is only 280 kilometers from Beijing and has impressive scenery with ancient city walls, buildings, and temples with unusually shaped Buddhist pagodas. More than 170 history movies and serials were made in the "Chinese Hollywood" district and about 1.5 million tourists visit Zhengding each year.

20 世纪 80 年代，在中国找到一个穷地方并不难，福建宁德就特别贫穷。福建省与台湾地区、东南亚的华侨社团建立了密切的贸易关系，产业规模不断扩大，但宁德是中国 18 个集中连片贫困区之一，与该省其他地方的差距非常明显。习近平在正定主政两年并在经济繁荣的厦门担任副市长三年后，被派往宁德工作。

宁德的民众与梁家河很不一样，彼此之间都是使用难懂的方言交流，但面对的问题很类似——世代穷困。扶贫脱困成了习近平未来 5 年的主要任务。他经常徒步深入山村，与农户在泥房中同吃同住；他还探访了许多渔民，这些人世世代代都生活在船上。在宁德，习近平亲自制订了贫困人口搬迁安置计划。在宁德，习近平要求党员干部和地方官员签订扶贫责任状；在宁德，成百上千的腐败官员因挪用扶贫资金而受到了严厉惩处。

在我走访陕西、河北、福建、浙江和上海的过程中，还听到了很多其他关于习近平亲自参与扶贫工作的故事。10 天来，我追随着习近平主席的足迹，重温了他 40 年来工作过的一些重要地方。在职务升迁的同时，他必须解决各种政治问题，制定农业和工业发展决策，满足广大人民群众的生活需求。

根据之前对习近平主席简历的研究及最新的感悟，我得出了三个结论。他自从政之初开始就推出了大大小小各种改革措施。他喜欢以小计划起步——如《1985—2000 年厦门经济社会发展战略》，然后再制定宏大战略——如"中国梦"发展战略。此外，习近平主席这些年来对扶贫工作投入了大量心血。显然，贫困给他留下了深刻印象，他一直将扶贫脱困当作头等大事来抓。

2012 年中国共产党第十八次全国代表大会召开之后，习近平主席进一步完善了邓小平的"改革开放"发展战略，并提出了打造"中国梦"的长期发展计划（2012—2049 年），其第一阶段是到 2021 年实现脱贫。

In the 1980s, it was not very difficult to find a poor place in China. Ningde Prefecture of Fujian Province was an outstanding example. It was one of the 18 most impoverished Chinese areas and a stark contrast with other parts of the province already pretty rich with expanding industries and close trade ties with the Taiwan region and overseas Chinese communities in Southeast Asia. Xi Jinping went to work in Ningde after two years of success in his governorship in Zhengding and three more years as a mayor of prosperous Xiamen City in Fujian.

People of Ningde and Liangjiahe looked different and spoke mutually incomprehensible dialects. But they had similar problems – they were destitute for many generations. Poverty alleviation was the primary responsibility of the Party Secretary for the next five years. He traveled to mountain villages, sometimes on foot, and stayed in mud houses. He visited fishers living on their boats for many generations. It was in Ningde where Xi Jinping personally drew up programs of resettlement for poor people. In Ningde, he started to use a system of personal responsibility of Party cadres and local officials for poverty alleviation. In Ningde, hundreds of corrupt officials were punished by misappropriations of money and property allocated to the poor.

There were many other examples of Xi Jinping's involvement in poverty eradication on my journey across Shaanxi, Hebei, Fujian, Zhejiang and Shanghai. It took me ten days to follow President Xi's steps in the key parts of China where he had spent 40 years of his life. On his road of promotion, he had to solve different political problems, make decisions on agricultural and industrial development, and meet the needs of thousands of people.

Based on previous research on President Xi Jinping's resume and the latest insights, I have come to three conclusions. Since the beginning of his administration, he has introduced various reform measures, large and small. He liked to make small plans at the early stages and great strategies later on – from the "Xiamen Development Program 1985−2000" to "Chinese Dream" strategy for the entire nation. Besides, President Xi Jinping has invested a lot of efforts in poverty alleviation over the years. Apparently, Liangjiahe's poverty left him such a big impression that he has made poverty alleviation his priority forever.

After the 18th CPC Congress in 2012, Xi Jinping has made improvements to Deng Xiaoping's "reform and opening-up" strategy, put forward his own "Chinese Dream" long-term plan for 2012−2049, and made poverty alleviation by 2021 the

2020 年建成小康社会之际，就是这一伟大胜利与习近平的名字载入史册之时。就像秦始皇第一次统一中国、孙中山推翻清朝统治、毛泽东建立新中国、邓小平开启改革开放一样，中华文明将再次为世界提供一个富于创造、足智多谋和艰苦奋斗的新典范。各国领导人和人民将会再次探讨"中国奇迹的奥秘"。

中国奇迹的奥秘

当向莫斯科语言大学的学生或通过电视广播脱口秀介绍中国的扶贫状况时，我总会得到两种反应。第一种是："这是谎言，地球上没有哪个国家能做到这一点！"第二种是："中国奇迹的奥秘是什么？俄罗斯也有类似的创举吗？"我通常会开玩笑说：要复制中国奇迹也行，只可惜俄罗斯没有那么多中国人。随后，我讲了一个非常严肃的故事，它分为两个方面。

首先，中国人探索、试验并发展了一种新的经济社会体制，即"中国特色社会主义"。1978 年，邓小平推出了对内改革和对外开放的新政策。他设法把社会主义计划经济、国有经济的优点与自由市场满足消费者需求的能力结合在一起，在市场发挥决定性作用的同时，强调政府和公共部门的主导性作用。

这一新体制的两个部分有时相互矛盾，给经济和整个社会都带来了问题。幸运的是，这一体制当中还有第三个关键角色——中国共产党。这一"计算机网络"的成员有 9000 多万人，能够收集各种信息，党的基层组织达到 400 多万个，就像 5G 通信蜂窝一样发挥着作用，而网络中心是一台超级计算机——中国共产党中央委员会。它借助学术机构和智库来分析信息，在制定决策时考虑社会主义和市场部门的需要，同时将国家利益放在首位。

first stage of this plan. When the goal of building a moderately prosperous society is achieved in 2020, this great victory will become inseparable from Xi Jinping's name in the history of China. It is comparable to the first unification of China under First Emperor of Qin, the overthrowing of the Qing Dynasty by Sun Yat-sen, the founding of New China by Mao Zedong, and the masterminding of the "reform and opening-up" policy by Deng Xiaoping. Simultaneously, the Chinese civilization will offer the world a new example of creativity, resourcefulness, and hard work. World leaders and ordinary people once again will start talking about the "secret of Chinese miracle."

The Secret of the Chinese Miracle

When I tell my students in Moscow Linguistics University and audiences on TV or radio talk shows about poverty alleviation in China, I always see two reactions coming one after another. First: "It cannot be true. No country on Earth can achieve it!" Second: "What is the secret of the Chinese miracle? Can we have something similar in Russia?" I usually start answering their questions with a joke: to recreate the Chinese miracle, we don't have enough Chinese in Russia. But then I tell a serious story. It comes in two chapters.

First of all, the Chinese have invented, tested, and developed a new economic and social system called "socialism with Chinese characteristics." In 1978, Deng Xiaoping started new policies of domestic reforms and openness to the outer world. He managed to combine the best socialism features with its planned and state-owned economy with a free market and its ability to follow consumers' needs. The market plays a decisive role while emphasizing the positive functions of the government and public sector.

The two parts of the new system sometimes contradict each other and bring problems to the economy and society in general. Fortunately, there is the third part in the design – the Communist Party. This "computer network" of 90 million members can collect various information. Then there are 4 million local cells functioning like 5G "clever houses." The central part of the network is a supercomputer called CPC Central Committee. It analyses the information using academic institutes and think tanks. It formulates decisions considering the needs of socialist and market sectors

1978 年，中国共产党十一届三中全会做出了第一个具有历史意义的决定，实行邓小平提出的"改革开放"政策。40 多年来，中国正是在这一政策的指引下快速发展，成为世界第二大经济体。这项政策还帮助很多中国人摆脱了贫困，改善了生活，甚至步入了"中产阶级"之列。1978 年至 2012 年，中国共产党还阶段性地推出了五项有关减贫的重要方案，提出要促进农村地区的发展，完善灌溉、道路、供水和教育基础设施，以及对贫困村庄和地区提供财政援助。

中国梦始于"小康"

2012 年 11 月下旬，中国共产党第十八次全国代表大会结束后不久，中国政府做出了第二个具有历史意义的决定。在此期间，习近平主席首次提出了"中国梦"。这项长期发展规划独具特色。当时，美国通过了"重返亚太"军事战略和反华《跨太平洋伙伴关系协定》，加强对华战略遏制。贸易战呼之欲出，但中国共产党十分明智，在"中国梦"的口号下进行了全国动员。

从国内的角度来看，国家制定新的长期目标，并将几个不同的社会阶层团结在民族复兴的伟大旗帜下非常重要。到 2049 年，要把中国建设成为富强、民主、文明、和谐的社会主义现代化强国！这一理念非常伟大，它以爱国主义填补了自由经济条件下长期不平等和腐败所必然导致的意识形态真空。

"中国梦"总体规划包含几个主要战略。"新常态"经济战略旨在平衡国内外市场，以最大限度地减少对外贸的过度依赖，同时更加注重质量、科学和生态。"依法治国"战略旨在最大限度地减少腐败，以免伤害经济、激起民愤或为外部颠覆活动提供温床。"一带一路"倡议不仅能与其他发展中国家分享中国的经验与资源，还有助于确保中国的市场和原材料不受西方控制。

while putting the national interests above all.

The first decision of historic significance was taken in 1978 at the Third Plenary Session of the 11th CPC Central Committee. It gave the green light to the reform and opening-up policy proposed by Deng Xiaoping. For almost 40 years, it allowed China to develop with the unthinkable speed and become the second-largest economy globally. It also helped millions of Chinese get out of poverty, improve their livelihood, and even turn them into "middle class." From 1978 to 2012, the Communist Party of China also introduced five important poverty reduction programs in stages, proposing to promote rural areas' development; improve irrigation, roads, water supply, and education infrastructure; and provide financial support to impoverished villages and regions.

Chinese Dream starts with "moderate prosperity"

The next, second historic decision was made in late November 2012, soon after the end of the 18th CPC Congress. President Xi Jinping first presented his "Chinese Dream". This unique long-term plan made some corrections to the concept of "socialism with Chinese characteristics" under new international and domestic circumstances. By then, the USA had intensified their containment of China's strategy with a "Pivot to Asia" military build-up program and anti-Chinese Trans-Pacific Partnership Trade block. The trade war was only looming, but CPC was wise enough to prepare for the national mobilization drive under the "Chinese Dream" slogan.

From the domestic point of view, it was imperative to give the nation a new long-term goal and unite several quite different social strata under the great banner of National Rejuvenation and turn China into a powerful socialist country of a prosperous, democratic, civilized, and harmonious society by 2049! It uses patriotism to fill the ideological vacuum inevitably caused by long-term inequality and corruption under free economic conditions.

The "Chinese Dream" master plan contains several major strategies. The economic strategy called "new normal" aims to balance external and domestic markets to minimize overdependence on foreign trade, emphasizing quality, science, and ecology. The second strategy, "governance by law," aims to reduce corruption that harms the economy, angers people, and gives external subversive activities an

在我看来，"中国梦"发展计划的关键战略是扶贫和全面建设"小康社会"，这些成为整个计划的首要目标绝非偶然。随着经济的发展，亿万中国人的生活得以改善。

习近平亲身经历了贫穷。"文革"期间，他曾在贫穷的陕西梁家河村工作了7年，后来又在福建和浙江任职，努力帮助那里的渔民和农民摆脱贫困。走上新岗位后，他明白是时候报答长期受苦的中国人民了。在实施新常态战略的同时，扩大国内市场也很重要，这样可增加一亿多的消费者。显而易见，在全球化和争夺消费者市场的时代，拥有14亿消费者的市场有多么宝贵。中国商品的三个主要市场（美国、欧洲和东南亚）加在一起也比不过即将形成的"庞大的小康市场"。

为在2021年实现既定目标，帮助1亿人口脱贫，习近平承受着相当大的政治风险。经济持续放缓，国内生产总值增速越来越低，国民经济从外部市场重新转向国内市场引发了许多意想不到的问题。不过，贫困人口的确是在不断减少。截至2017年11月和中共十九大，中国贫困人口数量为4300万，而到2019年年底（距离最后期限仅剩一年）这一数字只有550万。显然，小康社会将在2021年年初如期实现。

"黑天鹅"事件无法阻止小康社会建设

2020年年初，新冠肺炎疫情在中国暴发，许多地方阻断了交通，工厂生产陷入停顿。显然，这场疫情成为到年底消除极端贫困的一大阻力。现在，中央政府已加强对省市地方的控制并为疫区提供额外资助，这成了实现既定战略目标、防止百姓返贫的主要策略。

opportunity. The "Belt and Road" Initiative not only shares Chinese experience and resources with other developing economies but also guarantees markets of China and sources of raw materials beyond the control of the West.

To my mind, the key strategy of the "Chinese Dream" plan is poverty alleviation and building a "comprehensive moderately prosperous society." It is no coincidence that it is the first opening chapter of the entire program. Parallel with economic development, hundreds of millions have improved their lives.

Xi Jinping knew well what poverty is from his personal experience. During the Cultural Revolution, he had spent seven years toiling in the impoverished village of Liangjiahe in the underdeveloped Shaanxi Province. Later he tried to help homeless fishers and poor peasants in Fujian and Zhejiang provinces as a Party official. After taking up his new position, he knew it was time to repay the Chinese people who have suffered for a long time. It was also essential to enlarge the domestic market along with the "new normal" strategy, to add 100 million new consumers. It is evident that a market of 1400 million consumers is an invaluable asset in our times of deglobalization and competition for consumer markets. Three major markets for Chinese goods — the USA, Europe, and Southeast Asia combined — are smaller than the soon-to-be "massive *moderately properous* market."

As early as 2012, President Xi Jinping proposed to "build a well-off society in all respects." To achieve the set goal in 2021 to lift 100 million out of poverty, Xi Jinping took considerable political risks. China's economy continued to slow down, GDP figures were becoming lower and lower, and resetting the national economy from external to domestic markets brought unexpected problems. Still, the number of poor people was decreasing. By November 2017 and the CPC 19th Congress, there had been only forty-three million poor people left and, by the end of 2019, one year before the deadline, there had only been 5.5 million. It was evident that "*moderate prosperity*" will be realized as planned by the beginning of 2021.

Black swans cannot stop "moderate prosperity"

But then, in early 2020, the outbreak of COVID-19 happened. It has brought traffic and factory production to a standstill in many parts of China. Closing off roads and other lockdown measures to contain the outbreak. It was evident that this epidemic became a significant obstacle to eradicating extreme poverty by the end

习近平主席掌控全局。2020 年 3 月 6 日，他在决战决胜脱贫攻坚座谈会上发表重要讲话，明确了到 2020 年现行标准下的农村贫困人口将全部脱贫，这是党中央向全国人民做出的郑重承诺，必须如期实现。采取的措施首先包括财政援助。在 2020 年的前三个月，中央政府已向贫困地区拨款 1396 亿元（约合 210 亿美元），其中包括西藏、新疆、四川、青海、甘肃和云南。与此同时，中国还拨款 1030 亿元（约合 157 亿美元）帮助民众渡过疫情难关，并要求地方政府为民众提供更多援助。疫情过后如何攻克最后的贫困堡垒是一个令人关注的问题。在此，我分享《环球时报》2021 年 3 月 31 日发表的一篇有关新疆的报道，这篇报道给我留下了深刻的印象。

中国西北部的新疆维吾尔自治区依托脱贫攻坚大数据平台，健全、完善了四色信号灯分级预警机制，以快速发现扶贫工作中的问题，防止出现返贫。这一机制将登记在册的贫困户分为四类，分别以红、橙、黄、绿标识。

对年收入超过 5000 元（约合 700 美元）且"两不愁三保障"（不愁吃、不愁穿，义务教育、基本医疗、住房安全有保障）全部达标的，用绿色信号灯标识；对年收入低于 5000 元高于 4500 元的，用黄色信号灯标识，各级政府采取针对性措施多渠道增加贫困人群收入。

南疆地区（那里的贫困村更多）的基层公务员告诉《环球时报》，驻村帮扶干部更关注橙、红两类人员。新疆扶贫办官员马缨说："对因失业、创业失败等原因导致收入较大幅度下滑、年收入 4000 ～ 4500 元的家庭，用橙色信号灯标识。县乡两级综合分析收入下滑具体原因，并根据家庭实际情况和意愿，采取转移就业、公益性岗位安置等针对性帮扶措施。"

of the year. Strict control over provincial and rural governments from Beijing and additional funds for affected regions are now a primary method of achieving the strategic goal and preventing people from slipping back to poverty.

Speaking at the special conference in Beijing on March 6, Xi Jinping stressed that the CPC's promise to the nation to lift all rural residents living below the current povrty line out of poverty by 2020. These means include, first of all, financial assistance. During the first three months of 2020, the Central Government has allocated RMB 139.6 billion (around US $21 billion) to local administrations of the poverty-stricken areas. They include Tibet, Xinjiang, Sichuan, Qinghai, Gansu, and Yunnan. Simultaneously, the government has also allocated an additional RMB 103 billion (US $15.7 billion) for people's short-term needs seriously affected by the epidemic. The Central Government required that the local authorities allocate more resources to help their people. How to overcome the last bastion of poverty after the epidemic is a matter of concern. I want to share a story on the situation in Xinjiang that impressed me very much. It was published on March 31 by *Global Times*.

In northwest China, Xinjiang Uygur Autonomous Region has completed a four-level early warning system based on its big data platform to spot problems in poverty alleviation work quickly and to avoid a slide back to poverty. The system classifies residents who have been registered as "poverty-stricken" into four levels color-coded with green, yellow, orange, and red.

Green represents households that have more than RMB 5,000 (around US $700) of yearly income, which means they have no worries about food and clothing and have access to compulsory education, basic medical services, and safe housing; yellow represents those with a yearly income of RMB 4,500 to 5,000. Governments at different levels would help find solutions to increasing their income.

The grassroots public servants in southern Xinjiang, where there are more poverty-stricken villages, told the *Global Times* that working groups stationed in the villages give more attention to people marked with orange and red. According to Ma Ying, an official from the Poverty Alleviation Office of Xinjiang, the color orange represents households that suffer from unemployment or business failures and have an annual income of RMB 4,000 to 4,500. The county and village administrations would thoroughly study the reasons for their income decline and offer targeted assistance policies, including job transfer and public welfare job placement based on the family's actual situation and expectations.

对因重大自然灾害、重大疾病等特殊原因导致家庭年收入下滑至4000元以下的，则用红色信号灯标识。

当地政府的工作人员告诉《环球时报》，这一贫困监测预警机制有助于发现可导致返贫的问题，及时提供援助，从而确保扶贫工作的顺利开展。1月以来，新疆已在10个深度贫困村实施了针对性帮扶政策，确保165800人到2020年年底摆脱贫困。中国新冠肺炎疫情得到控制后，新疆成为中国最早复产复工的地区之一。新疆正在帮助当地居民和外出务工人员重新返回工作岗位，确保个人收入。

2017年10月，习近平主席在党的十九大报告中引用了这样一句话："大道之行，天下为公。"这种"大道"超越了国界，希望天下和谐、和平。实现这一目标有很多方法，很多"大道"。

今年（2020年），中国摸索出了"疫情防控之道"，并与世界分享；今年年底实现"小康"后，中国将会分享另一伟大创举，即"扶贫脱困之道"。人类社会的确需要掌握这种方法，以便在未来消除贫困。目前的状况丝毫不容乐观。根据联合国发布的《2019年可持续发展报告》，全球仍有8.6%的人口生活在贫困线以下，而且状况变得越来越复杂。2015年，全世界长期挨饿的人口数量为7.84亿，而两年后（2017年）这一数字增长到了8.21亿！甚至在美国和俄罗斯，贫困人口也在增加。对于世界许多国家，新冠肺炎疫情将会带来严重后果，贫困将进一步加剧。

显然，在2016年，联合国提出的可持续发展目标将无法像2000年的千年发展目标那样顺利实现。"消除极端贫困和饥饿"是这两项行动计划的首要任务。这一目标在2016年仍未实现，到2030年也将无法实现，这一点联合国已正式承认。联合国193个成员国中，只有中国（2020年）履行了消除贫困和饥饿的承诺。

Poverty-stricken households marked red usually face severe problems, including suffering from natural disasters or having family members with severe illnesses. The income of the whole family is less than RMB 4,000.

A public servant from the local government told the *Global Times* that this poverty monitoring and early warning mechanism helps identify problems that could lead to poverty and provide timely assistance, thereby ensuring smooth progress of poverty alleviation. Starting from January, Xinjiang has implemented targeted policies in ten severely poverty-stricken villages to ensure that 165,800 people could get out of poverty at the end of 2020. Xinjiang is among the first regions in China to resume work after the COVID-19 pandemic was put under control. Xinjiang is helping local residents and migrant workers return to work to ensure personal income.

In the report of the 19th CPC National Congress in November 2017, General Secretary Xi Jinping said emotionally: "When the *Dao* prevails under heaven, it is for the public." The *Dao* or Way also goes beyond the Chinese borders and brings harmony and peace to everyone in the world. There are many Ways to achieve this goal.

This year (2020), China has found the "*Dao* of controlling the pandemic" and shared it with the world. After "moderous prosperity" is achieved by the end of this year, China will share another great undertaking, the "*Dao* of poverty alleviation." The human society really needs to master this *Dao* or Way to eradicate poverty in the future. At present, the situation allows no optimism at all. According to *Sustainable Development Report 2019* issued by the United Nations, 8.6% of the world population still lives in poverty. The situation becomes increasingly complicated. 784 million people suffered from constant hunger in 2015, and two years later, in 2017, the number was 821 million! Poverty population grows even in the U.S. and Russia. Many countries of the world will see poverty growth as the grave consequence of COVID-19.

It is quite evident the Sustainable Development Goals proposed by the UN in 2016 will never be achieved as smoothly as the Millennium Development Goals of 2000. "To eradicate extreme poverty and hunger" was the priority in both global programs. This goal was not achieved by 2016 and will not be achieved by 2030. This was officially admitted by the UN. Only one country among the 193 United Nations member states that has fulfilled its promises to eradicate poverty and hunger: that is China, who did it in 2020.

中国特色社会主义的大道

对于中国取得的扶贫成就，其他国家做出了两种反应：第一种是忌恨加深，加大贸易战，禁用中国技术，试图破坏中国的政治经济稳定；第二种是承认并且越来越重视中国社会制度和治理方针的有效性。我希望俄罗斯及其他国家能做出第二种反应。

中国特色社会主义所具有的全球意义比以往任何时候都更加明显，为追求自主快速发展的国家提供了借鉴。过去 70 年来，中国始终致力于带领贫困人口脱贫致富，8 亿多人由此摆脱贫困。中国共产党自 1921 年成立之初就将此作为自己的使命，并一直坚持到现在。只有社会主义才敢做出带领亿万人口摆脱贫困的承诺，并确保其最终得以实现。

今年（2020 年），中国和中华民族所取得的两次重大胜利向世界证明中国的政治制度具有强大的生命力和影响力。中国已向发展中国家表明，西方的政治制度不是实现现代化的唯一途径。中国还有其他经验可以分享，其中包括社会主义市场经济体制、大众创业、包容性社会保障制度以及扶贫制度。

更为重要的是，这两次胜利证明了中国特色社会主义制度优于自由资本主义制度。任何一个资本主义国家都未能像社会主义中国一样迅速而有效地遏制新冠病毒的传播，也未能带领绝大多数人口摆脱贫困。

显然，弗朗西斯·福山（Francis Fukuyama）提出的"历史终结论"是完全错误的。历史的车轮滚滚向前，我们现在正在掀开新的篇章。我认为这一篇章应被称为"人类命运共同体"。习近平主席几年前提出这种理念时，曾引发一些质疑。一些专家就此大做文章，热炒"修昔底德陷阱"，称中国要称霸世界。

The Great *Dao* of socialism with Chinese characteristics

There are two reactions from other countries to China's achievement in poverty alleviation: The first is the intensified envy and hatred, which have led to the increase of trade wars and stepping up the efforts to ban Chinese technology and undermine China's political and economic stability; The second is to admit the efficiency of the Chinese social system and governance, which is already increasingly valued by the rest of the world. I want my country Russia and other countries to choose the second reaction.

The global significance of socialism with Chinese characteristics is more evident than ever, providing a reference for countries pursuing independent and rapid development. In the past 70 years, China has carried out a continuous mission of lifting poor residents out of poverty, which has helped over 800 million people get rid of poverty. That was the The Communist Party of China mission from the very start in 1921, and it is still true to the mission 100 years later. Only socialism can promise eradication of poverty to hundreds of millions of people and guarantee it will be realized finally.

This year (2020), the two great victories achieved by China and its people have proven to the World the strong vitality and strength of China's governance system. China has shown to the developing nations that Western ideas about political systems are not the only way to achieve modernization. China can also share other experiences on the socialist market economic system, the mass employment system, the inclusive social security system, and the poverty alleviation system.

Maybe even more important is that these two triumphs have also demonstrated that socialism with Chinese characteristics is superior to the liberal capitalist system. No capitalist country can put the COVID-19 pandemic under control as quickly and efficiently as the socialist China has done. No capitalist country can eradicate the poverty of the great majority of its people like the socialist China has done.

Obviously, Francis Fukuyama was entirely wrong with his "end of the history" idea. History goes on, and we are now opening an entirely new chapter, which, I think, we will call "a community with a shared future for mankind" put forward by President Xi Jinping just a few years ago. This idea was at first met with some skepticism and even suspicion. Some experts started to write stories and books about

这种观念极其错误，毫无意义可言，对信奉者只是一种误导。首先，中国并未主导成立任何新的组织，也未强迫其他国家信奉这一理念。它提供的只是一种主动思考，没有统一世界的其他理念。如今，人类社会通过技术和贸易密切联系在一起，但仍存在着一些非常危险的消极趋势，比如去全球化、摧毁当前世界秩序、破坏国际组织和废除协定。在西方，单边主义甚嚣尘上，多边主义受到压制，而且这种趋势在全球愈演愈烈。在这种局势下，世界各国都需要积极向上的理念和实例来效仿。

"人类命运共同体"就是这样一种理念，遏制疫情和消除贫困则是对这一理念的践行。

the "Thucydides' trap" or even "Chinese plans of world hegemony."

It is a very wrong perception that leads them astray and fraught with grave mistakes for the followers. First of all, Beijing does not start any new organization under its control and does not press other nations to join or even share the idea. It offers the initiative to think about because there are now no other ideas to unite the world. Human society nowadays is being united by technology and trade. Simultaneously, there is a very dangerous negative tendency of deglobalization, breaking the current world order, damaging international organizations, and scrapping agreements. Unilateralism is prevailing over multilateralism in the West and is spreading worldwide. Under such circumstances, world nations need positive ideas and examples to follow.

"A community with a shared future for mankind" is precisely such an idea. Stopping the COVID-19 pandemic and eradication of poverty are exactly such examples.

穆罕默德·哈利勒
Mohammed Khalil

我眼中的中国扶贫

China's Poverty Alleviation in My Eyes

穆罕默德·哈利勒博士，于 1954 年 3 月 28 日出生于摩洛哥的卡萨布兰卡。1978 年至 1986 年在北京医科大学和北京中医药大学学习，是第一位从中国毕业的摩洛哥学生。2002 年至 2007 年，曾任摩洛哥众议院议员，自 2012 年起担任中摩友好交流协会主席、中阿友好协会会员、外交事务委员会办公室成员等。2016 年荣获习近平主席颁发的"中阿友谊贡献奖"。

Dr. Mohammed Khalil was born in Casablanca, Moroccoo on March 28, 1954. He studied at Peking University Health Science Center and Beijing University of Chinese Medicine from 1978 to 1986 and was the first Moroccan student who graduated in China. From 2002 to 2007, he served as a Moroccan member of the House of Representatives. Since 2012, he has been the chairman of the China-Morocco Friendship and Exchange Association, a member of the China-Arab Friendship Association, a member of the Office of the Foreign Affairs Council, etc. He was awarded the "Outstanding Contribution Award to China-Arab Friendship" awarded by President Xi Jinping in 2016.

1978 年，作为第一个赴中国留学的摩洛哥人，我选择了学习医学。当我抵达中国首都北京的时候，它给我的印象就是一个庞大的村庄，彼时北京最高的建筑物是北京饭店。

那时的街道，到处都是自行车。除了公交车以外，自行车是中国人最常用的交通工具，很少能见到汽车，人们的衣着风格很统一。我在中国获得的奖学金，相当于我中文老师一个月的工资。

那个时期，我了解到中国领导人邓小平执政，掀开了中国改革开放的序幕。

邓小平的脱贫路

邓小平是第一个提出让中国摆脱贫困的人，他也是第一个用中国的方式诠释"小康社会"概念，明确"建设小康社会"目标的人。所采取的主要举措之一是四个现代化政策：

- 农业现代化
- 工业现代化
- 国防现代化
- 科学技术现代化

当时，在我们这些生活在中国的外国人看来，这一计划是一种很难实现的幻想，认为只是一种党派宣传。但是，中国人民的决心、纪律和领导力正在促使这些不可能的事情慢慢实现。

根据邓小平提出的新政策，数百万中国农民可以拥有自由耕种的土地，自由出售多余的农作物，并把钱投资到村里的工厂。对 80% 的常住农村户口居民来说，这一改变十分大。不再有饥荒，也不再缺乏粮食，甚至农民也开始拥有自己的房子和舒适的家具。改革开放政策的实施，也改变了一些年轻人的行为方式。在一些大城市，陆续出现了舞厅。这些变化引起了保守主义者的不满和当时所谓的"清除思想污染"行动，对此，领袖邓小平回应道：不要因为害怕苍蝇飞进来就把窗户紧闭，我

In 1978, as the first Moroccan to study in China, I embarked on my journey to China to study medicine. When I arrived in Beijing, the capital of China, it impressed me as a huge village. Back then, the tallest building in the city was Beijing Hotel.

At the time, the streets were teeming with bicycles, the most common means of transportation for Chinese people except buses. The cars were rarely seen. The people were dressed in a quite uniform style. The scholarship I received in China was equivalent to the monthly salary of my Chinese teacher.

I learned that the Chinese leader Deng Xiaoping came to power and initiated China's reform and opening-up.

Deng Xiaoping's way to get out of poverty

Deng Xiaoping was the first to propose to lift China out of poverty. He was also the first to interpret the concept of a "moderately prosperous society" in Chinese style and clarify the goal of "building a moderately prosperous society." To this end, one of the key measures taken was the implementation of the policy of the Four Modernizations.

- Modernization of industry;
- Modernization of agriculture;
- Modernization of national defense;
- Modernization of science and technology.

The Four Modernizations sounded like an illusion almost impossible to come true in the eyes of foreigners living in China back then. The goal was deemed to be a kind of partisan propaganda. However, the Chinese people's determination, discipline, and leadership have been gradually turning the impossible into a reality.

Under the new policy introduced by Deng Xiaoping, millions of Chinese peasants can own the land they are free to cultivate, freely sell their surplus crops, and make an investment in the villages' factories. This meant a fundamental change for 80% of the permanent rural residents. As time went by, there was no more famine or food shortages, and the farmers even began to have their own houses and fine furniture. The implementation of the reform and opening-up policy also transformed some young people's way of living. Ballrooms began to emerge in some big cities. These changes led to the conservatives' dissatisfaction and protests from the so-

们应当打开窗户，并把飞进来的苍蝇清除掉。

1980年，中国政府颁布了独生子女生育政策，这是政府为控制人口增长采取的一项措施。

1986年，中国实施了另一项创造就业机会、减少失业和贫困的政策，即对外国投资实行开放政策，并在中国特色社会主义背景下鼓励市场经济和私营企业的发展。

深圳，曾是毗邻香港的小渔村，自1979年邓小平提出要将其划为经济特区以来，发生了翻天覆地的变化。1984—1992年，邓小平两次视察深圳，为将深圳建设成可媲美香港的现代化城市指明方向，以期吸引来自香港及西方国家的投资者。改革发展已延伸至中国东海岸一带，例如上海的浦东及山东省，吸引了来自中国台湾地区、日本、韩国和西方国家的许多投资者，并建立了能创造大量就业机会的大型企业，这鼓励了大批农村的年轻人到东南沿海地区工作，以获得更高的收入和更好的生活。改革开放政策旨在吸引外资，鼓励市场经济和私营企业的发展。

对集体农业的限制和吸引外资的支持等初期改革措施，引起了包括国家制度规范化、部分公司私有化以及市场贸易自由化在内的诸多改变，这对降低失业率和减少贫困人口大有裨益。

中国的GDP从1978年的1500亿美元左右增至2004年的1.6万亿美元。1986年，极端贫困标准为206元，改革之后，贫困线分别提高到2008年的1067元、2009年的1186元和2010年的1247元。

亚洲开发银行首席经济学家在评价中国经济迅速增长时说道："这表明中国政府在经济急剧增长的过程中应对困难和挑战的方法是务实的。"中国人口与发展研究中心主任马力表示，这一阶段中国经济的发展反映出中国政府对提高个人收入以适应国家经济增长速度的关切。这意味着更多的低收入者将从中国的经济繁荣中获益。

中国脱贫的另一项重要举措是大力发展教育。中国有一句谚语："授人以鱼不如授人以渔。"中国式脱贫不是给予贫困者金钱的扶持，而是

called "anti-ideological-pollution" groups at the time. In response, Deng said that we shouldn't shut the windows for fear of letting the flies in, but instead, we should keep the windows open and get rid of the flies.

In 1980, the Chinese government introduced the one-child policy to curb population growth.

In 1986, with the aim of creating job opportunities and reducing unemployment and poverty, China adopted an open policy towards foreign investment and encouraged the development of the market economy and private enterprises in the context of socialism with Chinese characteristics.

Once a small fishing village adjacent to Hong Kong, Shenzhen has undergone radical changes since Deng Xiaoping designated it as a special economic zone in 1979. Between 1984 and 1992, Deng Xiaoping visited Shenzhen twice and charted a road map to develop Shenzhen into a modern city that can rival Hong Kong to attract investors from Hong Kong, and Western countries. As the reform extended to the east coast of China, such as Pudong in Shanghai and Shandong Province, a large number of investors from the Taiwan region, Japan, South Korea, and Western countries were drawn there to establish large enterprises that provided plenty of job opportunities. Against this backdrop, a lot of rural young people went to Shenzhen and other cities along the east coast for a higher income and better life.

The initial reform measures involving the restrictions on the collective agriculture and the support for attracting foreign investment have brought about a series of changes, such as the standardization of national systems, the privatization of some companies, and the liberalization of market trade. They played a significant role in reducing unemployment and poverty.

China's GDP had increased by 9.4% from around US$150 billion in 1978 to US$1.6 trillion in 2004. Through the reform and opening-up, the extreme poverty line has risen from RMB 206 in 1986 to RMB 1,067 in 2008 before hitting RMB 1,186 in 2009 and RMB 1,247 in 2010.

The chief economist of the Asian Development Bank made the following remarks on China's rapidly growing economy. "It indicates the Chinese government's pragmatic approach to the difficulties and challenges arising from the rocketing growth of the economy." According to Ma Li, director of China Population and Development Research Center, China's economic growth at this stage demonstrated the Chinese government's intention to increase people's income to adapt to the

提供就业机会。通过扫除文盲、普及文化教育等工作的开展，使大学里来自贫穷地区的学生人数逐年递增。

1986 年，我在获得医学博士学位后，离开中国回到摩洛哥。中国的变化发展和中国人民的善良执着给我留下了深刻的印象，这促使我加入了"中摩友好交流协会"，相信我们可以从中国的探索经验中受益，通过发展摆脱贫困，让人民的温饱问题得以解决。

1998 年，离开中国 12 年之后，我有幸成为前首席部长阿卜杜拉赫曼·优素福先生率领的摩洛哥代表团成员之一前往中国。当我们抵达北京时，我感到非常惊讶，北京已经蜕变成一座现代化大都市，拥有宽阔的街道，鳞次栉比的摩天大楼，街头小巷遍布各式各样的汽车、摩托车和自行车。人们的习惯和服饰也发生了变化，变得更为丰富时尚。中国人均收入较以前提高很多。由于我精通汉语，并且熟悉中国的习俗，经常会有记者询问我关于中国现状的问题。我告诉他们，北京发生了翻天覆地的变化，它已经从一个大村庄变成了一个可以与西方最新城市媲美的现代化城市，我甚至不知道我曾经学习的学校要怎么走。我们还去了山东省青岛市，那也是一座现代化城市，我们参观了当地一些新兴的工厂，比如海尔生产基地。我们见证了中国近几年取得的巨大成就。

中国共产党在脱贫工作中的作用

毫无疑问，中国共产党在领导国家走向发展、引领人民创造美好生活方面发挥了显著作用。值得注意的是，尽管国家领导人几经变化，但

country's economic growth. It means that more low-income people will benefit from China's economic prosperity.

Another key measure of China to get rid of poverty is to develop education vigorously. As a Chinese proverb goes, "Give a man a fish, and you feed him for a day; teach a man to fish, and you feed him for a lifetime." China doesn't lift people out of poverty by providing financial support but rather job opportunities. Thanks to the campaigns of eliminating illiteracy and promoting universal education, the number of university students from poverty-stricken areas has been increasing year by year.

In 1986, I went back to Morocco after graduating with a doctorate in medicine in China. However, China's booming development and the Chinese people's kindness and perseverance have left me a deep impression. That's why I joined the China-Morocco Friendship and Exchange Association. I believe that Morocco can benefit from China's pioneering experience to get rid of poverty through development and provide adequate food and clothing for people.

In 1998, twelve years after leaving China, I had the pleasure of joining the Moroccan delegation headed by the former Minister Mr. Abdourahmane Yusuf to visit China. When we arrived in Beijing, I was amazed to find that Beijing has transformed into a modern metropolis with broad streets, row upon row of skyscrapers, as well as a myriad of cars, motorcycles, and bicycles running through the streets and alleys. People's life and dressing styles have become far more varied and fashionable. The per capita income in China has increased significantly. Since I am proficient in Chinese and familiar with Chinese customs, reporters in China often asked me about the situation. I told them about the radical changes in Beijing and how it has transformed from a huge village to a modern city that can rival the West's newest cities. I didn't even know how to get to the school I used to study. We also went to Qingdao in Shandong Province, also a modern city, where we visited some novel factories, such as the Haier production base. We witnessed the tremendous achievements of China in recent years.

The role of the CPC in poverty alleviation

There is no doubt that the Communist Party of China (CPC) has played a significant leading role in the national development to create a better life for people. What's worth mentioning is that despite the changes of state leaders, the decisions

中共会议的决定和长期计划仍能持续下去，每一任接替的领导人都沿着中国共产党的指导方向在脱贫致富中留下足迹。我们已经看到中国东部沿海地区发展所取得的成就，但中国共产党面临的挑战是如何发展和开发中国中西部地区，以及如何带领大批乡镇走出贫困。

以邓小平为主要代表的中国共产党建立的建设小康社会的目标，在全党和全国各民族人民共同努力下实现。2002 年举行的中国共产党第十六次全国代表大会，明确了 20 世纪前 20 年内达到全面建成小康社会的总体目标。

1994 年，中国公布了《国家八七扶贫攻坚计划》，力争用 7 年左右的时间基本解决全国农村 8000 万贫困人口的温饱问题，这是中国首次制定具体的减贫目标。2001 年，中国发布了《中国农村扶贫开发纲要（2001—2010 年）》，强调需要通过发展项目减少贫困。时任总理温家宝在全国减贫会议上表示，中国在减贫方面投入了巨额预算，中国的扶贫支出从 2001 年的 127.5 亿元增加到 2010 年的 349.3 亿元，年均增长11.9%。数据显示，2001—2010 年的扶贫总支出达到 2043.8 亿元。通过不懈努力，1978 年以来，中国的贫困人口减少了 2.5 亿，提前 5 年实现联合国制定的贫穷人口比例减半的目标。

2011 年，中国政府颁发的《中国农村扶贫开发的新进展》白皮书显示，中国农村贫困人口数量从 2000 年年底的 9422 万减少到 2010 年年底的 2688 万。

前任联合国开发计划署驻华副国别主任拿破仑·纳瓦罗说："中国的减贫历程是历史性的，意义非凡的。没有国家能像中国一样，短时间内帮助大量贫困人口脱贫。"

and long-term plans adopted at the CPC meetings go on in the same line. Each succeeding generation of leaders has followed the CPC's direction and made their contributions to poverty alleviation and development. Everyone has witnessed the achievements in the development of the eastern coastal areas of China. Today, the challenge facing the CPC is how to develop the central and western regions of China and how to help a large number of villages and towns get rid of poverty.

The goal of "building a moderately prosperous society" set by the CPC with Deng Xiaoping at the core is to be achieved through the concerted efforts of the whole Party and the people of all ethnic groups in China. In 2002, the 16th CPC National Congress made it clear to fulfill the overall goal of building a moderately prosperous society in all respects within the first 20 years of the century.

In 1994, China launched the Seven-Year Priority Poverty Alleviation Program (1994–2000) in a bid to basically ensure adequate food and clothing for 80 million poor people in rural China within seven years. This is the first time that China has set a specific goal in poverty alleviation. In 2001, China issued the Outline for Poverty Reduction and Development of China's Rural Areas (2001–2010), laying the stress on poverty alleviation through the development projects. At the National Conference on Development-driven Poverty Alleviation, then-Premier Wen Jiabao said that China had made a heavy investment in poverty alleviation, registering an average annual increase of 11.9% from RMB 12.75 billion in 2001 to RMB 34.93 billion in 2010. Relevant data showed that the total spending on poverty alleviation between 2001 and 2010 amounted to RMB 204.38 billion. As a result of unremitting efforts, China has reduced the poor population by 250 million since 1978 and achieved the United Nations' goal to halve the poor population five years ahead of schedule.

According to the white paper titled *New Progress in Development-oriented Poverty Reduction Program for Rural China* issued by the Chinese government in 2011, the rural poor population in China dropped from 94.22 million at the end of 2000 to 26.88 million at the end of 2010.

Napoleon Navarro, former deputy country director for UNDP China, said, "China's poverty reduction drive is historic and extraordinary. There are no other countries like China that can bring so many people out of poverty in such a short time."

During Jiang Zemin's presidency, he attached great importance to the

江泽民任国家主席期间，十分重视城市及沿海地区的发展。沿海地区在引进外资方面取得的巨大成就，不仅创造了繁荣向好的经济环境，还为大量从业者提供了劳动机会。胡锦涛主席力求协调中国的东部沿海和中、西部地区之间区域发展问题，努力缩小中国城乡差距。胡锦涛主席曾在中国的贫困地区积累了许多工作经验：年轻时曾在贫困的甘肃省工作两年；在西藏工作四年，任西藏自治区党委书记。

在 2010 年 11 月举行的全国减贫会议上，胡锦涛主席说："中国在减贫方面取得的显著成就，在促进世界经济增长、政治稳定、民族团结、边境安全、社会和谐、消除贫困等方面做出了巨大贡献。"他还表示，确保到 2020 年实现全面建成小康社会的奋斗目标。

胡锦涛主席在脱贫路上采取的重要举措还包括免征农民税收，加强公民与社会思想道德建设，进行反腐倡廉工作，建立健全社会公平保障体系。

2004 年 4 月，胡锦涛主席在陕西省考察时强调，各级党委和政府必须全面贯彻落实中央关于发展粮食生产、增加农民收入的政策措施，稳定农业在国民经济中的主要地位。

胡锦涛还表示："我们的总体目标是确保到 2020 年，我国的贫困人口不会再因吃不饱、穿不暖而发愁；确保他们有获得义务教育、基础医疗及住房保障的权利。"

如今，中华人民共和国能够稳步发展，中国共产党发挥了至关重要的作用：通过走进城乡，实地考察，倾听人民群众的诉求，结合理论与实践，制订出精准的解决方案；通过教育、媒体、讲座、宣讲等宣传方式，基本扫除文盲；加强政府与民众之间的凝聚力，从而更好地落实各项发展规划。

development of cities and coastal areas. The tremendous achievements in attracting foreign capital to the coastal areas have created a prosperous economic environment and provided job opportunities for a large number of workers. President Hu Jintao was committed to coordinated development between eastern coastal, central, and western regions and a narrower gap between urban and rural areas. President Hu Jintao accumulated rich experience from his work in impoverished areas of China. For instance, when he was young, he worked in the poverty-stricken areas in Gansu Province for two years and in Tibet for four years as the Party Secretary of the CPC Committee of the Tibet Autonomous Region.

At the National Conference on Development-driven Poverty Alleviation in November 2010, then-President Hu Jintao said, China's remarkable achievements in poverty reduction have contributed to economic growth, political stability, national unity, border security, and social harmony, and poverty eradication across the world." He also showed that efforts would be made to ensure that the goal of building a moderately prosperous society in all respects would be achieved by 2020.

Then President Hu Jintao adopted a host of other important measures for poverty alleviation, such as exempting farmers from taxation, raising intellectual and moral standards of citizens, combating corruption and promoting integrity, and establishing a system for guaranteeing fairness in society.

During his inspection tour in Shaanxi Province in April 2004, President Hu Jintao emphasized that party committees and governments at all levels must fully implement the central government's policies and measures for increasing food production and farmers' incomes, with the aim of consolidating the primary role of agriculture in the national economy.

Hu also noted that our overall goal is to ensure that by 2020, the poor people in our country will no longer worry about food or clothing and will enjoy compulsory education, basic medical care and housing security.

The steady growth of the People's Republic of China today should be attributed to the CPC's vital role. They went to urban and rural areas to conduct on-spot investigations, listen to the people's appeals, and develop targeted solutions through the combination of theory and practice. They eliminated illiteracy through education, media, lectures, presentations, and other means. They enhanced the cohesion between the government and the people and thus better implemented various development plans.

It is not difficult to see that China has followed an incremental approach to

我们不难看出，中国在实现改革开放和脱贫的目标上，采取的是循序渐进的策略。最初的改革只限定在一个区域，先试验，后推广。如先从深圳开始，再到上海浦东和山东。正所谓"摸着石头过河"。

关于中国的变化，我们还可以看出，中国城乡之间发展始于农民。改革开放初期，即20世纪70年代末、80年代初，我在中国读书的时候，邓小平决定以农村为发展中心，将土地从人民公社体制中解放出来，按照普遍公认的市场原则运作，既可以产生巨大的生产能力，又能带来迅速增长的经济收益。事实证明他的决定是正确的，在此期间农民的收入年增长率为18%。

自1996年中共中央、国务院决定尽快解决农村贫困人口温饱问题以来，中国就致力于推动扶贫协作，让发达的东部沿海地区带动落后的西部地区经济协作发展。

2000年，中国开始发展其西部地区，涉及甘肃、贵州、青海、陕西、四川、云南、宁夏、西藏、新疆、广西、内蒙古以及重庆。这些地区占中国国土总面积的70%，占中国总人口的30%，拥有丰富的土地和矿产资源，与十多个国家接壤，是对外开放的重要地带。中国政府在制订区域开发规划时，出台了一系列优惠政策，鼓励和引导外商到这些地区投资。跨国公司也已进入中国各主要领域，如商品贸易、信息技术、货运物流、金融和银行信贷等。

2003年，中共中央、国务院发布《关于实施东北地区等老工业基地振兴战略的若干意见》，社会保障试点、增值税转型、豁免企业历史欠税、国有企业政策性破产等各项振兴战略政策已付诸实施。

achieving the goals of reform and opening up, and poverty alleviation. The reform was initially piloted in a particular area before being extended to other areas. For example, the reform was first piloted in Shenzhen before being carried out in Pudong of Shanghai and Shandong. As the saying goes, "We wade across the river by feeling the stones."

Regarding the changes in China, we can also see that China's urban and rural development began with farmers. At the beginning of the reform and opening up in the late 1970s and early 1980s, when I was a student in China, Deng Xiaoping decided to center on the rural development and liberate the land from the people's commune system for operations in line with the widely acknowledged market principles. In this way, it could produce huge production capacity and rapidly increase economic benefits. His decision has been tried and trusted, as evidenced by an annual increase of 18% in the farmers' income.

Since 1996 when the CPC Central Committee and the State Council decided to meet the basic living needs of the poor in rural areas as soon as possible, China has been committed to promoting cooperation on poverty alleviation and mobilizing the developed eastern coastal areas to assist the western regions towards coordinated economic development.

In 2000, China began to step up efforts in the development of the western region, involving Gansu, Guizhou, Qinghai, Shaanxi, Sichuan, Yunnan, Ningxia, Tibet, Xinjiang, Guangxi, Inner Mongolia, and Chongqing. The region covers 70% of China's total land area and has 30% of China's total population, boasting abundant land and mineral resources. Bordering more than a dozen countries, the region is an important area to open up to the world. The Chinese government issued a series of preferential policies in the regional development plan to encourage and attract foreign investment in the region. Transnational companies have entered almost all major sectors in China, such as commodity trade, information technology, freight logistics, finance, and bank credit.

In 2003, the CPC Central Committee and the State Council issued the *Opinions on Implementing the Strategies for the Revitalization of Old Industrial Bases in the Northeast and Other Parts of the Country*. Various revitalization strategies related to the pilot projects of social security, transformation of value-added tax, exempting companies from outstanding taxes, and the policy-mandated bankruptcy, had been put into practice.

2004 年，为促进中国中部省份（河南、湖北、湖南、江西、安徽和山西 6 省）经济发展，中国政府提出了中部崛起战略。

中国中部地区是连接中国东西部、南北方的枢纽。此外，中部地区人口密度大，拥有全国约 10.7% 的土地，却承载全国约 28.81% 的人口，创造全国约 19.5% 的 GDP。中部崛起战略的重点是加强中部地区的粮食生产能力，培育全国煤炭基础和优质的原料基础，建立全面的运输系统。

为建设和谐社会，创新区域发展方法，提高各地区及全国综合实力，2012 年 4 月，国务院批准了 11 个综合配套改革试点地区。

1996—2016 年，20 年间，中国东部沿海 9 个省、直辖市向内地的 10 个省、自治区、直辖市累计提供 137.2 亿元的经济援助；在山区修建 21500 公里道路；建造共计 1690 个医疗中心。

改革开放的进程为年轻人创造了更多新动力。改革开放期间，成千上万的年轻人投身创业浪潮，这种行为又被称作"下海"。这批青年建立了约 43.5 万家私营企业，其中不少人成为"百万富翁"。在 1993 年，仅有 10 万余人放弃政府机构或事业单位的工作，建立公司或从事海外工作，而在 1992 年，这个数字超过 60 万。其中大多数人凭借"下海"使自己和家人摆脱贫困，也有不少人带领自己所在的村庄摆脱了贫困。

每年都有数以亿计的外国游客到中国旅游，这要归功于中国多个省市国际机场的普及，以及建在崎岖地形之上，连接各省市、城乡的铁路。交通的连通与便捷有助于消除城乡之间的差距，促进旅游业的发展，直接或间接地创造更多就业机会，从而使许多城镇和村庄摆脱贫困。

In 2004, in order to facilitate the economic growth in central China, involving six provinces of Henan, Hubei, Hunan, Jiangxi, Anhui, and Shanxi, the Chinese government introduced the strategy to develop the central region.

Central China is a hub connecting eastern, western, southern, and northern regions. Besides, the densely-populated central region is home to 28.81% of China's population with merely 10.7% of the country's land, contributing about 19.5% of the national GDP. The key to developing the central region is to increase the food production capacity, develop it into the national base for coal and high-quality raw materials, and establish a comprehensive transportation system.

In April 2012, in a bid to build a harmonious society, explore innovative approaches for regional development, and improve the overall strength of various regions and the country, the State Council approved eleven pilot areas for comprehensive and integrated reform.

During the two decades from 1996 to 2016, nine provinces and municipalities along the eastern coast of China provided a total of RMB 13.72 billion in economic assistance to help build 21,500 kilometers of roads in mountainous areas and a total of 1,690 medical centers in 10 provinces, municipalities, and autonomous regions in the central and western areas.

The reform and opening up provides even greater impetus for young people. Thousands of young people joined in the wave of entrepreneurship, which was also dubbed the "plunge into the commercial sea." These young people founded about 435,000 private enterprises, and many of them turned into "millionaires." In 1993, only more than 100,000 people gave up their work in government bodies and public institutions for entrepreneurship or overseas employment. The number was over 600,000 in 1992. Most of them got themselves, their families, and even their hometown out of poverty by venturing into business.

China receives hundreds of millions of foreign tourists every year. This should be attributed to the establishment of international airports in many provinces and cities in China and the railways running through the rugged terrain that connect provinces and cities. The connectivity and convenience of transportation shorten the distance between urban and rural areas; facilitate the development of tourism in multiple regions; create job opportunities directly or indirectly; and boost the development of tourism culture. All these play a part to help many towns and villages get rid of poverty.

所有这一切的结果是，在过去的 20 年中，中国十几亿人的生存状况发生了不可思议的变化。为低收入人群提供更全面的生活保障这一目标仍在进行，这是时代的奇迹。

我眼中的中国扶贫

中国人民对外友好协会

通过"中摩友好交流协会"与"中国人民对外友好协会"，我们常受邀前往中国不同的地区参观访问，了解中国的成就，特别是那些曾经贫困的农村地区。"中国人民对外友好协会"与其他中国民间组织一样，积极参与减贫工作。

宁夏回族自治区

宁夏是我在中国访问次数最多的地区之一。"宁夏人民对外友好协会"与"中摩友好交流协会"达成合作协议，我于 2012 年当选"中摩友好交流协会"会长，并应"宁夏人民对外友好协会"邀请参加在宁夏举办的"中国—阿拉伯国家博览会"和中阿经贸论坛。2016 年，我很荣幸获得摩洛哥—宁夏荣誉大使奖。每一次抵达宁夏省会银川市的时候，我都会被这座城市变化之快所震惊。中阿博览会是推动中国与"一带一路"沿线国，特别是阿拉伯国家经贸交流与合作的重要平台，对促进经济发展，提高宁夏地区的对外开放水平，为全省打赢脱贫攻坚战具有十分重要的作用。这也是中国为扶贫减贫、发展地区经济开展的又一举措。展览每两年举行一次，由中国商务部、中国国际贸易促进委员会和宁夏回族自治区地方政府共同主办。

As a result, the living conditions of hundreds of millions of Chinese people have undergone incre-dible changes over the past two decades. Currently, China is still striving toward the goal of providing more comprehensive life security for low-income people. China has made a miracle of the era.

China's poverty alleviation in my eyes

The Chinese People's Association for Friendship with Foreign Countries (CPAFFC)

As part of the exchange programs between China-Morocco Friendship Association and CPAFFC, we were invited to visit different regions of China to learn about China's achievements, especially those rural areas that were once in dire poverty. Like other non-governmental organizations in China, the CPAFFC has played an active part in poverty alleviation.

Ningxia Hui Autonomous Region

Ningxia is one of my most-visited regions in China. The Ningxia People's Association for Friendship with Foreign Countries reached an agreement with China-Morocco Friendship and Exchange Association. Having been elected as the Chairman of China-Morocco Friendship and Exchange Association in 2012, I was invited by the Ningxia People's Association for Friendship with Foreign Countries to attend the China-Arab States Expo and the China-Arab States Economic and Trade Forum held in Ningxia. In 2016, I was honored to receive the Morocco-Ningxia Honorary Ambassador Award. Every time I arrive in Yinchuan, the capital of Ningxia, I was amazed by the rapid changes in this city. The China-Arab States Expo is an important platform for promoting economic and trade exchanges and cooperation between China and the countries along the "Belt and Road," especially Arab states. It plays a significant role in promoting economic growth, expanding the opening-up of Ningxia, and winning the fight against poverty in the region. This is also another step taken by China to alleviate poverty and develop the regional economy. The biennial expo is co-sponsored by the Ministry of Commerce of China, the China Council for the Promotion of International Trade, and the Ningxia Hui Autonomous Region's local government.

福建省与宁夏的扶贫协作是中国东部沿海与西部扶贫合作的典范。自1996年福建省与宁夏决定开展扶贫合作以来,两地在各领域开展合作,建立两岸城市结对子关系,促进企业间合作与经验交流。2019年,多项协议已签订,多个项目投资共计131.2亿元,其中福建贡献3.5亿元。自2016年起,在福建省的支持下,5600多家福建企业和客商落户宁夏。

四川省

"中国人民对外友好协会"和"中摩友好交流协会"携手四川省政府,每年在四川和摩洛哥分别举办一次题为"中外历史文化名城对话会"的论坛,摩洛哥和四川的多个城市通过讲座和商务会议等活动进行文化商贸交流。上一次论坛是在成都举办的,论坛后我们前往雅安市,参观了当地茶田和村庄。在那里,我们了解到农民如何通过种茶脱贫致富,向导还向我们介绍了当地的旅游业发展。我们得知,雅安附近有一些山,那里的贫困居民使用铁矿石来建造住所,政府已将18多万人安置到山脚下的新居里。我们沿着山间的公路,从成都到雅安,再到眉山,之后返回成都,沿途有许多隧道。在过去,因为大山之隔,交通十分不便。如今道路畅通,促进四川开发旅游业,也为地方产品的销售提供了便利,以此带动区域经济协调发展。我们还参观了一个曾遭受2008年大地震重创的贫困市,如今已重建为一个现代化城镇。中国通过电视台举办的抗震救灾大型募捐活动筹集款项超过15亿元,这充分表明了中国政府和人民在抵抗自然灾害、攻克脱贫难关方面的团结力量是坚不可摧的。

众所周知,四川是大熊猫的故乡,除了欣赏自然风光,也有许多游客怀着对大熊猫可爱形象的好奇和向往前往四川,四川旅游业的发展也顺势蓬勃起来,这对摆脱贫困和提升居民收入有着很大的作用。

The Fujian-Ningxia cooperation on poverty alleviation is an example of such collaboration between the eastern coastal areas and western regions in China. Since Fujian and Ningxia decided to cooperate in poverty alleviation in 1996, they have carried out cooperation in various fields, established sister-city ties, promoted cooperation between enterprises, and shared experience. In 2019, a number of agreements were signed, and an investment of RMB 13.12 billion was made in multiple projects, of which Fujian contributed RMB 350 million. As of 2016, with Fujian Province's support, more than 5,600 enterprises and merchants from Fujian have settled in Ningxia.

Sichuan Province

The CPAFFC and China-Morocco Friendship and Exchange Association joined hands with Sichuan Provincial Government to hold the Forum on "Dialogue Between Renowned Historical and Cultural Cities in China and Foreign Countries" in Sichuan Province and Morocco every year. Multiple cities in Morocco and Sichuan conducted cultural and business exchanges through lectures, business meetings, and other activities. The latest forum was held in Chengdu in October. After the forum, we visited the tea fields and villages in Ya'an City to see how local farmers got rid of poverty by growing tea. The tour guide also told us about the tourism development in the city. We learned that in some mountainous areas near Ya'an, the impoverished residents use iron ore to build their dwelling houses. The government has relocated more than 180,000 residents to their new homes at the foot of the mountains. We drove along the mountainous roads and passed through many tunnels on our way from Chengdu to Ya'an, Meishan, and then back to Chengdu. In the past, transportation was very inconvenient because of the mountains. Today, convenient transportation has promoted tourism development in Sichuan and facilitated local products' sales, thereby boosting the regional economy's coordinated development. We also visited a poor city almost devastated by the 2008 earthquake, but now it has been rebuilt into a modern town. China once raised more than RMB 1.5 billion through large-scale fund-raising activities organized by TV stations for earthquake relief. This fully demonstrates that the unity of the Chinese government and people in resisting natural disasters and overcoming poverty is impregnable.

It's well known that Sichuan is the hometown of giant pandas. Apart from the

政府"两会"报告显示，2019 年，四川省投入 1500 亿元，共帮助 50 万人脱贫，31 个计划摘帽贫困县达到退出标准。目前，尽管面临新冠肺炎疫情的考验，四川省仍继续跟进实施减贫计划，帮助贫困人口脱贫，以使他们不重返贫困。

山东省

继我随摩洛哥总理访问团首次访华之后，山东省成为我到访次数最多的一个省份。山东省的飞速发展、日新月异的变化以及大量项目的实施都让我震惊。其中变化最大的要数完成脱贫的日照市。30 年前，日照还是山东一个贫穷的小城。为了脱贫，当地领导从中国南方引进一批茶树进行种植试验，试验的成功带动了大量贫困家庭脱贫致富，旅游业也应运而生，昔日的日照如今已成为现代化大都市。

2015 年，我前往临沂参观新临沂市场，市场内出售上万家工厂的产品，这个市场为临沂市的城市发展做出了巨大的贡献，因此也被称为临沂商城。临沂有 568 个贫困村庄，25.5 万户贫困家庭，24.2 万贫困人口，占全省贫困人口的六分之一。2016 年，市县财政共设立扶贫开发专项资金 3.71 亿元，脱贫 29 万人，帮助 255 个贫困村摘下贫困帽子。

甘肃省

2017 年，应甘肃省政府邀请，"中摩友好交流协会"派出两人前往甘肃进行了为期一个月的考察学习。这不仅是了解甘肃情况的机会，也是对甘肃在兰州、张掖、嘉峪关、敦煌等地发展经济成功经验的一次

natural scenery, many tourists were attracted to Sichuan out of curiosity by the cute giant pandas. As a result, tourism in Sichuan has also flourished as a great boon for the locals to get rid of poverty and increase income.

According to the government work report, in 2019, Sichuan Province invested RMB 150 billion to help 500,000 people get out of poverty, and 31 counties have met the criteria for being deregistered as impoverished counties. Currently, despite the COVID-19 pandemic, Sichuan Province continues to follow up the implementation of poverty reduction plans to help the poor people get rid of poverty and make sure that they won't return to poverty.

Shandong Province

Following my first visit to China with the delegation headed by the Prime Minister of Morocco, Shandong Province has been my most visited place. I was astonished at the rapid development, drastic changes, and the progress of many projects. Rizhao City has undergone the most fundamental changes brought by eradication of poverty. Thirty years ago, Rizhao was still a poor town in Shandong. In order to get rid of poverty, local leaders introduced a batch of tea trees from southern China for trial plantation. The success of the experiment helped many low-income families get rid of poverty and become rich. As tourism gradually thrived, Rizhao has developed into a modern metropolis.

In 2015, I went to Linyi to visit the new Linyi market that sells products from tens of thousands of factories. The market has made great contributions to the development of Linyi City, and thus it is also called Linyi Mall. In Linyi City, there are 568 impoverished villages, 255,000 impoverished families, and 242,000 poor people, accounting for one-sixth of the province's total poor population. In 2016, the municipal and county governments allocated RMB 371 million as the special fund for poverty alleviation and development. The fund lifted 290,000 people out of poverty and helped 255 villages get deregistered from the list of poor villages.

Gansu Province

In 2017, at the invitation of Gansu Provincial Government, the China-Morocco Friendship and Exchange Association sent two people to Gansu Province for a one-month study tour. It's an excellent opportunity to get to know about Gansu's

学习。代表团受到当地政府和人民的热情接待，我们对甘肃省的稳定安全印象深刻，当地居民认真工作的精神也让人念念不忘。甘肃省因沙漠和缺水成为中国最贫穷的省份之一，为此甘肃省政府采取了许多扶贫措施，全面精准扶贫。2012 年至 2018 年间，甘肃成功地将省内贫困人口从 692 万减少至 111 万人，全省贫困人口比例从 33.2% 下降到 5.6%，75 个贫困县区中有 36 个已经完成脱贫。甘肃凭借其处于丝绸之路枢纽地带的优势，发展农业，并向丝绸之路沿线国家和地区出口苹果、小番茄、草莓等产品，并通过扩大农田的方式防治荒漠化。另外，由于其地形和历史遗迹的多样性，旅游业得以发展，甘肃成为一个重要的旅游目的地，从而促进了该省的发展。

习近平主席的脱贫攻坚路

每当我访问中国，目睹中国是如何实现飞跃式变化时，都会想起曾在北京语言大学学习汉语期间，读过毛泽东一篇题为《愚公移山》的文章。这也更加印证了一句话：对于坚持的人来说，没有什么是不可能的。

自习近平领导中国共产党以来，我每年访问中国的次数都在三次以上。我注意到，在中国不同城市的街道上，都能看见关于习近平中国梦理念的宣传标语。我问过很多人这标语的含意，得到的是不同的回答。起初，我对"中国梦"的理解是，实现每个中国人的梦想。后来我阅读了 2013 年 3 月 23 日习近平主席在俄罗斯莫斯科国际关系学院发表的演讲稿，他对中国梦的概念解释如下："实现中华民族伟大复兴，是近代以来中国人民最伟大的梦想，我们称之为'中国梦'，基本内涵是实现国家富强、民族振兴、人民幸福。"我才知道，

situation and draw on the economic success in Lanzhou, Zhangye, Jiayuguan, Dunhuang, and other places in the province. The local government and people warmly received the delegation. We were deeply impressed by the stability, security, and hard-working people in the province. Due to the deserts and water shortage, Gansu was one of the poorest provinces in China. Therefore, the local government adopted a host of measures for targeted and all-around poverty alleviation. From 2012 to 2018, Gansu reduced its poor population from 6.92 million to 1.11 million and the ratio of the poor people in the province from 33.2% to 5.6%. In addition, 36 of the 75 impoverished counties have been lifted out of poverty. Located at the hub of the Silk Road, Gansu Province was able to develop agriculture and export apples, small tomatoes, strawberries, and other products to the countries and regions along the Silk Road. Meanwhile, it could combat desertification through the expansion of farmland. Furthermore, thanks to its varied topography and historic sites, tourism has flourished, making it an important tourist destination. All these have boosted the development of the province.

Chinese President Xi Jinping's way out of poverty

Every time I visited China and witnessed the revolutionary changes, I would recall the article by Mao Zedong entitled *Foolish Old Man Who Removed the Mountains* that I read during my Chinese stay at Beijing Language and Culture University. It also lends substance to the argument that nothing is impossible for those who persevere.

Since Xi Jinping served as the CPC leader, I've visited China more than three times every year. Along the streets in different cities, I noticed the posters about the "Chinese dream" proposed by Xi Jinping. I inquired many people about the meaning of the Chinese dream and got diverse answers. Initially, I thought the Chinese Dream meant to realize the dream of each one of Chinese people. One day, I read the manuscript of Xi's speech at the Moscow State Institute of International Relations, in which he interpreted the Chinese dream as follows. "Achieving the rejuvenation of the Chinese nation has been the greatest dream of the Chinese people since the start of modern times. We call it the Chinese dream. Essentially speaking, it pertains to making China prosperous and strong, rejuvenating the nation, and bringing happiness to the Chinese people." That's when I realized that the Chinese dream is

中国梦是领导和人民的梦想并存。脱贫攻坚，正是实现中国梦的重要行动。这就是习近平自执政以来一直为之奋斗的目标。

习近平在其青年时期就奋战在脱贫战役中。20 世纪 60 年代末、70年代初，习近平曾在陕西省延川县文安驿公社梁家河大队工作，致力于发展生产力，改善人民生活条件；80 年代初在河北省正定县工作期间，大力推行家庭联产承包责任制；80 年代末、90 年代初，习近平曾在福建省任宁德地委书记一职。

习近平在《摆脱贫困》一书中分享了他关于脱贫的经验，他总是将发展经济作为首要目标。他喜欢"滴水石穿"这个理念，他在书中写道："滴水穿石的自然景观，我是在插队落户时便耳闻目睹，叹为观止的。直至现在，其锲而不舍的情景仍每每浮现在眼前，我从中领略了不少生命和运动的哲理。"他还用"弱鸟先飞"来激发贫困地区的人民摆脱贫困的自信心。

习近平为此做的"四个尝试"分别是：

- 鼓励领导干部深入基层倾听百姓意见和心声
- 深入基层处理民生问题
- 与基层组织机构合力调查、研究、解决问题
- 深入基层研究如何完善和落实党的原则和政治要求

习近平在邓小平"一个中心，两个基本点"（以经济建设为中心，坚持四项基本原则，坚持改革开放）理论指导下，将主要工作集中在发展农业和扶贫上。其中一项成就是"闽宁协作"，建立东西部合作模式，帮扶脱贫。在他担任浙江省委书记时，发起了"千村示范，万村整治"美丽村庄建设工程。

shared by both Chinese leaders and the Chinese people. Poverty alleviation is an important move towards achieving the Chinese dream, as well as a goal that Xi has been pursuing since he took office.

Xi Jinping has been dedicated to poverty alleviation since he was young. In the late 1960s and early 1970s, he served as the leader of several areas in dire poverty. He once worked in the Liangjiahe production team of Wen'anyi Commune, Yanchuan County, Shaanxi Province, committed to increasing productivity and improving people's living conditions. During his work in Zhengding County, Hebei Province, he vigorously promoted the system of household contract responsibility. In the late 1980s and early 1990s, Xi Jinping served as the CPC Ningde Prefectural Committee secretary in Fujian Province.

In the book *Up and Out of Poverty*, Xi shared his firsthand experience in poverty alleviation. He always regards economic development as the primary goal. He likes the idea that constant dripping wears away a stone. He wrote in the book, "Constant dripping wears away a stone. I witnessed this natural phenomenon as early as when I was working in the production team in the countryside. It's breathtaking. Until now, the scene of persistent dripping always swirls in my mind. I've learned a lot of the philosophy of life and motion from the phenomenon." Xi also said that "a slow sparrow should make an early start," in a bid to boost the confidence of the people in the impoverished areas to get rid of poverty. To this end, Xi Jinping made the following "four attempts:"

- Encourage the leading cadres to go to the grassroots to listen to the ideas and opinions of the people
- Go to the grassroots to address the problems concerning the people's livelihood
- Cooperate with the grassroots organizations to investigate, study and solve problems
- Go to the grassroots to study how to improve and implement the Party's principles and political requirements

Under the guidance of Deng Xiaoping's theory about "one central task; two basic points" (the central task of economic development and the two basic points of adhering to the Four Cardinal Principles and the policy of reform and opening up), Xi Jinping focused on the main work on agricultural development and poverty alleviation. The "Fujian-Ningxia Cooperation" is an achievement in this regard that

79

习近平主席曾在国际减贫与发展高层论坛上深有感触地说："40多年来，我先后在中国县、市、省、中央工作，扶贫始终是我工作的一个重要内容，我花的精力最多。"

2013年，习近平主席前往中国南方湖南省进行考察，首次提出"精准扶贫"。他指出，每个贫困个体之间生活情况存在差异，要因地制宜、精准扶贫，在2020年彻底消除贫困，全面建成小康社会。截至2014年，全中国有14个集中连片特困地区，12.8万个贫困村庄和近3000万个贫困家庭。截至2015年，仍然有5575万人处于贫困状态。要完成2020年农村贫困人口全部脱贫的任务，根据测算平均每年必须使1200万人摆脱贫困，即每月要有100万人脱贫。而这些地区大都是地形复杂的农村及少数民族聚居地，生存环境艰难，发展成本高昂。

数据显示，2013年至2018年，中国贫困人口减少6800多万，这是摩洛哥人口的两倍，贫困发生率由10.2%下降到3.1%。2012年年底，中国贫困人口为9998万；2017年年底，中国成功降低了这一数字，贫困人口降至3046万人；到2019年年底，贫困人口进一步下降至551万人。贫困县区由832个减少到52个，贫困人口的收入大幅增加，生活得到改善。为进一步发展，防止返贫，中国政府在教育、医疗、技术、基础设施等领域及相关产业方面出台了一系列措施，旨在让贫困人口参与各种项目，为失业者提供更多就业机会。

established a cooperation model between the eastern and western regions for poverty alleviation. When he served as the party secretary of the CPC Zhejiang Provincial Committee, Xi initiated building beautiful villages that aimed for 1,000 new demonstration villages and 10,000 more improved ones.

While addressing the Global Poverty Reduction and Development Forum, President Xi Jinping once said with deep feelings that "For more than 40 years, I have worked in counties, cities, provinces, and the central government in China. However, poverty alleviation has always been an important part of my work. I've dedicated most of my energy to the work."

During his visit to Hunan Province in southern China in 2013, President Xi Jinping put forward the concept of "targeted poverty alleviation" for the first time. He noted that each case of poverty is different. We must tailor measures to local conditions and target poverty alleviation to eradicate poverty and to build a moderately prosperous society in all respects by 2020. As of 2014, there were 14 contiguous impoverished areas, 128,000 impoverished villages, and nearly 30 million needy families in China. By 2015, there were 55.75 million people still living in poverty. Calculations showed that to fulfill the task of lifting all rural poor people out of poverty by 2020, we must lift 12 million people out of poverty every year on average or 1 million people each month. What made it more difficult is that most of these areas are villages with complex landforms and settlements inhabited by ethnic groups where the environment is harsh, and development costs are high.

The latest data shows that from 2013 to 2018, China reduced its poor population by more than 68 million, which is twice the Morocco population. During the same period, the incidence of poverty in China dropped from 10.2% to 3.1%. The poor people in China dropped from 99.98 million at the end of 2012 to 30.46 million at the end of 2017, before reaching 5.51 million at the end of 2019. The number of poverty-stricken counties fell from 832 to 52. The income of the poor has increased substantially, and their lives have improved significantly. To promote further development and prevent a relapse into poverty, the Chinese government has introduced a series of measures in education, medical care, technology, infrastructure, and related industries, to engage the poor in various projects and provide more job opportunities for the unemployed.

Since the start of reform and opening up in China, human history has witnessed

自改革开放政策实施以来，人类历史见证了中国文明的迅速崛起。随着改革开放政策的实施，中国经历了人类历史上规模最大、最为迅速的城市化进程，取得了令人瞩目的成就。截至 2015 年年底，中国城市人口达到 7.71 亿，常住人口城镇化率达到 56.1%，超过了全球历史平均水平。与一些发达国家相比，城市居民人口比例从 20% 上升到 40%，英国用了 120 年，法国用了 100 年，德国用了 80 年，美国用了 40 年，而中国只用了 22 年（1981 年至 2003 年）。

脱贫取得的阶段性胜利，得益于中国政府在习近平主席领导下付出的巨大努力，是所有基层组织和人民群众团结协作的结果。习近平主席曾这样说："人心齐，泰山移。脱贫致富不仅仅是贫困地区的事，也是全社会的事。"

在东西部地区扶贫协作的问题上，2016 年 7 月 20 日，习近平主席主持召开"东西部扶贫协作座谈会"，并发表重要讲话。他指出，东西部扶贫协作，是推动区域协调发展、协同发展、共同发展的大战略，是加强区域合作、优化产业布局、拓展对内对外开放新空间的大布局，是实现先富帮后富、最终实现共同富裕目标的大举措。

习近平多次深入贫困地区走访考察，为各级领导干部树立榜样。2012 年，在担任中共中央总书记不到一个半月之后，他走访了河北省阜平县，深入了解当地乡民生活状况。这是当时中国最贫困的地区之一，习近平说："如果我们想了解贫困状况，就必须了解到真实情况，我们可以通过走访最贫困的地方来了解这一点。"在过去的 5 年中，习近平主席进行了 30 多次实地考察，几乎所有考察都涉及贫困这一话题，中国最贫穷的 14 个地区无一落下。

the rapid rise of Chinese civilization. Meanwhile, China has experienced the most massive and fastest urbanization in human history and made remarkable achievements. By the end of 2015, China's urban population reached 771 million, and the urbanization rate of permanent residents hit 56.1%, higher than the global historical average level. As for some developed countries, it took 120 years for Britain, 100 years for France, 80 years for Germany, and 40 years for the United States to raise the proportion of urban residents from 20% to 40%, but it took merely 22 years (1981-2003) for China.

The phased victory in poverty alleviation should be attributed to the Chinese government's tremendous efforts under the leadership of President Xi Jinping, as well as the concerted efforts and cooperation of all grassroots organizations and people. President Xi Jinping once said, "When people work with one mind, they can even remove Mount Taishan. Poverty alleviation is not merely a concern of the poverty-stricken areas, but of the whole society."

Regarding the collaboration on poverty alleviation between the eastern and western regions, President Xi Jinping presided over the Symposium on the Collaboration on Poverty Alleviation between the Eastern and Western Regions and delivered an important speech. He pointed out that the collaboration on poverty alleviation between the eastern and western regions is an important strategy to promote coordinated, synchronized, and joint development of various regions. It's a grand plan for strengthening regional cooperation, optimizing the industrial layout, and creating new spaces for expanding the opening up at home and abroad. It's an important measure to mobilize the rich to help the poor and finally achieve the goal of shared prosperity.

As the Chinese President, Xi Jinping has made multiple visits to poverty-stricken areas and set an example for officials at all levels. Less than one and a half months after assuming the General Secretary of the CPC Central Committee's role in 2012, Xi visited Fuping County in Hebei Province to learn about the local people's living conditions. It was one of the most impoverished areas in China at the time. Xi Jinping said, "To know about poverty, we must learn the truth and facts. To this end, we could visit the most impoverished areas." Over the past five years, President Xi Jinxing made more than 30 fact-finding trips, and poverty has been a concern of each trip. He has visited all of the 14 poorest areas in China.

Moreover, we must mention a vital initiative proposed by Xi Jinping in 2013 —

这里我们必须提到习近平在 2013 年发起的一项重要举措，即"一带一路"倡议。包括摩洛哥在内的很多国家参与了这项倡议。这一举措对增加人们收益和脱贫产生了巨大影响：为中国人开辟了许多市场；良好的投资环境让不少中国企业从中受益；创造出更多的中国境内外就业机会。很多中国工厂面向贫困地区开放，鼓励他们从事一些家庭生产和简单的工业劳动，帮助许多村庄摆脱贫困，并改善了许多家庭的收入状况。

最后的话

中国政府的基本目标是在 2020 年摆脱贫困，即实现两项保证：确保贫困人口摆脱贫困，确保所有贫困县摘帽。在全球遭受新冠肺炎疫情考验的情况下，中国这一目标的实现，意味着中国将创造史无前例的经济奇迹。目前，中国取得的脱贫成绩已经比世界银行所预估的提前了 10 年。阿拉伯经济专家阿布·加扎利集团主席塔拉勒·阿布·加扎利，是中国提名的十位中阿友谊的重要贡献者之一（我很荣幸也成为其中之一），他曾说："没有中国，整个世界的经济都将处于低迷状态。"中国摆脱贫困的经验是历史上前所未有的独特经验，世界将从中受益。

the Belt and Road Initiative. Many countries, including Morocco, have participated in the initiative. It played a huge role in increasing people's income and eliminating poverty. It opened up more markets for the Chinese people. It facilitated the construction of a good business environment that benefited many Chinese firms. It created more job opportunities in China and other countries. Many Chinese factories opened their doors to the poor areas, encouraged the poor people to engage in household production and simple industrial work, helped many villages get rid of poverty, and increased many families' income.

Epilogue

The Chinese government's fundamental goal is to eliminate poverty in 2020, which means to ensure that the impoverished population is lifted out of poverty and poor counties rid themselves of the poverty tag. While the world is undergoing the test of the COVID-19 pandemic, China will create an unprecedented economic miracle to achieve the goal. Currently, China's progress in poverty alleviation has been ten years ahead of the schedule as predicted by the World Bank. The economic expert Talal Abu-Ghazaleh, Chairman of Talal Abu-Ghazaleh Global, is one of the ten important contributors to China-Arab friendship nominated by China (I am honored to be one of them as well). He once said, "Without China, the entire global economy will be in a downturn." China's experience in poverty alleviation is unique and unprecedented in history, and the world will benefit from it.

安东篱
Antonia Finnane

脱贫致富

Out of Poverty

安东篱，法国人，毕业于巴黎狄德罗大学和巴黎索邦大学，主攻人文和文学，现任中法文化交流协会主席，巴黎国立东方语言文化学院讲师、语言学院法语教师，并为多位研究生辅导方法学。研究涉及"一带一路"项目中的文化、经济和地缘政治层面。曾参加国际写作大赛并获得奖项，多年来持续参加国际著名期刊的撰写工作。曾为国家大剧院翻译戏剧作品《人生天地间》和姚国强的纪录片《拉法兰：我看了西安》，译有雪漠的短篇小说《新疆爷》，将在《塞纳河上的中国》文学期刊刊登，即将翻译《莎尔娃蒂的情书，见信如面》。

Antonia Finnane is a French, who has graduated from Paris Diderot University and Paris Sorbonne University, majoring in humanities and literature. Currently, he is chairman of the Sino-French Cultural Exchange Association, a lecturer at the Paris National Institute of Oriental Languages and Culture, a French teacher of the Institute of Languages, and tutoring many graduate students on methodology. His research involves the cultural, economic, and geopolitical aspects of the "Belt and Road" Initiative. He has participated in the international writing contest CastelDi and is an award winner. He has been contributing to internationally renowned journals for many years. He has translated the drama *Life Between Heaven* and *Earth* for the National Center for the Performing Arts and Yao Guoqiang's documentary *Raffarin: I Saw Xi'an*. He has also translated Xue Mo's short story *Sir Xinjiang* to be published in the *Chine-sur-Seine* literary journal. He is going to translate *Salvathi's Love Letter*, *Seeing Like Seeing You*.

导言：全球背景、框架和国际目标

在对"一带一路"倡议进行了长期研究并观察中国在过去 10 年内发生的巨大变化后，我们很高兴对 CCSTT 的提议做出积极回应，尽我们所能，阐明减贫这一至关重要的问题。中国在减少世界贫困和极端贫困方面的直接与间接参与，是学术界重点研究的现象，也是人类历史上的一项独特事业。在过去 25 年里，中国的脱贫人数超过同期全球脱贫人数的三分之二，中国对非洲交通基础设施的投资（2015 年正式通车的亚的斯亚贝巴轻轨，2016 年 10 月正式通车的亚的斯亚贝巴—吉布提铁路，2017 年竣工的蒙巴萨—内罗毕标准轨距铁路，以及 2018 年正式启动的吉布提自由贸易区）为当地居民提供了就业机会，促进了流动性。这些项目对于帮助非洲实现繁荣具有重要意义，世界银行报告《2018 年贫困与共享繁荣：拼出贫困的拼图》指出，到 2030 年，近90% 的贫困人口将来自非洲撒哈拉以南地区。中非关系历史悠久，目前正处于重大发展时期。2019 年 11 月，塞内加尔经济展望办公室主任穆巴拉克·罗提出，非洲人民应以中国模式为榜样并从中获取灵感。罗赞扬了中国政府数十年来坚持的战略，并说："中国抗击贫困 30 年取得了真正的成功，是值得称赞的。"

因此，我们不能仅关注扶贫本身，更要关注扶贫过程的时间及范围。中国仅经历了一代人的时间就实现全球超过十分之一的人口（按净值计算）摆脱赤贫。此外，在意识形态上，如果没有代代努力和自我牺牲的精神，中国是不可能获得成功的。《摆脱贫困》（1990 年 3 月）一书介绍了这一点，书中使用了一个形象的比喻：滴水穿石。的确，历史、经济和地理等因素往往具有悠久的历史，它们对人类的命运及发展愿景具有持久的影响。然而，我们不可能"一直等待确保条件成熟或者以牺牲必要的基础设施为代价来一味地追求结果，而是要牢牢把握现实，努力

Introduction: Global Context, Framework, and International Targets

We have conducted long-term research on the "Belt and Road" Initiative and observed the tremendous changes that have taken place in China in the past ten years. Based on that, we are happy to respond positively to CCSTT's proposal and do our best to clarify the vital issue of poverty reduction. China's participation in reducing poverty and extreme poverty in the world, both direct and indirect, is a well-documented phenomenon within academia.[1] It is also a unique undertaking in the history of humanity. China reduced more than two-thirds of the global poverty within its territorial boundaries over the past 25 years. Simultaneously, its investments in transport infrastructure in Africa (Addis Ababa Light Rail in 2015, Addis Ababa–Djibouti Railway inaugurated in October 2016, Mombasa–Nairobi Standard Gauge Railway in 2017, and Djibouti Free Trade Zone in 2018) have provided local employment opportunities and new mobility. These projects are essential for helping Africa achieve prosperity. According to the recent World Bank report[2], *Poverty and Shared Prosperity 2018: Piecing Together the Poverty Puzzle*, nearly nine out of ten needy people will have been in sub-Saharan Africa by 2030. The long-standing Sino-African relations are now undergoing significant development. In November 2019, Mubarack Lo, Director-General of the Economic Foresight Office of Senegal, invited Africans to take the Chinese model as an example and inspiration. Mr. Lo praised the strategies that the Chinese government has put in place for several decades, saying, The PRC has to its credit, a real success in its fight against poverty for three decades now.

Therefore, we must focus not only on poverty alleviation itself but also on this process's time and scope. China has helped lift more than a tenth of the world's total population within a generation, in net terms, out of the harshest and most exiguous economic thresholds. Moreover, ideologically, China could not have achieved this success without the spirit of hard work and self-sacrifice from generation to generation. The book *Up and Out of Poverty* has shed light on this achievement, with an evocative metaphor that drops of water could drill a piece of rock in due course (March 1990). It is true that historical, economic, and geographical factors, which

---

[1] SACHS, Jeffrey D. (2005). *The End of Poverty: Economic Possibilities for Our Time*. Penguin Press, New York, 396 pp.
[2] World Bank. (2018). *Poverty and Shared Prosperity 2018: Piecing Together the Poverty Puzzle*. Washington, DC: World Bank, 201 pp.

实现长期目标"。中国扶贫与人类发展的现象是如此独特，使中国能够完成世界上其他国家今后几十年里仍需面临的任务。中国的扶贫事业以及在林业、教育系统化、交通基础设施等领域的杠杆效应，将国内外实践相结合，实现了快速／原创／独特／开拓性的成功。一些时间和范围因此被纳入对曲线变化的理解中，即从青藏高原开始，北至黑龙江，南至珠江和中国南海的贫困曲线向下移动的拐点。

因此，自邓小平在 1978 年 12 月中共十一届三中全会上做出改革开放的伟大决策，直至 2012 年 11 月中共十八大——以及 2013 年 11 月习近平主持的中共十八届三中全会——扶贫与抗击极端贫困一直是中国的一个重要目标。世界银行报告称，10 年来，经济学家和社会学家已经一致认可并强调这一历史性变化。经济与政策研究中心首席经济学家、社论作家马克·维斯布罗特指出："中国对全球减贫做出了最大贡献。"

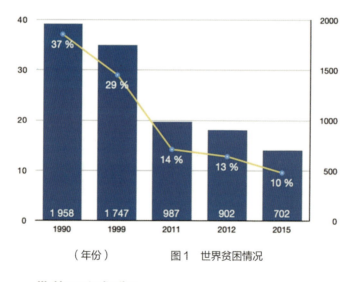

（年份）　　　图 1　世界贫困情况

World poverty situation
Source : worldbank.com

■ Number of people living in poverty (in millions)　○ Poverty rates (%)
　贫困人口（百万）　　　　　　　　　　　　　　　贫困率（％）

来源：worldbank.com

are often ancient, have a lasting influence on human beings' future and the horizons to which their hopes and development are anchored. However, it is "impossible to wait until conditions are perfect enough to ensure success or to concentrate on spectacular results at the expense of the necessary infrastructure but to have a firm grip on reality and make concrete progress towards long-term objectives." This singular phenomenon of poverty alleviation and human development in China is such that it has made it possible to accomplish a challenge that remains to be met in other areas of the world in a few decades. This experimentation and the leverage effects set up in fields as diverse as forestry, systematization of education, and transport infrastructures have combined domestic and foreign practices to achieve an upstart, original, unique, and trailblazing success. Several temporalities and scales are thus summoned to understand this inflection point which has led to a downward shift in the poverty curve from the Qinghai-Tibet Plateau to Heilongjiang in the north and the Pearl River and the South China Sea in the south.

Alleviating poverty and fighting extreme poverty have been an important goal of China since Deng Xiaoping decided on reform and opening up at the 3rd plenary session of the 11th Congress of the CPC in December 1978, [①] the 18th Congress of the CPC in

Figure 1 *Evolution of Global Extreme Poverty* (1990–2015).

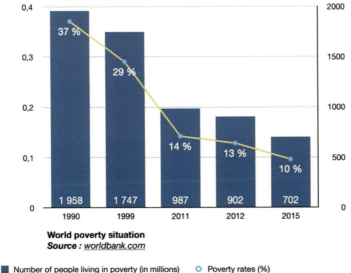

① TISDELL, Clement. (2009). "Economic Reform and Openness in China: China's Development Policies in the Last 30 Years", *Economic Analysis and Policy* (39:2), pp. 271-294.

如果从量化角度分析这一情况，在 1990 年至 2015 年近四分之一个世纪中，世界上约有 11 亿人（按净额计算）摆脱了极端贫困，生活水平得到了提高。

2015 年年初，中国在此期间的脱贫人口占全球同期脱贫人口的三分之二以上。尽管扶贫事业依然任重道远，但这一成果值得赞赏，鼓舞人心。1990 年，中国 61% 的人口生活在极端贫困线以下。这一年，习近平（现任中国国家主席）担任福建省宁德地委书记，"经济建设"与"改革开放"是当时的两大任务。到 2016 年，仅有 0.5% 的中国人生活在极端贫困中。

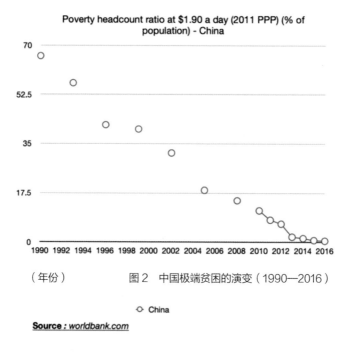

图 2　中国极端贫困的演变（1990—2016）

日均 1.90 美元（2011 年购买力平价）贫困发生率（人口 %）– 中国
来源：worldbank.com

November 2012, and the 3rd plenary session chaired by Xi Jinping in November of the following year. As a result, the World Bank report stated that economists and sociologists have unanimously recognized and emphasized this historical change in the past ten years. Mark Wisbrodt, chief economist and editorial writer of the Center for Economic and Policy Research, points out: "The greatest contribution to global poverty reduction has come from China." Let's analyze this situation from a quantitative perspective. It appears that in almost a quarter of a century, between 1990 and 2015, around 1.1 billion people in the world (in net terms) got rid of extreme poverty and experienced an improvement in their standard of living.

The number of Chinese lifted out of poverty during this period accounts for more than two-thirds of the total global record at the beginning of 2015.[①] Although poverty alleviation still has a long way to go, this achievement is commendable and inspiring. In 1990, 61% of China's population lived below the extreme poverty line. That year, Xi Jinping, currently President of China, served as Secretary of the Ningde Prefecture CPC Committee of Fujian Province. "Economic construction" and "reform and opening up" were the two major tasks at the time. Only 0.5% of the Chinese population fell below this threshold in 2016.

Figure 2   *Evolution of extreme poverty in China* (1990-2016).

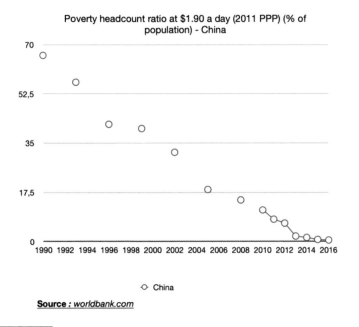

① LI, Y., SU, B. & LIU, Y. (2016). "Realizing targeted poverty alleviation in China: People's voices, implementation challenges and policy implications", *China Agricultural Economic Review* (8:3), pp. 443-454.

然而，除了定量分析对中国扶贫成就的有力印证之外，这种成功更多地体现在精神状态上，即中国在发展、全球化和人权方面的特殊理念。中国的扶贫战略深深根植于"实践是检验真理的唯一标准"这一理念中，任何对中国扶贫成就的歪曲、质疑和抹黑注定都是徒劳无益的。中国共产党把人权问题同建设小康社会、实现中国梦的发展实践逻辑紧密结合起来，这是一种创新的、有组织的、系统的主张。

然而，这些为数不多的初步判断，无论是统计的还是定量的，都未能充分反映中国扶贫战略的范围和相关重要问题。它们似乎也很难对贫穷的概念及其后果做出宽泛、宏大的理解，导致这一现象的原因五花八门、多变不定。如果用第一个定义，即经济上的定义，会由于门槛问题而有待商榷。如果弃用单一变量来定义贫穷，那么可能会产生其他的概念，从而避免一味地依赖国际标准。出于实际和比较的目的，在规划和融资方案中，我们通常采用世界银行日均 1.90 美元的贫困标准及 2030 年目标。然而，这一经济维度仅仅揭示了部分问题。我们必须始终把贫困理解为一种复杂的、多变的、多因素的和多维度的现实。

贫穷，是介于绝对门槛和相对或关系定义之间的多变概念

经济学家习惯在研究中保留收入贫困，将处于某一特定界限以下的个人均纳入"穷人"范畴。从这个意义上说，贫穷是绝对的。这种方法论和统计方法自 19 世纪末在英国发明以来一直在官方统计中盛行。中国的 10 年减贫目标的制定与规划隐晦而自动地强化了这一概念定义的绝对性，联合国国际发展目标和千年发展目标（MDGs，2000—2015）均采用这一定义，可持续发展目标（SDGs，2015—2030）作为"实现所有人类更美好和更可持续未来的蓝图"，在提出的 17 个全球目标中也

However, in addition to the strong confirmation of China's poverty alleviation achievements by quantitative analysis, this success is more reflected in the state of mind, that is, China's special concepts in development, globalization, and human rights. China's poverty alleviation strategy is deeply rooted in the idea that "practice is the only criterion for testing truth." [1] Any distortion, questioning and smearing of China's poverty alleviation achievements are bound to be futile. The Communist Party of China closely integrates human rights issues with the development and practical logic of building a moderately prosperous society and realizing the Chinese Dream. This is an innovative, organized, and systematic proposition.

However, these few initial assertions, both statistical and quantitative, do not fully capture the scope of China's strategy and the issues at stake. It also seems difficult to avoid an extensive and great apprehension of the concept of poverty and its ramifications, resolutely diverse and shifting in the meanings often given to this phenomenon. If the first definition, the economic one, raises the question of the threshold, and for this reason seems questionable and to stop the definition of poverty at a single variable, other possible conceptions have developed, freeing themselves from the sole prism of international standards. For practical and comparative purposes, for planning and financing programs, the poverty criterion of $1.90 per day has generally been used in World Bank studies and the objectives set for 2030. However, this economic dimension reveals only part of the problem. Poverty must always be understood as a complex, protean, multifactorial, and multidimensional reality.

Poverty, a protean concept, between an absolute threshold and a relative or relational definition

Traditionally, economists have retained income poverty in their research. Below a specific limit, the individuals taken into account belong to the category of "poor." In this sense, poverty is thus considered absolute. This methodology and statistical method, invented in England at the end of the 19th century, prevails in official statistics. The setting of 10-year poverty reduction target and planning reinforce almost implicitly and automatically this absolute conceptual definition. It can be found in the International Development Goals, the Millennium Development Goals [2] (MDGs, 2000-2015) and the Sustainable Development Goals (SDGs, 2015-

---

[1] XI, Jinping. (2017). "Secure a Decisive Victory in Building a Moderately Prosperous Society in All Respects and Strive for the Great Success of Socialism with Chinese Characteristics for a New Era", Delivered at the 19 th National Congress of the Communist Party of China, October 18, 2017.

[2] LIU, Qian-Qian, YU, Man & WANG, Xiao-Lin. (2015). "Poverty reduction within the framework of SDGs and Post-2015 Development Agenda", *Advances in Climate Change Research* (6), pp. 67-73.

采用该定义。可持续发展目标与千年发展目标的首要目标都是消除贫困，而前者的前十个目标都与抗击贫困（消除饥饿，良好健康与福祉，优质教育，清洁饮水与卫生设施，廉价和清洁能源，体面工作和经济增长，工业、创新和基础设施……）有关，从而使这一现象的相互关联得到强化。国际社会认识到，通过广泛而务实的效应融合，消除文盲和降低儿童死亡率同样有助于减少贫困。

为了在社会学和经济学的交叉范围内从概念的角度理解贫困概念的构建，我们需要回溯 19 世纪，当时的贫困往往与工人阶级相关。因此，马克思等学者对工人贫困给予了特别的关注，甚至专门研究贫困现象，恩格斯也在《英国工人阶级状况》（1844）中描述过这一现象。在这部作品中，恩格斯支持 19 世纪初的社会改革尝试，批判绝对贫困使人们衣、食、住等最基本的生理需求无法得到满足。然而，随着生活水平逐渐提高和集体保障的出现，对贫困现象的定义与分析也发生了变化。但反观中国，中国主要是农村社会，不能从一开始就使用这种方法。1949 年，几乎 90% 的中国人口是农村人口。尽管城市化进程加快，但在 1993 年，仍有 70% 的中国人生活在农村。据估计，到 2020 年上半年，仍有 40% 的中国人生活在农村。因此，习近平主席在 2012 年 12 月 29 日和 30 日发表讲话《推动贫困地区脱贫致富、加快发展》，称"革命老区和老区人民为中国革命胜利做出了重要贡献，党和人民永远不会忘记"，同时必须意识到，中国自古以来就是一个农耕社会，这深刻影响了中国特色社会主义建设。

2030) of the United Nations, which are defined as a collection of 17 global goals designed to be a "blueprint for achieving a better and more sustainable future for all." This definition is also used in the 17 proposed global goals. The primary goal of the Sustainable Development Goals and the Millennium Development Goals is to eradicate poverty. Simultaneously, the first ten goals also seem to be incidentally correlated with poverty (fight against hunger, access to health care, quality education, drinking water, clean and affordable energy, decent work, infrastructure...). The international community recognizes that eliminating illiteracy and reducing child mortality can also help reduce poverty through comprehensive and practical integration of effects.

To understand the construction of this notion of poverty from a conceptual perspective, within the intersection of sociology and economics, we need to go back to the 19th century, when poverty was often related to the working class. Authors such as Marx thus paid particular, if not exclusive, attention to workers' poverty, as Engels also described it in *The Situation of the Working Class in England* (1844). In this work, Engels supports social reform attempts in the early 19th century and criticizes that absolute poverty makes it impossible for people to meet their basic physical needs, such as clothing, food, and housing. However, the gradual increase in living standards and the emergence of collective protections have transformed the definition and analysis of the phenomenon of poverty. On the other hand, Chinese society is primarily rural, and the same categories cannot be used from the outset. In 1949, almost 90% of the Chinese population was rural. Despite an increase in urbanization, 7 out of 10 Chinese still lived in the countryside in 1993 [1], and 4 out of 10, according to estimates, for the first half of 2020.[2] Therefore, President Xi Jinping delivered a speech on December 29 and 30, 2012,[3] *Eliminate Poverty and Accelerate Development in Impoverished Areas*. He states that "the old revolutionary base areas and the people there made an enormous contribution to the revolution's victory, which the Party and the people will never forget." At the same time, we must realize that China has been an agrarian society since ancient times, and it has profoundly affected the construction of socialism with Chinese characteristics.

[1] LARIVIERE, Jean-Pierre. (1995). "L'urbanisation en Chine", Espace Populations Sociétés (2), pp. 249-258.
[2] 陈金永 . (2014). "China's Urbanization 2020: A New Blueprint and Direction", *Eurasian Geography and Economics* (55:1), pp. 1-9.
[3] XI, Jinping. (2014). *The governance of China*, Foreign Language Press, Beijing, pp. 209.

20 世纪下半叶出现了新的、更加多样化的社会类别。从那时起，贫困似乎从绝对概念变为相对概念，并成为特定社会中背离健康生活方式、无法获得商品、服务与财产的同义词。"门槛"这个概念最早出自英国改革者查尔斯·布斯。他发起的这场重大变革改变了我们对穷人的分类方式和贫困的概念。20 世纪初，他以算术方式提出了贫困线的概念。格斯林（2004）指出，这件新的工具和对相对贫困现象的解读成为工业社会和后工业社会的特征。在大部分前工业社会中，财富与收入呈双峰分布形式，贫穷是一种普遍的必然结果，其分布呈两极化：少数非常富有的人和大多数下等阶层。在这种情况下，划定贫困线是无意义且无效的。只有当一个社会以中产阶级为主体，这个衡量工具才有其意义。中国正在走向中产阶级社会，建设"小康社会"、追求"中国梦"也印证了这一点。近几十年来，贫困线也被用来进行国际对比，评估公共政策的效果，制订 10 年长期规划目标。但每个社会在使用贫困线概念时也会根据自身情况进行调整，以便更恰当、更准确地评估相对贫困（与其他人口对比）。也正因为如此，2017 年，中国共产党决定将 70% 的扶贫资金直接投入县级基层，因为基层更接近、更了解具体情况。法国采用收入中位数作为一般衡量框架。因此，法国将收入不足中位数的一半设定为贫困门槛。在加拿大，贫困线的设定注重衣、食、住等基本需求。如果一个家庭的消费水平仅达到全国平均水平的 20%，那么这个家庭就会被视为贫困户。中国的贫困门槛一直在增高，2008 年为每年 1067 元，2009 年为每年 1196 元，到 2010 年上调至 1274 元。温家宝曾在报告中指出，从 2009 年至 2011 年，贫困线的总增幅为 92%，至 2011 年上调至 2300 元。2015 年，贫困线继续增高，年收入低于 2800 元即属于贫困人口。

In the second half of the 20th century, new and more diverse social categories emerged. From then on, poverty seemed to become relative rather than absolute and synonymous with deviation from a healthy lifestyle, access to goods, services, and possessions in a given society. The very notion of 'threshold' comes from the English reformer Charles Booth [1]. He initiated a significant transformation in the way we categorize the poor and the concept of poverty. In an arithmetical way, he developed the poverty line concept at the beginning of the 20th century. According to Gueslin (2004), this new instrument and reading of the phenomenon of relative poverty then became characteristic of our so-called industrial and post-industrial societies. In most pre-industrial societies, there was a form of the bimodal distribution of wealth and income, and poverty seemed to be a universal, inevitable result. This distribution was polarized: the very rich few and a majority of the lower class. In such a context, the poverty line would have been meaningless and ineffective. Only when the middle class dominates a society does this measurement tool have its meaning. China is moving towards a middle-class society, which is confirmed by China's effort to build a "moderately prosperous society" and pursue its "Chinese Dream." In recent decades, the poverty line has also been used to make international comparisons, assess the consequences of public policies, and set ten-year targets. However, when each society uses the poverty line concept, it will also adjust it according to its own situation to assess relative poverty more appropriately and accurately (compared with other populations). This is why the CPC decided in 2017 to directly allocate 70% of the poverty-alleviation funds to the local authorities at the county level because these grassroots have proximity to and intimate knowledge of the concrete situation. If we take our gaze away from China for a moment to observe the French case, we will find the median income as the general measurement framework. The threshold thus corresponds to having less than half of the median income. In Canada, the calculation focuses on basic needs centered on housing, food, and clothing. Once a family spends just over 20% of the national average, it is considered poor. In China, the threshold has been continuously raised from RMB 1,067 per year in 2008 to RMB 1,196 per year in 2009 and to RMB 1,274 in 2010. According to a state report given by Wen Jiabao, between 2009 and 2011, the total increase in this poverty line was 92% to RMB 2,300 in 2011. In 2015, the poverty line continued to rise, and an annual income of less than 2,800 yuan was considered poor.

---

[1] SPICKER, Paul. (1990). "Charles Booth: the examination of poverty", *Social & Policy Administration* (24:1), pp.21-38.

中国内陆省份的发展水平不同，单凭经济标准并不能客观地反映实际情况。此外，社区面临的困难及其自身的历史背景和地理条件各不相同，需要有针对性地、合理地回应，因此不能采用单一的贫困衡量标准。在西藏最贫困的县，高海拔和植被稀少是问题所在。在宁夏南部，缺水则是关键问题。在这方面，我们必须意识到，要研究中国的情况，首先要明白中国的地理和人口差异远远大于欧洲，其地表结构也与欧、美大陆截然不同，不能以国家—大陆的角度去解释中国的情况。

贫困线及其测量工具的选择也引发了一些理论问题：如果个人、家庭或群体的生活水平仅略高于贫困线，其生活环境和生活标准是否与贫困家庭有很大差距？习近平主席曾含蓄地指出，设定单一的经济标准和绝对门槛都很容易陷入从量化角度看待贫困现象的弊端。我们可以在《摆脱贫困》一书的结语中看到，闽东地区居民跨越贫困门槛、摆脱贫困状态包含着两个不同的目标。同样地，相同收入水平也可能反映出获得基础设施、教育、家庭内部关系、文化、遗产以及国家结构性扶贫投入等方面的现实差异。贫困的定义本身就带有政治色彩，例如，我们认为贫困是应由个人负主要责任的现实结果（许多自由主义社会即是如此），还是认为贫困有复杂的形成原因，因而需要制定社会保障制度？中美在新冠肺炎疫情应对措施上的差异刚好说明了这一点。

在国际统计中，财富往往不被考虑在内，但它对生活条件有重大影响。最重要的是，贫困线是线性的，它只考虑收入水平，但不包含非货币资源（家庭和社区人际网、消费、社会地位）。贫困的定义往往也来自外界，而不是由有关行动者制定。而且，我们还应当从内部评估贫困，

Therefore, the economic criterion alone is not always an objective reflection of the situation since China's inland provinces have different levels of development. Moreover, each community faces its difficulties and its own historical and geological context, requiring targeted and appropriate responses, diminishing the utility of one sole measure of poverty. In the poorest Tibetan counties, the altitude and the rarefaction of more luxuriant vegetation below the plateaus tended to pose a problem. In the south of Ningxia, it is a scarcity of water. In this regard, we must realize that to study China's situation, we must first understand that its geographic and demographic differences are far more significant than that of Europe, and its surface structure is also completely different from that of Europe and the United States. So, we cannot explain the situation in China from a country-continent perspective.

Such a poverty line and the setting of a measuring instrument also raise several theoretical questions. Can it be considered that an individual, a family, or a group placed slightly above this poverty line really experiences conditions and standard of living very different from those of a "poor" family? The only economic criterion and the definition of an absolute threshold have the disadvantage, as President Xi Jinping implicitly reminds us, of taking a strictly arithmetical look at the phenomenon. [1] However, as we can read in the conclusion of *Up and Out of Poverty*, residents in eastern Fujian have two different goals in crossing the poverty threshold and getting rid of poverty. Similarly, the same income level may reflect quite the different realities in terms of access to infrastructure, education, intra-family relations, culture, heritage, and the State's structural commitment to combatting the phenomenon. The definition of poverty itself has a political color. For example, do we believe that poverty is the actual result of the individual's primary responsibility (as is the case in many liberal societies)? Or do we think that poverty has complicated causes and therefore needs to develop a social security system? We see the differences in performance again, between Chinese and American societies, in managing the COVID-19 crisis [2].

In international statistics, wealth is often not considered, yet it has a significant influence on living conditions. Above all, the poverty line is unidimensional. It only takes into account income levels but not non-monetary resources (family and community networks, self-consumption, social status). Often, the definition of

---

[1] XI, Jingping. (2016). Op. Cit., pp. 140.
[2] HIRO, Dilip. (2020). "Comparing the US' and China's Response to Covid-19", The Nation.

即直接针对有关行动者，并尽可能注重他们的需要。个别评估结果可能会令人惊讶，例如，偶尔会有一些低收入者主观感觉自己比其他高于平均收入水平的人更富有。无法达到理想的生活标准，无法应对基本的生活开支，这些都会强化主观的贫困感。家庭团结则可以消除或减轻家庭成员的贫困感。家庭因素对中国的影响尤其大，"孝"包含了一系列相互的义务与责任，构成了中华文明的基础。因此，收入只能被视为贫穷的一个方面，尽管是一个基本方面。从这个意义上讲，贫困是一个多变的概念，往往涉及社会、教育和职业上的不平等与剥夺，导致穷人的生活和看法受到影响。

此外，从这个意义上说，尽管需要将"贫困"视作全球现象，但要精确地描述贫困和恶劣的生活条件，往往是行不通且难以令人满意的。我们通常喜欢使用"不平等"和"排斥"等词语来详细描述贫困的后果：住房条件变差，难以获得体面住房，地理隔离，通勤时间很长，难以获得优质公共服务（要等待很长时间，服务质量差），难以获得教育、健康和休闲资源。"排斥"一词将完全不同的现实进行匹配与结合，即便在这种认识论背景下也值得商榷。为此，塞吉·鲍姆于 1991 年提出"社会失格"的概念。同年，罗伯特·卡斯特尔提出"孤立"的概念。被孤立的人经济贫困，他们还缺乏融入工作场所和"社会—家庭"的社交能力。因此，孤立和失格是两个累积过程，导致在所有社会领域的脆弱。关于这一点，毛泽东的《关于正确处理人民内部矛盾的问题》（1957）和习近平的《摆脱贫困》（2016）都倡导各民族团结统一，这样才能有效克服这种孤立感。

poverty also comes from outsiders rather than being formulated by relevant actors. Conversely, we can also use another method to assess poverty internally, i.e., by addressing the actors concerned directly and targeting their needs as carefully as possible. Indeed, some results may sometimes appear singular and surprising, as some people with low incomes may occasionally feel subjectively wealthier than other individuals with more comfortable means thanks to an above-average income. The feeling of an inability to achieve or claim a desired standard of living, the difficulty of honoring the most common expenses can also reinforce this subjective perception of being poor. Family solidarity can erase and blur the phenomenon for others. This element was notably to be taken into consideration in China, as the concept of filial piety contains a whole series of reciprocal obligations and duties, which are the very foundation of Chinese civilization. Therefore, income can only be seen as one aspect of poverty, albeit an essential dimension. In that sense, poverty, being understood as a protean phenomenon, tends to encompass social, educational, and professional inequalities and deprivations, whose result is always to constrain the existence and perspectives of those considered poor.

Moreover, in this sense, although "poverty" needs to be regarded as a global phenomenon, it is often impossible and unsatisfactory to accurately describe poverty and poor living conditions. The terms "inequality" or "exclusion" are often preferred and allow us to detail the consequences of poverty: degraded housing or difficulty in accessing decent housing, geographical isolation and long commuting time, reduced quality public services (including long waiting time, reduced quality of services), more difficult access to education, health and leisure. Even in this epistemological context, the term exclusion could be questioned because of the disparate realities it endeavored to match and bring together. For this reason, Serge Paugam proposed the notion of "social disqualification" in 1991.[1] Then the same year, Robert Castel[2] suggested the concept of "disaffiliation." The isolated person is economically poor, but his or her situation is explained by the lack of integration in the workplace and "socio-familial" sociabilities. Disaffiliation and disqualification are, therefore, two cumulative processes linked to vulnerability in all social spheres. On this particular point, solidarity and unity of all ethnic groups

---

[1] PAUGAM, Serge. (2009). *La disqualification sociale: Essai sur la nouvelle pauvreté*, PUF, Paris, 256 pp.
[2] CASTEL, Robert. (1991). "De l'indigence à l'exclusion, la désaffiliation" in DONZELOT, J., (dir.), *Face à l'exclusion, le modèle français. Éditions Esprit*, Paris, pp. 137-168.

此外，有两种情况都体现出逐渐失去联结的过程：失业、疾病。一个中国男孩的故事在网上曾引起反响：居住在云南省鲁甸县鱼池麻村的男孩王福满为了上学，不得不在冰天雪地中步行前往学校。这个小男孩的故事在网上广泛传播，他也由此获得"冰花男孩"的绰号。这个故事让我们意识到，距离也是一种贫困现象：上学的距离、获得医疗服务的距离、工作的距离（同样属于通勤流动范畴内，此外还包括偏远郊区的居民，考虑到中国都市的巨大规模，这是一个特别引人关注的现象）。因此，中国自 2013 年以来进行的许多投资都发挥了双重影响。第一个范畴是具体而实际的，例如让全国各地，特别是生活在偏远省份和最严酷条件下的儿童能够使用更多教学设施。第二个范畴则相对隐性，在悬崖、峭壁等严苛条件下修建现代建筑，代表着中国整体水平的提升，这种进步已不再局限于沿海和港口等长期享受全球化优势的地区。以贵州省岩博村为例，20 世纪，村里没有水源，也未设立行政管理单位，最近的集市离村子大约有两小时的路程。除了一些农田以外，什么也没有。近 95% 的村民没有接受过正规教育，最近的学习中心距离村子四五小时的路程。距离再次成为一个现实难题，这有助于我们通过实践更好地理解贫困。无论从什么角度来说，修路都是连接偏远村庄的好办法，这也让我们想到《摆脱贫困》一书中通过"桥与路"解决贫困问题的段落（p.97）。现在，岩博村盖起了工厂，当地居民以股东身份分享财富。值得注意的是，2013 年至 2018 年，通过精准扶贫，全国农村贫困发生率从 10.2% 下降到不足 4%。

are advocated by Mao Zedong in *On the Correct Handling of Contradictions Among the People* (1957) and President Xi Jinping's survey, *Up and Out of Poverty* (2016), enabling to combat this feeling of disaffiliation effectively.[1]

Moreover, both cases have a path where a progressive loss of ties comes to exist: loss of employment and illness. A Chinese story recently affected social network users: the story of the young Wang Fuman, who had to walk from the village of Yuchima, in the southern region of Yunnan, along snowy paths to go to school. The story of this young schoolboy quickly went well-known, as did his nickname Ice boy. This story helps us understand that distance can also be used to describe poverty: the distance someone covers to learn, to receive medical care, to work (referring here also to the category of commuting flows, also including the inhabitants of the most remote suburbs, a particularly interesting phenomenon and one that needs to be put into perspective with the gigantic size of Chinese metropolises). Many of the Chinese investments undertaken since 2013 thus have this double impact. The first scope is concrete and practical and involves making educational facilities more accessible throughout the country, particularly in remote provinces and under the most restrictive conditions. The second dimension is relatively intangible, since through these modern constructions, on cliff sides, in the steepest regions, it represents China's general elevation, not merely of the coastal and port areas that have long been a figurehead of today's globalization. For example, let's analyze the situation of Yanbo's Village (in the province of Guizhou, China). It appears that before 2000, there was no access to water or administration, as the first market was also some two hours away. Apart from individual subsistence farming, nothing was present. Nearly 95% of the villagers had not received formal education, and the first study center was four to five hours away. Again, the distance posed a real and challenging question, making it possible to understand this conceptual issue in practice better. From a concrete and symbolic point of view, the construction of a road made it possible to connect the isolated village, reminding us of this emblematic section "the bridge and the road" in *Up and Out of Poverty* (p.97). In the factory then set up in Yanbo, the inhabitants now act as shareholders and share the wealth. It is worth noting that from 2013 to 2018, through targeted poverty alleviation, the national rural poverty incidence rate dropped from 10.2% to less than 4%.

---

[1] XI, Jingping. (2016). Op. Cit., pp. 140.

无独有偶，四川省凉山彝族自治州昭觉县支尔莫乡阿土勒尔村的"新天梯"也改变了当地72个家庭的儿童的生活，其象征意义获得了全世界关注。2018年，英国广播公司（BBC）在头条中报道了中国关于即将帮助4300万极端贫困人口脱贫的承诺。位于云贵边界的另一处工程在法国媒体引起极大反响。长江支流牛栏江流经威宁县和会泽县。几十年来，当地人一直使用简陋的小船运送学龄儿童、病人、流动工人和牲畜。然而，自2013年以来，当地政府做出重大承诺，用现代桥梁等基础设施取代原先的小船，这是一项重大工程，再次反映了消除贫困的重要性。总体而言，中国的交通运输行业正在发生整体性的变化。大多数内陆地区和偏远村庄都已与更有活力的地区相连接。例如，中国的高铁网络现已达到世界领先水平，全长3.5万公里（全球铁路总长13.9万公里）。再以湖北省渔山村为例，这是一个建在悬崖高空上的村子，村中孩子每天要坐在铁篮子里往返学校。当地政府在峭壁上开凿了一条20公里的水泥路，让村民走出大山。

距离的象征意义为理解贫穷提供了一个适当的切入点：远离好学校，远离重要的经济中心，远离有活力的市场。收入水平一样，但消费也可能不平等：正如詹姆斯·鲍德温在1961年写的，穷的代价反而高昂。大卫·卡普罗维茨在1963年的著作《穷人支付更多》中，阐述了导致最弱势群体被剥夺适当价格服务（全球速卖通、银行服务）的过程，而中产阶级很容易获得这些服务。他们只能妥协，前往集市、本地商店，并在银行市场以外的地方贷款。这样一来，拥有最少资金的人反而要付

Thus the improvement of a new ladder in the village of Atule'er, located in Zhaojue County of Liangshan Yi autonomous prefecture, has changed the lives of the children of the 72 families living in this remote area in Sichuan Province of southwest China. Its symbolism has attracted worldwide attention: China is vowing to wipe out extreme poverty for 43 million people, as was reported in the BBC headline news in 2018. In the same way, another construction site on the border of Yunnan and Guizhou has recently received significant resonance in the French press. The Niulan River, a tributary of the Yangtze river flows at the gap between the Weining and Huize counties. For decades, rudimentary gondolas have been used to ensure schoolchildren's passage, sick people in need of care, migrant workers, and livestock from one place to another. Since 2013, however, the local government has made a significant commitment to replace these old gondolas with modern bridges and infrastructure. Naturally, the project is a significant undertaking, but once again, it reflects the importance attached to the fight against poverty. Generally speaking, it is indeed the transport sector that is currently undergoing this change in China. The most landlocked regions and remote villages are served and connected to more dynamic regions. For example, the Chinese rail network's high-speed lines are now the world's leading network, with 35,000 km (of the 139,000 km of rail lines globally). Many other projects could still be mentioned: construction of a road to link the village of Yushan, located on a cliff (in the Hubei Province, China). An open-sided cable car was the only way for the children of Yushan to travel to and from school every day. Nevertheless, the new local government has carved a 20 km cement road out of the mountains.

The notion of distance as a metaphor could offer a suitable entry point for understanding the concept of poverty: distance from good schools, from essential and vital economic centers, from the most dynamic markets. Access to consumption can also be unequal for the same level of income: being poor is paradoxically expensive, as James Baldwin wrote in 1961[1]. David Caplovitz, in his famous 1963 text, *The Poor Pay More*, demonstrated the processes that led the most vulnerable populations to be deprived of modestly priced services that members of the middle class easily access (Aliexpress, banking services). They then retreat to markets, local shops, loans outside the banking market. Thus, access to money is often more expensive

---

[1] BALDWIN, James. (1961). *Nobody Knows My Name*, New-York, 190 pp.

出更多的金钱，这种现象在西方社会非常严重（次贷危机就非常直接地说明了这一点）。

当然，贫穷主要是经济问题。在这方面，中国的小额信贷战略在精准扶贫政策和地方举措中发挥着至关重要的作用。60 年来，学术界已经对这一方面进行了研究。尤其是 2008 年金融危机以来，学术界对这一问题表现出了浓厚的兴趣。特别是在全球新冠肺炎疫情期间，获得信贷的先决条件自然而然会对全球经济产生影响。法国学者乔治·格鲁科维佐夫已经论证了银行贷款排斥最贫困人口对国民经济产生的影响（2010）。正如世界卫生组织赞扬中国的危机应对能力，我们现在必须评估这场全球卫生危机引发的间接后果。世界银行的专家在预测全球经济放缓的后果及其对极端贫困的影响时持相对悲观的态度。

正如我们所看到的，上述对贫困的定义仍然主要是在经济层面。社会学也提供了另一种可行的分析。使用建构主义方法，我们也可以通过关系分析来理解贫穷。在这个框架中，研究者不再聚焦于收入或物质条件，而是更关注个人与社会之间联系的紧密性。格奥尔格·齐美尔在他的贫困社会学（特别是 1907 年的著作《穷人》）中提出了这样一种观点，即贫困的特征不仅仅是匮乏、难以或无法获得商品和服务，而是实际上依赖于某种形式的援助关系。社会反映的集体形象也有助于界定这一现象的概况。的确，贫困可能指的是一种相似的、同质的现象，但在这个概念中没有特别的独特性或凝聚力，它的表现形式多种多样。

朱力、毛飞飞在《中国城市底层群体的生存状态与救助机制》（2019）中借鉴了齐美尔的研究，用"相关概念的区别"恰当地描述了中国的概念边界，为我们提供了更好的见解。他们在研究中将底层群体划分为脆弱群体、弱势群体、被剥夺群体和边缘化群体。如今，在中国研究尤其

for those who paradoxically have the least money, particularly in Western societies (which is very directly illustrated by the subprime crisis).

Naturally, poverty also has a primarily financial aspect. In this respect, China's micro-credit strategy plays a vital role in the policy of targeted measures to combat poverty and launch individual local initiatives. For about six decades, academic studies have included this aspect of poverty in their research, with a wholly renewed interest in this issue since the 2008 financial crisis. The leonine prerequisites on access to credit, even more so in the wake of the global pandemic of COVID-19, naturally have consequences on the global economy. Among French researchers, Georges Gloukoviezoff has demonstrated the exclusion of the most impoverished populations from bank loans[1] and its implications on the national economy (2010). As the WHO has praised the management of the crisis in China, we now have to assess the indirect consequences of this global health crisis. Therefore, the World Bank experts are relatively pessimistic in their future prognosis on the effects of the global economic slowdown and its repercussions on extreme poverty.

As we have seen, the definitions of poverty mentioned above remain mainly economic. However, sociology offers another possible analysis. In a constructivist approach, poverty can also be apprehended by employing a relational analysis. In this framework, there is not much income or the material conditions of existence that hold the researcher's attention, but rather the more or less close ties that an individual maintains with society. In his sociology of poverty, Georg Simmel, particularly in his famous 1907 text *The Poor* — proposes the idea that it is not merely deprivation, difficulty in accessing goods and services, or lack that characterizes poverty, but virtually dependence on some form of assistance relationship.[2] It is also collectively the image that society reflects them that helps define the phenomenon's contours. Indeed, speaking of poverty might refer to a similar and homogenous phenomenon, but there is no particular uniqueness or cohesion within the concept; it is a collection of varied and odd situations.

In their recent publication, *Living Conditions and Targeted Aiding Mechanisms of the Urban Underclass in China* (2019), the two co-authors, Zhu Li and Mao

[1] GLOUKOVIEZOFF, Georges & REBIERE, Nicolas. (2014). "Le dispositif de microcrédit personnel garanti : une nouvelle forme de solidarité pour lutter efficacement contre la pauvreté et l'exclusion sociale ?", *Revue française des affaires sociales* (1-2), pp. 100-119.

[2] SIMMEL, Georg. (2001). Les pauvres, translated by CHOKRANE, Bertrand, PUF, Paris, 102 pp.

是次级研究的框架中，许多研究者都在关注这一具体现象。例如，徐振明在界定次级阶层或贫困群体时，主要从四个方面进行了研究。第一，他们被排斥在社会结构之外，有时与其他社会阶层的关系非常遥远，导致他们特别容易受到生活变故或经济危机的影响。他们的大部分收入都用来支付住房费用。第二，这些群体的年龄通常在35至40岁之间，从事技术工作，受过中等程度的教育。正如布迪厄在《继承者》（1964）中阐述的那样，这种情况形成了一种习惯，一种已被证实的代际再生产倾向，以及向年青一代的资本传递，这种资本无疑是经济的，但也涉及文化、教育和其他方面。第三，这个群体，特别是农村贫困群体，在世界加速抛弃他们的过程中正在失去参照点。在迁移和流动的过程中，他们感到不堪重负。第四，这些群体也在创造自身价值，他们无法彻底摆脱贫困。

此外，根据斯图尔特·麦克弗森和王海国在《社会发展与转型社会》（2019）一书中的观点，我们所从事的这种概念分析对于更好地理解中国的贫困状况确实至关重要。中国农村先后经历了"生产责任制""废除公社制度""农产品价格上涨"和"市场自由化"时期。尽管过去40年来农村地区的减贫工作取得了成功，但由于中国长期以农业和农村为主，其贫困形式也随城市化进程而不断演变，这与其他国家是一致的。据作者估计，区域内和区域间迁移有可能导致1.1亿波动人口没有登记在案，他们因此失去享受住房和社会福利援助计划的资格。正是由于这个原因，地方政府做好身份识别工作成为精准扶贫的首要步骤。早在20世纪下半叶，法国社会学家勒内·勒诺瓦就著书专门研究了这一现象及其在纲领性工作中的演变，并为这本书起了一个合适的名字：《排斥》。社会学家倾向于表明，后现代社会的快速城市化引发了新的贫困形式和新的边缘化现象，令这一概念的理解更加混乱。尽管住房危机在不同程

Feifei, study, in particular, in the wake of the work of Georg Simmel, the "distinction of relevant concepts" used in China to describe the conceptual boundaries of the notion properly, contributing to give us a better insight. In their study, they identify vulnerable groups, disadvantaged and deprived groups, and marginalized groups.[①] Today, in the framework of Chinese studies, and more precisely in subaltern studies, many researchers focus on this precise phenomenon. Xu Zhenming focuses, for instance, on four main aspects in determining groups belonging to these subaltern or poor classes. Firstly, they are excluded from the social structure and sometimes have very distant relationships with the rest of society, making them particularly vulnerable to the vagaries of life and economic crises. Most of their income hardly covers housing costs. Secondly, these groups are often between 35 and 40 years of age, occupy skilled positions, and have a moderate education level. As Bourdieu argues in *Les héritiers, Les étudiants et la culture* (1964), this situation has formed a habit, a proven tendency of intergenerational reproduction, and capital transmission to the younger generation. This kind of capital is undoubtedly economic but also involves culture, education, and other aspects[②]. Thirdly, this group, particularly in rural areas, suffers a loss of reference points in a changing world that sometimes seems to evolve without them. Caught up in movements of migration and mobility, these subordinate groups feel overwhelmed. Fourthly, these groups can create their own value and hinder a deep and lasting escape from poverty.

Moreover, according to Stewart MacPherson and Hoi-Kwok Wong (2019), in *Social Development and Societies in Transition*, it is indeed this conceptual analysis that we are engaged in is essential, facilitating us to better understand the new contours of poverty in China. Mostly rural, at the time of the "adoption of production, responsibility system," "the dismantling of the commune system," the "agricultural product price increases," and "the market liberalization." For the latter, while poverty reduction in rural areas has been successful over the last four decades, poverty in China has also changed in form due to the urbanization of this historically agricultural and rural nation—like many other nations. Thus, the authors estimate that, due to intra-regional and inter-regional migration, a fluctuating population of 110 million people may not always be registered and, therefore, eligible for the

---

① ZHU, Li & MAO, Feifei. (2019). Living Conditions and Targeted Aiding Mechanisms of the Urban Underclass in China, New-York, 214 pp.

② JOURDAIN, Anne & NAULIN, Sidonie. (2011). "Héritage et transmission dans la sociologie de Pierre Bourdieu", *Idées économiques et sociales* (166:4), pp. 6-14.

度上影响着全世界每一座城市，但在中国的某些大城市，住房问题似乎仍然是最不富裕社会阶层面临的一项严峻挑战。正如勒诺瓦所预言，我们不该严格地从个别现象的角度来研究城市贫困，而是要注意到复杂的社会进程，特别是过快的城市化可能对城市内部和城市周边产生的隔离效应。此外，社会学家倾向于主张这些困难群体的混合性质，因此并未将这种现象划入次无产阶级的边缘。过去 40 年里，他所宣称的结论经常被用来分析发达国家和发展中国家的贫困现象。

边缘化即社会学中的排斥现象。我们思考一下"贫困文化"这个概念。这个概念对于识别和理解当代社会学对贫困问题的研究方式以及"贫困文化"概念在中西方减贫工作中的重要性有着至关重要的意义。从一开始，"贫困文化"一词似乎就在学术界引起了激烈的争论。除了分类和现象外，这一概念还顺便提出了国家在（通过干预或观察）解决这一问题中的责任与角色。

首先，美国人类学家奥斯卡·刘易斯在 1959 年奠定了这一概念的基础，并对这一概念进行了限制。在研究了墨西哥城几个贫困群体和家庭的真实案例后，他得出结论，贫困是一个恶性循环，这使得对抗和消除贫困变得极为困难。事实上，他认为，贫困会促使生成一种价值体系，确保贫困群体在面对脆弱和困难的生活条件时产生凝聚力和组织

housing and social benefit assistance program. This is why local authorities' initial identification remains a fundamental issue to target poverty reduction as carefully as possible. As early as the second half of the 20th century, a French sociologist, René Lenoir, studied the phenomenon in particular and studied its evolution in programmatic work under the symbolic title of *Les Exclus*. The sociologist thus tended to show that our postmodern societies' rapid urbanization had led to new forms of poverty and new marginalization, managing to make the understanding of this concept even more confused. Although the housing crisis affects the different world metropolises to varying degrees, it appears that housing remains a challenge for the least well-off social categories in some large Chinese cities. As Lenoir anticipated, this urban poverty should not be studied from the perspective of a strictly individual phenomenon but as the result of complex social processes, particularly over-rapid urbanization, potentially generating intra-urban and peri-urban segregation effects.[1] Moreover, the sociologist tends to assert the diverse nature of the groups facing these difficulties and, therefore, does not reduce this phenomenon to a sub-proletarian marginality. The conclusions he announces have often been used over the last four decades to analyze poverty's consequences in developed and developing societies.

Marginalization parallels sociological exclusion. It seems appropriate to pause for a moment to reflect on the notion of the "culture of poverty." The latter is indeed essential to identify and understand how contemporary sociology has approached the subject of poverty and how this notion crystallizes a significant stake in the fight against the phenomenon in the West and the East. The term "culture of poverty" seems to have given rise to critical debates within academia from the outset. Beyond the categories and phenomena, this notion incidentally raised the question of the State's responsibility and role in addressing this issue, either through intervention or observation.

First and foremost, the American anthropologist Oscar Lewis laid the foundations and the limits of this concept in 1959. [2] After studying the practical cases of several groups and families in Mexico City, he concluded that poverty is a vicious circle, making it extremely difficult to fight against and eliminate poverty. According to him, poverty would bring the emergence of a value system, making

[1] LENOIR, René. (1974). *Les exclus*, Paris, 175 pp.
[2] LEWIS, Oscar. (1961). *The children of Sanchez. Autobiography of a Mexican family*, New York, 499 pp.

力——然而，这种价值体系最终会导致个人始终生活在贫困线以下。因此，贫穷或弱势群体与个人将通过三重行动维持其初始状态：远离有活力的中心（地理、空间、社会、教育距离），外部社会对这一群体的界定和与社区内其他人建立的援助关系，以及内部的因素，如使他们继续忍受匮乏的生活条件而不去摆脱其规则、规范、价值观和幻想。因此，这种"贫穷文化"的特点是边缘感、依赖性，以及只注重短期内的生活，从而导致视野受限。

在《摆脱贫困》一书中，习近平在 1988 年 10 月回答记者提问时，准确地指出了同样的现象。不可否认的是，当时贫困现象在寿宁、平南一带尤为突出。但是，"贫困文化心态"存在真正的危险和严重的后果，因此绝不能提倡或鼓励这种心态。相反，为了继续推进该地区的成果，需要始终保持现实但乐观的分析。中国的总体目标是建立一个以中产阶级为主体的小康社会。

尽管亨利·孟德拉斯确实曾预言未来几十年里中产阶级将不断扩大，全球社会也将"趋同"——通过进步运动或他口中的"自上而下的愿望"——但仍需注意到弱势阶层在获得社会流动机会方面仍面临的障碍。有学者在 2006 年的社会流动性研究中说明了贫困群体在教育、就业和住房竞争中的劣势。排斥的三个主要方面（它的三种当代形式），分别是"脆弱""边缘"和"贫困"三个经济层面的概念。朱力和毛飞飞（2006）在分析中详尽介绍了这些情况的共同特征的象征意义。我们将尝试评估它们是否适用于、在多大程度上适用于中国国情。"弱势"这一概念在语义上接近于脆弱性，这意味着在面对风险、冲击和变故时缺乏抵抗或保护能力。以河北省涞源县小关城村为例，我们可以看到一系列脆弱特征。朱力（1995）和毛飞飞（2006）总结了 6 项主要特征：

it possible both to ensure group cohesion and organization in the face of delicate and difficult living conditions. This value system ultimately contributes to keeping individuals below the poverty line. Poor or disadvantaged groups or individuals would thus be maintained in their initial condition by a three-fold movement: centrifugal (geographical, spatial, social, educational distance) from dynamic centers, by the external societal definition placed on this category and the relationship to aid established with the rest of community, and finally internal, by the construction of rules, norms, values and a fantasy/myth allowing them to exist in diminished living conditions but not necessarily to emerge from them. Therefore, this "poverty culture" is characterized by a sense of marginality, dependence, and only focusing on short-term life, which leads to limited vision.

In the book *Up and Out of Poverty*, Xi Jinping accurately identifies the same phenomenon while answering a journalist's questions in October 1988.[1] At that time, it was undeniable that precisely in the districts of Shouning and Pingnan, the poverty was striking (p.87). However, due to the real dangers and consequences of the "poverty cultural mentality," this mentality must never be promoted or encouraged. On the contrary, to forward the district's successes, this was always a realistic, albeit optimistic, analysis conducted. The general aim was already the constitution of a moderately prosperous society and the emergence of a middle class in China.

Henri Mendras (1988) predicted the constitution of a large middle class and the global "averaging" of our societies over the next few decades[2] through progressive movements or what he calls "aspiration from above." However, we still need to pay attention to the obstacles that disadvantaged groups still face in accessing social mobility opportunities. In their studies on social mobility, Huo Huang and Dawei Hou demonstrated, as early as 2006, the disadvantage of poor categories in the competition for education, employment, and housing. The three main dimensions, the three contemporary forms of this exclusion, today imply the notions of "vulnerability," "marginality," and "poverty" in the first and most economic sense of the term. In their analysis, Zhu Li and Mao Feifei (2006) exhaustively detail the typology of the features common to these different situations. We will attempt to assess the extent to which they may or may not apply to the Chinese space. The idea

---

[1] XI, Jinping. (2016). Op. *Cit., pp.* 86-87.
[2] MENDRAS, Henri. (1988). *La seconde Révolution française*, Paris, 329 pp.

（1）经济脆弱性：收入略高于或低于贫困线。

（2）食品和医疗脆弱性：收入不足以支付生活成本，或全部用于最基本的标准需求。

（3）文化和社会脆弱性：表现在难以获得文化和优质商品与服务。

（4）心理脆弱性：应对经济和职业变化的压力变大。

（5）存在的脆弱性：难以在生活中表现自己可以迅速和持续地改变一个人的状况。

（6）时间上的脆弱性：贫困很可能会持续或长或短的时间，甚至几代人。

从这个概念角度简单分析，我们会发现这些似乎正是小关城村的特征。这里是中国最贫困的村庄之一，其衡量标准为年收入（居民人均年收入）低于 3000 元（在本文写作时相当于 423 美元）。正因如此，这个北京以西仅 3 小时车程的村庄成为习近平主席到 2020 年全面消除贫困的一个重点。因此，我们可以毫不困难地得出结论，第一个特征是相关的。在一系列关于中国政府重点帮扶这些贫困地区的报告中，我们可以看到普通村民的生活。一些村民患有疾病或身体虚弱，这不是该地区的特点或与该地区明确相关的因素，但加剧了当地人的经济脆弱性。

同样，虽然随着生产队的参与，生活发生了变化，但许多人在冬天仍然没有真正的工作，只是在山里砍柴。根据这份文件，我们了解到，当地人就业和收入不稳定，种植作物或饲养动物品种单一（玉米、土豆、鸡），基础设施陈旧，难以参与文化活动，依赖集体慈善和援助项目，人口老龄化严重，教育负担重，心理压力巨大。从这一个例子就可以看出，贫困体现在农村、经济、社会、教育、医疗和财政等方方面面。

of vulnerability, semantically close to fragility, connotes the absence of resistance or protection to the most contrary risks, shocks, and inflections of existence. Take Xiaoguancheng Village of Laiyuan in Hebei Province, for example. We see the emergence of a certain number of characteristics of vulnerability. According to Zhu Li (1995) and Zhu Li and Mao Feifei (2006), six main features are :

（1）Economic vulnerability: income is slightly above or below the poverty line.

（2）Food and medical vulnerability: profit is not sufficient to cover their expenses or is entirely spent on the most basic and standard needs.

（3）Cultural and social vulnerability: reflecting more difficult access to culture and quality goods and services.

（4）Psychological vulnerability: with more significant pressure to cope with economic and occupational variations.

（5）Existential vulnerability: the difficulty of projecting oneself in life can change one's condition rapidly and sustainably.

（6）Temporal vulnerability: as poverty is likely to extend over a longer or shorter period, or even several generations.

From a simple analysis of this concept, we will find that these seem to be Xiaoguancheng Village's characteristics. In this impoverished area, one among the poorest in China, we tend to consider that the yearly income (yearly per capita income of the inhabitants) is below 3,000 yuan (which corresponds to US $ 423 at the time of writing). For this reason, the village, only three hours drive west of Beijing, has been targeted as part of President Xi Jinping's campaign to wipe out poverty across China by 2020. We can, therefore, conclude without difficulty that the first characteristic is relevant. In a series of reports, filmed to present the Chinese government's efforts in favor of these deprived regions, we discover the life of a modest family of villagers. Several members suffer from illness or infirmity, an element that is not characteristic of or attached explicitly to the region but reinforces these local populations' economic vulnerability.

Similarly, although life has changed with the production team's involvement, many men remain without real employment except chopping firewood in the mountains during the winter. Based on this document, we note the following: professional fluctuation, fluctuation of income, domestic agricultural specialization around a few plant and animal varieties (maize, potatoes, chickens), dilapidated infrastructure, the difficulty of access to culture, reliance on collective charity, and

贫困是一个需要全面反映的问题，既需要局部、具体和准确的反映，也需要大范围的反映。因此，对贫困的研究有时需要采取非常不同的路线。最初的"贫穷"一词已逐渐被弃用，因为它意味着财富水平是对人进行分类的首要甚至唯一标准。如果我们稍微思考一下，就会明白这样的方法本身在概念上是贫乏和不充分的。此处不再赘述相互冲突的表述，仅看奥利维耶·施瓦茨（2011）的说法，他提出，工人阶级这一类别更容易被用来定义贫困，他们是处于社会底层的人。在他看来，有两个方面可以说明这个概念：首先，作为一名初级技术工人，其地位往往体现在工作不稳定、薪酬低以及工作性质相对危险等。其次，我们可以看到文化分离会导致隔阂。这种文化分离的观念，在新疆目前开展的教育和就业项目中得到了体现。席勒研究所在 2019 年秋季开展的多项扶贫计划获得了一致好评，尕秀示范村建设正是其中一个项目。另外，这一政策还有一个目的，即打击和铲除该地区滋生的恐怖主义。正如孔子在《论语》中所言："好勇疾贫，乱也。人而不仁，疾之已甚，乱也。"

尕秀示范村，消除新疆极端贫困

对贫困的第一种概念和社会学分析的结论是，贫穷应当被视为相对的。同样，在许多社会中，贫困的衡量标准是与收入中位数的差距。在欧洲，家庭收入低于收入中位数（将人口分成相等两部分后，其平均工

assistance programs, aging of the population, substantial debt for studies, intense psychological pressure. Without aiming to be exhaustive, it would seem that this example perfectly illustrates the rural, economic, social, educational, medical, and financial dimensions that poverty can cover.

Poverty is a problem that needs to be fully reflected. It requires both a partial, specific, and accurate response as well as a large-scale response. For this reason, research on poverty has sometimes taken very different routes. The initial term "poor" has sometimes been discarded because it means that the level of wealth is the primary or even the only criterion for classifying people. Such an approach would itself be conceptually poor and inadequate if we can spin the metaphor for a moment. Without listing the competing expressions again, let us note for all intents and purposes that Olivier Schwartz proposes that the category of working classes be more readily used to define poverty, i.e., those at the bottom of the social ladder. [①] In his view, two aspects come together to illustrate this concept: status as a low-skilled worker, often marked by a form of instability, a low or shallow level of remuneration, access to solely precarious jobs. Secondly, we observe a cultural separation, which contributes to creating a climate of division. This notion and the idea of cultural separation are illuminated through the education and employment programs currently underway in Xinjiang. The many poverty-alleviation programs carried out at the Schiller Institute in the autumn of 2019 won unanimous praises, and the construction of the Gaxiu Demonstration Village is one of them. Besides, this policy has another purpose, which is to combat and eradicate terrorism that breeds in the region.

As Confucius stated in *The Analects*, "The man who is fond of daring and is dissatisfied with poverty will proceed to insubordination. The man who is not virtuous, when you carry your dislike of him to an extreme, will also proceed to insubordination."

脱贫致富
Out of Poverty

---

① SCHWARTZ, Olivier. (2018). "Les femmes des classes populaires, entre permanence et rupture ", *Travail, Genre et Société* (39), pp.121-138.

资即是中位数）的 60% 即被认为是穷人。在这种结构中，贫困是通过不平等指标来衡量的。另外，为消除发展中国家社会贫困而设立的国际机构和项目，则更多地使用了绝对贫困指数，如日均生活费不足 1.25 美元或 1.9 美元。但是，贫困的货币维度可以且必须有其他指标作为补充。印度经济学家阿玛蒂亚·森（1991）认为，需要考虑的不是手段，而是"能力"。显然，我们很难给出一个具有普适性的贫困定义。

在《2000/2001 年世界发展报告》关于减贫的章节中，我们发现，根据 10 年研究和数据收集所得的经验和理论见解，可以从三个标准来理解贫困。三个关键元素为理解贫困现象提供了一个更精确的框架：贫困人口对关乎他们存在的关键决策无能为力；最容易受到经济变化和衰退以及其他自然、流行病或农业灾害的冲击；缺乏参与经济增长与发展、为其做出贡献并从中受益的机会。联合国 2030 年可持续发展目标也围绕贫困制定了一系列目标。

因此，贫穷绝不是一种静止的现象。人们有可能在摆脱贫困后返贫，或者在某个特定时期经历贫困。在巴黎国家运输局组织的一次活动中，一个全国协会指出，摆脱贫穷可能需要六代人的时间。因此，贫困必须被视为与其他威胁相生相伴的一种风险。它的部分影响可能被文化、家庭、个人、社会和遗产指标抹去，因此，有必要制定有针对性的战略，中国在 2013 年正是采取了这种做法。

To conclude on this first conceptual and sociological analysis, poverty must therefore mainly be considered relative. Again, in many societies, poverty is measured by the gap with median income. In Europe, people living in households with incomes below 60% of the median income (the average salary separating the population into two equal parts) are considered poor. Poverty is thus measured in this configuration by an inequality indicator. In international institutions and programs to combat poverty in developing societies, on the other hand, more absolute poverty indexes are used, such as less than US $ 1.25 or US $ 1.90 per day for survival. However, the monetary dimension of poverty can and must be supplemented by other indicators. From the perspective of the Indian economist Amartya Sen (1991), it is not the means but the "capabilities" or capacities to do things that need to be taken into account.[1] As can be seen, a universally applicable definition of poverty is difficult to elucidate.

In the *World Development Report (WDR) 2000/01* and the section on poverty reduction, we find the idea, based on empirical and theoretical insights gained from ten years of research and data collection, that poverty could be understood in terms of three criteria. Three key elements are thus retained to provide a more precise framework for the phenomenon: the powerlessness of poor populations in the critical decisions governing their existence, the greatest vulnerability to all shocks, whether economic variations and recessions, as well as to all other disasters, natural, epidemic or agricultural, and finally a lack of opportunity to participate in, contribute to, and benefit from economic growth and development. In the same way, the objectives of the United Nations in its program for the year 2030 define a list of targeted purposes based on the concept of poverty (see Appendix 1: The ODD1, declined in 7 targets).

Poverty is, therefore, never a static phenomenon. It is possible to get out of and then return to poverty or experience it during a certain age. In a recent campaign organized by the Parisian national transport authority, a national association thus tended to emphasize that it could take up to six generations to get out of poverty. Poverty must, therefore, be perceived as a risk, concomitant, correlated with other threats. Its effects can be partially erased by cultural, family, personal, social, and heritage indicators, making a targeted strategy still necessary, as China put in place in 2013.

---

[1] SEN, Amartya. (1991). *Inequality Reexamined*, New York, 207 pp.

1949 年以后中国的扶贫阶段

在本节中，我们主要参考了扶贫白皮书与报告，以及中国国家统计局、中国国际扶贫中心和一些历史专著关于 1949 年 10 月 1 日以后实施的各种扶贫计划的资料。中国脱贫致富经历了不同的阶段。

在第一阶段，中国试图通过制度改革解决农村的普遍贫困问题（1949—1978）。在这个阶段，中国通过农村土地使用权制度改革消除了造成农民土地短缺的制度障碍。同时，通过改善农村基础设施、发展教育和卫生服务、革新农业技术和建立社会保障制度，农民的生活条件得到了极大改善。在这一阶段，谷物总产量增长了 2.69%，婴儿死亡率下降了 75%。同时，人口预期寿命增长了近 30 岁，农村赤贫人口比例减少一半。

在第二阶段，减贫和发展被紧密融入国家战略，地方全面治理贫困被证明非常有效（1978—2012）。中国颁布实施了《国家八七扶贫攻坚计划》和"扶贫开发、农村发展两项计划"（这是否意味着即将资本化？）。政府还制定了发展导向型扶贫政策，明确了贫困地区和集中连片特困地区，设立了从中央到地方的四级扶贫体系。中国在社会进步领域（如必要基础设施建设、农业技术、水、交通、电力、通信、教育、卫生、文化等领域）建立了协调机制。大规模、有计划、有组织的扶贫工作被纳入国家级战略。改革期间还划定了具体优先类别（如高山地区、少数民族聚居区）。

第三阶段以 2012 年中共十八大为起点，中国进入了精准扶贫新时代。以习近平同志为核心的党中央，把打好脱贫攻坚战作为全面建设小

The periodization of poverty reduction in China after 1949

In this section, we mainly rely on the White Paper on poverty and reports, as well as information from the National Bureau of Statistics of China, the International Poverty Reduction Center in China (IPRCC), and various historical monographs on the different plans launched after October 1st, 1949. The fight against poverty in China has gone through different stages.

During the first stage, China sought to solve general rural poverty through institutional reform (1949-1978). China removed the institutional obstacles that caused a land shortage for farmers by reforming the rural land tenure system. Simultaneously, it improved rural people's living conditions considerably by improving rural infrastructure, developing education and health services, generalizing agricultural technologies, and establishing a social security system. During this stage, total cereal production increased by 2.69%, and the infant mortality rate fell by 75%. At the same time, China extended its population's life expectancy by almost 30 years, and the proportion of the rural population without food and clothing reduced by half.

In the second stage, poverty reduction and development were tightly integrated into national strategies, and overall poverty governance at the regional level proved to be exceptionally effective (1978-2012). China has promulgated and implemented the Seven-Year Plan to Help 80 million Chinese people out of poverty and two *Programmes for Poverty Reduction and Rural Development* (are these intended to be capitalized?). The government has also established a development-oriented poverty reduction policy, defined poor districts and impoverished contiguous areas, and developed a four-level poverty alleviation system from the central government to the local governments. China has established a coordination mechanism in social progress, such as necessary infrastructure construction, agricultural technology, water, transportation, power, communication, education, health, culture, and other fields. Thus, a large-scale planned and organized fight against poverty has been promoted at a strategic national level. From the years of reform, specific priority categories in the fight against poverty have been identified (high mountain areas, ethnic groups).

In the framework of the third stage, beginning with 18th CPC National Congress held in 2012, China entered a new era characterized by targeted assistance to the

康社会的根本任务和先行指标,做出到2020年消除绝对贫困的庄严承诺。为了能够从根源上消除贫困,提出了向贫困群体提供有针对性的援助和精准扶贫的措施。这一政策的实施,使中国在扶贫领域取得了前所未有的成就。中国甚至已经成为脱贫人数最多的国家。尽管数据显示,自改革开放以来,中国已经消除80%以上的贫困,但剩余的贫困地区才是最困难、最艰巨的挑战。扶贫工作是构建和谐社会的重要前提。这一目标也符合联合国2030年可持续发展目标。这是中国早在10年前就做出的承诺,是中国对国际社会和中国人民的坚定承诺。2015年,中国脱贫攻坚步伐加快,以期在2020年全面建成小康社会。贫困的判断标准既包括人均收入标准,也包含人民生活标准(图3)。

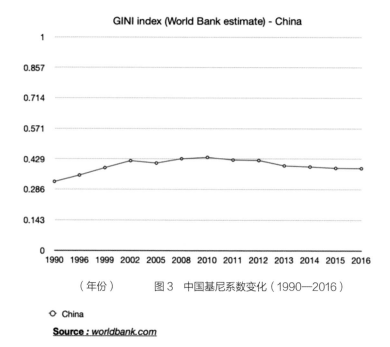

（年份）　　图3　中国基尼系数变化（1990—2016）

基尼系数（世界银行估算）- 中国
来源：worldbank.com

poor and the precise eradication of poverty.[①] Considering the decisive fight against poverty as a fundamental task and a leading indicator for the integral construction of middle-class society, the CPC Central Committee, with President Xi Jinping at the core of its leadership, has made a solemn commitment to eradicate absolute poverty as a whole by 2020. To this end, targeted assistance to the needy and precise eradication of poverty tend to eradicate poverty at its roots. As a result of this policy, China has achieved unparalleled results in the history of national poverty reduction. It has even become a country that has lifted the most significant number of people out of poverty. Although from a strict numerical point of view, more than 80% of poverty has been eradicated since the reform and opening up, the remaining deprived areas are, in fact, the most ambitious and difficult challenges. It is a campaign, a

Figure 3   Evolution of China's GINI coefficient (1990-2016).

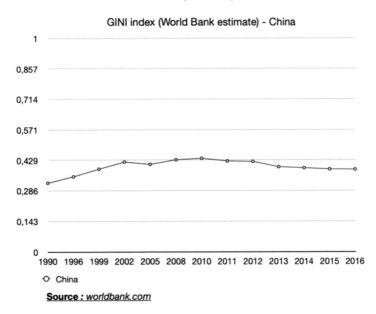

priority mission to build a harmonious society. This objective is in line with the Sustainable Development Goals in 2030. China set itself to achieve this commitment ten years earlier, so it is a strong commitment for the international community and its

① ZHOU, Yang, GUO, Yuanzhi, LIU, Yansui, WU, Wenxiang & LI, Yurui. (2018). "Targeted poverty alleviation and land policy innovation: Some practice and policy implications from China", Land Use Policy (74), pp. 53-65.

自中国提出"一带一路"倡议以来，下一个发展阶段已经不言自明。在这一背景下，中国已与非洲国家（比如位于非洲之角和沿海地区的埃塞俄比亚、吉布提、肯尼亚等国家）建立了长期贸易关系并加深了友谊。中国甚至提出在新冠肺炎疫情结束后免除部分非洲国家债务，续借部分发展贷款，这有力反驳了国际社会关于"一带一路"成员国可能被迫陷入债务螺旋的说法。在人类命运共同体中，共同发展模式既是"一带一路"的核心，也是全球化新范式（图4）。

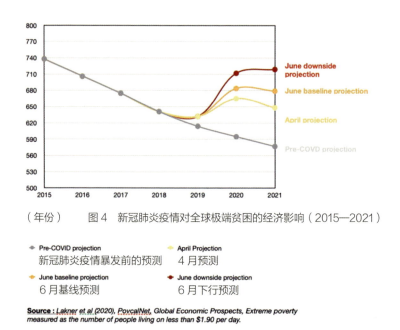

（年份）　　图4　新冠肺炎疫情对全球极端贫困的经济影响（2015—2021）

- ●— Pre-COVID projection
  新冠肺炎疫情暴发前的预测
- ●— June baseline projection
  6月基线预测
- ●— April Projection
  4月预测
- ●— June downside projection
  6月下行预测

Source: *Lakner et al (2020), PovcalNet, Global Economic Prospects, Extreme poverty measured as the number of people living on less than $1.90 per day.*

来源：拉克纳等人（2020），ProvalNet，全球经济预测，生活在极端贫困（日均低于1.90美元）中的人数

在这个框架下，我们提出一个假设：第四阶段是中国传播自身扶贫模式。中国提供的不是援助，而是发展。"授人以鱼，不如授人以渔"（经常被误认为出自《论语》，但其实出自《淮南子》）充分体现了这种长远眼光。中非合作论坛约翰内斯堡峰会以来，非洲

people. In 2015, therefore, we had seen an acceleration in this fight against poverty. The idea is for China to enter fully and ultimately into a moderately prosperous society. There is a criterion of per capita income to understand the phenomenon of poverty, but the indicators also include human standards (see Figure 3. Evolution of China's GINI coefficient).

Since China put forward the Belt and Road Initiative, the next development stage has been self-evident. In this context, China has established long-term trade relations and deepened friendship with African countries such as Ethiopia, Djibouti,

Figure 4 *The economic impact of COVID-19 on Global Extreme Poverty* (2015-2021).

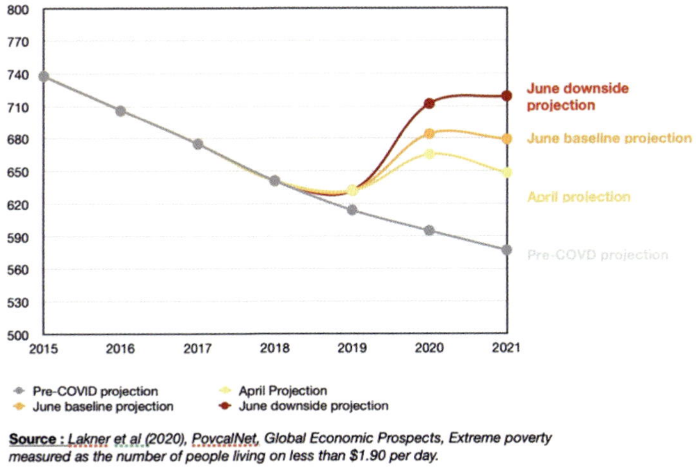

Source : *Lakner et al (2020)*, *PovcalNet*, *Global Economic Prospects, Extreme poverty measured as the number of people living on less than $1.90 per day.*

Kenya, to name but a few, in the Horn of Africa and coastal states. At the end of the COVID-19 crisis, China even canceled some African countries' debts and renewed some development loans, thus forcefully refuting the international community's claim that the member countries along the Belt and Road may be forced into a debt spiral. In a community with shared future for mankind, the joint development model represents the heart of the project and this new paradigm of globalization.

Within this framework, we can develop the hypothesis that the fourth stage will be disseminating China's poverty alleviation model. Rather than assistance, China offers development. The saying "It is better to teach people how to fish than to give people fish" from *Huainanzi*, though often mistakenly ascribed to *The Analects*, perfectly illustrates this long-term thinking philosophy. Since the

大陆启动了许多意义重大的项目，曾在 20 世纪 90 年代缺水缺电的闽东的脱贫经历刚好可以提供借鉴和参考。我们一直在讨论中非合作，但中阿合作也值得探讨。《习近平谈治国理政》对"一带一路"倡议的原始精神给出了明确的定义："弘扬丝路精神，就是要坚持合作共赢。中国追求的是共同发展。我们既要让自己过得好，也要让别人过得好。"中国在提出这一政治和道德理念的同时，还计划分享其扶贫经验。

从这个角度来看，我们可以说中国的扶贫工作是彻底的（"彻底"的词源意义 = 根源、初因、首要原因、问题的本质）。中国的举措并不是针对结果做出处理，而是从根源入手，调整因果结构，这也正是中医的理念。因此，在愚公移山精神的指引下，中国共产党绝不畏惧发展必要的意义深远的事业，其成果不一定能在一代人之后显现，但终将会在长期过程中逐渐显现。

历史悠久的发展范式和以人为本的原则

多年来，中国古代的一些文化理念一直被官方沿用，作为民族话语的基础。《摆脱贫困》一书中引用了大量相关内容，如杜牧、苏轼、白居易、丘迟等文人，孟子等思想家，甚至《管子》《道德经》《大学》《左传》《论语》《墨子》等著作。这些著作和思想对于执政进行了思考，并对

Johannesburg summit of the Forum on China-Africa Cooperation, many emblematic projects have been launched on the African continent,[1] and the experience of eastern Fujian, without water or electricity in the 1990s, now serves as a model and reference[2]. We talked about Sino-African cooperation, but it also seems right to say a word about Sino-Arab cooperation. In the book *Xi Jinping: The Governance of China*, a definition of the original spirit of the Belt and Road Initiative is given unequivocally: "To promote the Silk Road spirit, we need to focus on mutually beneficial cooperation. China pursues common development, which means we are aiming for a better life for the Chinese people and the people of other countries.[3]" In addition to this political and moral philosophy, the Chinese government intends to share its poverty reduction experience. In the same speech, President Xi Jinping pledges to "share experiences of development and poverty alleviation with the Arab states, and introduce those of advanced technologies that are suited to their needs."

From this point of view, we can say that China is radical in its fight against poverty, in the etymological sense of the term "radix," which means "roots," the "first cause," the "essence of a problem." In this approach, China seeks to tackle the causes rather than the results, starting from the root cause and adjusting the causal structure, which is also the philosophy of Chinese medicine. Therefore, under the guidance of the spirit of "Foolish Old Man Removes Mountains," the Communist Party of China is absolutely not afraid to develop necessary and far-reaching undertakings. The results may not appear after a generation but will gradually appear in the long-term process.

An ancient paradigm of development and the axiom of the people as a core foundation

For several years now, certain ancient Chinese cultural substratum elements have been enameling the official national discourse. *Up and Out of Poverty* has cited numerous ancient writers and thinkers, including Du Mu, Su Shi, Bai Juyi, Qiu Chi, and Mencius, involving such texts as *Guanzi*, *Daode Jing*, *The Great Learning*, *The Commentary of Zuo*, *The Analects*, and *Mozi*. Many of these texts and thinkers

[1] XI, Jinping. (2014). Op. Cit., pp. 333-341. ("Be Trustworthy Friends and Sincere Partners Forever", March 25, 2013).

[2] EDEH, Emmanuel Chidiebere. (2018). "Poverty alleviation in Africa: The impact of China's Aid", *International Journal of Arts and Social Science* (1:4), pp. 23-39.

[3] XI, Jinping. (2014). Ibid., pp. 347. ("Promote the Silk Road Spirit, Strengthen China-Arab cooperation", June 5, 2014).

相应时代的治国理政提出了建议和告诫。在当代民族话语中，这些元素承担了象征价值。儒家思想对人民的重视也再一次得以借鉴和思考。

因此，我们可以采取两种立场，一种是历史的，另一种是哲学的。第一个解释因素是历史的，是中国特色社会主义政治的有机组成部分。习近平主席对这一因素做了明确解释，指出"消除贫困、改善民生、逐步实现共同富裕是社会主义的本质要求"。2012 年，习近平主席宣布已在"社会主义初级阶段"获得成功，接下来将全力推进"全面建成小康社会"。第二种立场是哲学立场，在提交联合国教科文组织的人权哲学基础调查中，提出要继续参考 Zhang Yinde（2007）和陈明（2008）的研究工作，继承 Xiaoping Li（1997）和中国哲学家罗忠恕（1947）的古老传统。这位哲学家在分析中特别指出："中国社会政治关系的基本伦理概念是履行邻里义务，而不是要求权利。相互义务观念被视为儒家的基本观点。"这些儒家经典向我们讲述了哪些道理？《孟子》中说"民为贵"，并说"得天下有道：得其民，斯得天下矣；得其民有道：得其心，斯得民矣"，与法国哲学家、经济学家让·博丹的名言"人是真正的财富之源"不谋而合。

当我们漫步在曲阜孔子博物馆，还可以在墙壁上看到这样的愿景:"天下一家，四海一家。"赵汀阳正是受到这些文字的启发，在《天下体系：世界制度哲学导论》中指出，国际学者们应当深刻理解中国的多边全球化新范式 。从这个角度出发，脱贫致富必须是一项集体行为。贫困涵盖了多变的现实和不同的生存风险，我们已经对此做出详尽的阐释，

proposed a pragmatic reflection on good government and, in their time, gave their respective rulers advice and admonishments. In contemporary state discourse, these elements have symbolic values. Confucian notions are also mobilized, thought out, especially in the importance given to the people.

We can, therefore, adopt two positions, the first historical and the second philosophical. The first explanatory factor is historical and is an integral part of political socialism with Chinese characteristics. This factor is notably explained to us by Xi Jinping, recalling that "this is the essential requirement of socialism to eradicate poverty, improve people's livelihood, and achieve common prosperity." In 2012, President Xi Jinping presented the successes of "this first stage of socialism" and promoted "the building of a moderately prosperous society in all respect." The second position, philosophical, postulates a return to the work of Zhang Yinde (2007), Chen Ming (2008), taking up the older traditions of Li Xiaoping (1997) or the Chinese philosopher Lo Chung-shu (1947), in a survey submitted to UNESCO's survey on the philosophical foundations of human rights. In this analysis, the philosopher notably argues, "The basic ethical concept of Chinese social-political relations is the fulfillment of the duty to one's neighbor, rather than the claiming of rights. The idea of mutual obligations is regarded as the fundamental teaching of Confucianism." What exactly these ancient and canonical Confucian classics tell us? According to Mencius, "The people are the most precious treasure", adding that "there is a way to win the Empire: win the people and you will win the Empire. There is a way to win the people: win their hearts, and you will win the people", evoking us in a sense the French philosopher and economist Jean Bodin, stating that "the only wealth is men."

So when we walk around the Confucius Museum in Qufu, we can still read on some walls these words of hope: "The whole world is one family; the whole country is one family." Inspired by these words, Zhao Tingyang points out in his *The Tianxia System: An Introduction to the Philosophy of a World* that international scholars should deeply understand China's new paradigm of multilateral globalization. [1] In this respect, the fight against poverty has to be collective. Covering protean realities and different risks of existence, poverty, of which we gave an exhaustive definition, thus took on a new color and

---

[1] LIU, Weidong & DUNFORD, Michael. (2016). "Inclusive globalization: unpacking China's Belt and Road Initiative", *Area Development and Policy* (1:3), pp. 323-340.

Out of Poverty 脱贫致富

131

而在习近平主席的笔下，它又呈现出新的色彩和范畴："贫困思维"和"意识形态贫困"也是集体进步和进化的障碍。

清华大学当代哲学家陈来在分析中指出，中国长期坚持"以人为本"。这公认的观念可追溯至中国古代著作《管子》。陈来详细阐述了这项原则对中国思想世界和一种社会乌托邦的影响。正是这项原则，将务实、重视内在的中国与"以神为本"的其他国家区分开来。根据这一理念，习近平主席发表了题为《始终把人民生命安全放在首位》的讲话（收入《习近平谈治国理政》）。

陈明（2008）认为，这些哲学概念与哲学文本的交汇体现了东西方的文化差异。继承希腊哲学的文明强调城市作为一个政治组织的"城邦"概念，而儒家学说则以人和亲属关系为中心。城邦是一种"契约协议"，而亲属关系则以谱系和人与自然的和谐相处为基础。在政治学方面，哲学家亚里士多德主要关注权利和义务的概念。蒋庆（2003）在认真分析这些概念后提出："自由民主的主要问题在于，它将追求私欲作为政治的优先事项。一个目标自私的本质是不会改变的，无论它是基于个人、群体、国家或全人类的目标。自由民主把政治和道德完全分割了，这是一个主要问题。"因此，有必要在道德层面上考虑政治、改革的目的和国际关系。正是哲学和历史的这种多样性，孕育了闽东地区的长期分析解决方案。对中国现代性的这一探索已在国际学术界获得越来越多的认可。

scope under the pen of Xi Jinping: "the poverty of ideas" and "ideological poverty" have also been considered as an obstacle of collective progress and evolution.[①]

Chen Lai, a contemporary philosopher of Tsinghua University, pointed out in his analysis that China has long adhered to the philosophy of "putting people first." This axiom can be traced back to the ancient Chinese classic *Guanzi*. Chen Lai elaborated on this principle's influence on the Chinese ideological world and a kind of social utopia. This principle distinguishes China, which is pragmatic and values immanent moral integrity, from the "God-oriented" countries. In line with this axiom, President Xi Jinping published a speech entitled "Always Put the Safety of People's Lives First" in his book *Xi Jinping: The Governance of China* (November 24, 2013, p.215).

According to Chen Ming (2008), this melting pot of philosophical concepts and texts sometimes explains the cultural difference between the West and the East.[②] Civilizations that have inherited the Greek philosophy have emphasized the Polis, the city as a political organization, while Confucian philosophy is centered on man and kinship. The Polis is a "contractual agreement," kinship is based on genealogy and harmony between man and nature. In Politics, the philosopher Aristotle is mainly concerned with the notions of rights and obligations. Based on an excellent analysis of these concepts, Jiang Qing (2003) argued that "the main problem with liberal democracy is that it considers the pursuit of selfish desires as the priority of politics. A selfish goal does not change in nature, whether based on an individual, a group, a nation, or humanity. The major problem with liberal democracy is that it completely separates politics from ethics." Therefore, it is imperative to think about politics, the purpose of reforms, and international relations under this ethical dimension. In this regard, this philosophical and historical diversity has nourished the analysis and solutions implemented over the long term in eastern Fujian. The search for this Chinese modernity finally finds its completion and recognition within an ever-growing circle of international organizations.

[①] XI, Jinping. (2016), Op. Cit., p. 249.

[②] CHEN, Ming. (2008). "La philosophie politique confucéenne face à la globalisation", *Diogène* (221:1), pp. 128-145.

从闽东的例子到中国近期成就的新经验：撇开开拓精神重新理解农村扶贫实例

《习近平谈治国理政》对发展、教育和党中央扶贫工作做了一定介绍。在这部著作出版的同时，另一部作品也得以发行，书中介绍了改革开放 10 年后（1988 年至 1990 年间）闽东九个县市的经验。在强调中国传统象征、格言和智慧的同时，这本书提到了试验中出现的几个核心要求。第一，必须摆脱"贫困思维"，关于这一点，我们已在关于概念方法的部分通过"贫困文化"概念做了阐述。正是出于这个原因，我们认为有必要在对不同的认识论潮流进行早期反思时就提出这一概念，以便全面看待本书中提出的试验。第二，这本书倡导一种工业和生产的规范形式，注重借助特定产品、林业、畜牧业、食品加工、巨峰葡萄种植、茶叶种植脱贫致富。第三，脱贫还必须与农村社会主义文化建设相结合，从而消除剥夺感。扶贫工作还必须防范贫穷所固有的风险，如健康风险、闭塞和疾病。第四，必须投入部分资金鼓励农村集体经济。

在这个框架内，扶贫工作还必须考虑到民族维度，特别是在闽东的九个县市，这个问题格外重要。 因此，这里也体现出习近平主席所说的平等和民族团结等根本问题。民族问题在书中其他章节（如《畲族经济要更开放些》一文）继续作为分析对象，这一问题的重要性进一步凸显。"畲族文化节"也体现了对民族维度的重视，强调畲族民族文化、歌曲、民俗、谚语、音乐、民间舞蹈、流行故事、艺术、工艺……对地

From the example of eastern Fujian to the new experiences of China's recent achievements: Rereading a rural illustration of a way out of poverty, athwart the expression of a pioneering spirit as a driver for opening up horizons

In *Xi Jinping: The Governance of China*, Xi Jinping gives a certain introduction to the development, education, and the central fight against poverty. Simultaneously another book was also released to introduce the two years (1988 to 1990) of experiences in the nine counties and cities in eastern Fujian, in the wake of the reform and opening up undertaken a decade earlier. While echoing traditional Chinese metaphors, aphorisms, and wisdom, this book mentions several central requirements that emerged from the experiments. First of all, it is crucial to get rid of any "poverty mentality," which we had defined in our conceptual approach through the "culture of poverty" concept. For this purpose, we felt it necessary to say a word in our early reflection on the different epistemological currents to put it into perspective with the experiments presented in this book. Secondly, this work advocates a form of industrial and productive specification, focusing the way out of poverty on a specific product, forestry, livestock, food processing, Kyoho reasoning, tea cultivation. Thirdly, poverty reduction must also be accompanied by rural socialist cultural construction, making it possible to combat any desire for disaffiliation. This support must also prevent the risks inherent in poverty, such as health risks, obsolescence, and disease. Fourthly, part of the funds must be invested in encouraging the collective rural economy. [1]

Within this framework, the poverty alleviation work must also consider the ethnic dimension, especially in the nine counties and cities in eastern Fujian, where this issue is significant. Therefore, it also reflects the fundamental problems of equality and national unity mentioned by President Xi Jinping. (p.10; p.141). Other chapters of the book continue to analyze the ethnic issues, such as the article *The She Ethnic Economy Should Be More Open*, which further highlights the importance of this issue.[2] The "Ethnic She Cultural Festival" also emphasizes the importance of ethnicity (p. 30). It highlights the She ethnic culture, songs, customs, proverbs,

---

[1] For further informations, see: XI, Jinping. (2016). *Up and Out of Poverty*, Beijing, pp. 9-10.
[2] Ibid., pp. 131-132.

方文化的重视还必须伴随着市场经济意识的发展，畲族人应意识到自身拥有丰富的资源。此外，本书在第一部分提出了对年轻管理人员和领导干部的实践指导形式，倡导集体经济，建立廉政的历史维度。

针对贫困现象，这本书分析了闽东地区的劣势（缺乏电力和交通）和优势，并特别分析了依托当地企业、林业（包括茶园和果园）、渔业和海洋资源大规模开发农业的可能性。从这一点出发，这本书提出了合理的计划，并呼吁停止一切"盲目、鲁莽的投资"，告诫人们不要寄希望于突然出现"金矿"，而是要通过有针对性的重新造林来重现闽东山区古老的辉煌，制造机遇。这本书不仅是对当地经验的简单见证或反馈，还是一本关于地方官员行政、经济和政治道德行为的精简手册："绝不允许个人通过他们手中的权力来谋取私利，行政人员的主要任务是贡献和服务。"习近平主席强调地方层级的重要性，认为地方政府在采取具体行动、付诸实践、与当地群众建立"亲密"关系方面具有唯一性：在"亲密接近人民"方面，"基层政府承担巨大的责任"。鉴于此，六份报告的内容得到进一步发展。这些报告涉及短期和长期目标之间的时间性问题，还指出了经济增长速度与经济效益、资源开发与产业结构调整等方面的现实经济问题。福建省土地利用规划以及沿海地区和山区之间的平衡问题也需要得到进一步解决，还要考虑到早期改革和联合扶贫中的意识形态问题。最后一份报告涉及教育、技术和科学对经济发展的连锁影响。

music, folk dance, folktales, art, and crafts... This enhancement of local culture must also be accompanied by the development of an awareness of the market economy. The wealth of resources and raw materials postulates that this awareness should be developed within the She ethnic group (p.131). Besides, by advocating a collective economic chorus (p.12-12), as well as the historical dimension postulating the establishment of an honest government, this work proposes in the first part a form of a practical guide for young executives and officials.

In response to poverty, this book analyzes the eastern Fujian region's disadvantages (lack of electricity and transportation, p.83) and its advantages. It mainly explores the possibility of large-scale agricultural development based on developing local enterprises, forestry (including tea gardens and orchards), fisheries, and marine resources. For this reason, the book proposes reasoned planning and to stop all "reckless investment," carried out as if "blindly." Rather than relying on the sudden appearance of a "gold mine[1]", the book proposes to restore the ancient glories and create opportunities of the mountainous districts in eastern Fujian through targeted reforestation (p.134). This book is not only a simple testimony or feedback on local experience. It is also a condensed manual on the administrative, economic, and political ethics for the local officials with warnings such as "We absolutely cannot allow individuals to seek personal gain through the powers vested in them," "The main purpose of an executive is to contribute and serve," and "One cannot eat his cake and have it." President Xi Jinping emphasizes the importance of the local authorities and believes that local governments are unique in taking specific actions and practices to establish "intimate" relationships with local people. In terms of "close proximity to the people" (p.78), "basic-level governments have a huge burden of responsibility" (p.38). The management of the "six reports" is thus further developed.[2] These reports concern questions of temporality between short-term and long-term objectives. There are also practical and economic issues between growth and economic performance and between resource exploitation and industrial restructuring. Land use planning and the balance between the coastal and mountainous districts of the province also need to be developed. The ideological question is also to be taken into account in disseminating the first reforms and the

脱贫致富
Out of Poverty

---

[1] *Ibid.,* pp. 88.

[2] *Ibid.,* pp. 112-123.

经过三年的艰苦奋斗，"将近87%的闽东居民摆脱了贫困，走上了繁荣之路"。然而，书中更详细的分析显示，该省的平均生活水平与畲族的具体情况差距明显。事实上，在1985年，半数以上的畲族家庭（约1.6万户）生活在贫困中。三年后，只有4000户家庭仍在接受扶贫援助，即75%的家庭已经脱贫。尽管成功是巨大的，但我们仍要注意到，省级平均水平与民族间平均水平的差距接近12%。习近平主席还强调了群体内部的贫困转移和波动，即人们在脱贫之后在面临疾病、自然灾害或失业风险时可能重返贫困。

中国的扶贫工作很大程度上是在解决农村贫困问题。中国政府始终把减贫作为国家发展的首要目标和使命。中国政府坚持以人为本，努力使经济社会发展成果惠及全体人民。习近平主席在《摆脱贫困》一书中对闽东地区的发展（特别是对农村的发展机遇）提出了一些看法：选择闽东发展道路的关键在于工农业，闽东人民主要以农业为生，虽然我们因为务农而贫穷，但我们也可以通过发展农业而变得富裕起来。习近平主席认为：以小规模农业为基础的经济不能让人变富裕……它也没有真正的未来。因此，我们必须转向大规模农业，在保障粮食生产的同时，还要依靠山、海、河，发展农村企业，统筹发展农、林、畜、副产品、渔业。

例如，黑龙江山区的榛树种植业和江西昌平的渔业使许多家庭摆脱了贫困。在福建省北部的下党村，旅游和茶叶种植已经成为当地特产和收入来源。在贵州省华茂村，通过修建道路，当地悠久的文化遗产（特别是陶器制造）得以被外界所知。建设陶艺博物馆不仅方便保存并展示

joint fight against poverty. Finally, the last report concerns education, technology, and science and their knock-on effect on the economy's development.

After only three years of hard work, "nearly 87% of the inhabitants in eastern Fujian had managed to rise out of poverty and take the road to prosperity". However, a more detailed analysis in the book shows more significant disparities between the provincial average and the condition of the She ethnic group. Indeed, in 1985, more than half of the She households (about 16,000 households) lived in poverty.[1] Three years later, only 4,000 households are still receiving assistance for the poverty-stricken population, which means, a total of 75% households have been lifted out of poverty. Despite this success, we nevertheless note a differential of nearly 12% between the provincial and the intra-ethnic average. President Xi Jinping also underlines the shifting nature of the phenomenon of poverty and the fluctuations within groups, between those who get out of and return to poverty, faced with the risks of illness, natural disasters, or loss of employment (p.141-143).

Reducing poverty in China is, to no small extent, a matter of addressing poverty in rural areas. The Chinese government has always regarded poverty reduction as the primary goal and mission of national development. While putting people at first, the Chinese government strives to ensure that economic and social development results can benefit everyone.[2] In his book *Up and Out of Poverty*, President Xi Jinping put forward some views on the development of eastern Fujian, especially its rural areas: "The key to choose the development path lies in industry and agriculture. The people of eastern Fujian are mostly rural residents. Although we are impoverished because of farming, we can also become rich by developing agriculture." President Xi Jinping believes: "An economy based on small-scale agriculture cannot make people rich...it also has no real future. Therefore, we must turn to large-scale agriculture. While ensuring food production, we must rely on mountains, seas, and rivers to develop rural enterprises and coordinate agriculture, forestry, livestock, by-products, and fishery."

For instance, it is the cultivation of Hazel trees in the mountainous regions of Heilongjiang and fishery in Changping, Jiangxi Province, which have lifted many families out of poverty. Tourism and tea planting have become local specialties and income sources in Xiadang Village in northern Fujian Province. The time-honored,

脱贫致富
Out of Poverty

---

[1] *Ibid.,* pp. 142.
[2] XI, Jinping. (2014), Op. Cit., pp. 215-217.

这一文化财富，也促进了旅游业的发展。然而，有些村庄地处偏远、条件艰苦，有时最好的解决办法是重新安置居民。甘肃省王府沟村正是选择了这种方案。这些遍布全国的示范村使最贫困人口能够彻底脱离贫困。在离四川省巴中市（红四方面军长征前驻扎的地方）不远的南江县李寨村，贫困人口重新安置也有助于维持该地区的繁荣。目前，仍未脱贫的往往是少数民族地区。位于新疆西北部阿克陶县的克孜尔托村是柯尔克孜少数民族聚居地。在195户人家中，有132户生活在贫困线以下，这使得阿克陶高原成为中国最贫困的地区之一。在这种情况下，重新安置再次成为解决困难的办法。还有气候和农业条件恶劣的兰坪县吾马普村，2018年11月，这里92.89%的家庭生活在贫困线下，但在过去两年里，他们被陆续安置在兔峨乡示范村内。

中国的扶贫工作取得了举世瞩目的进步，近几十年来，农村地区的贫困率逐渐下降。自20世纪80年代中期以来，中国政府开始大规模、有组织、有计划地推进贫困农村的发展，已先后制定和实施了《国家八七扶贫攻坚计划》（1994—2000年）、2001—2010年和2011—2020年《中国农村扶贫开发纲要》，通过共识和社会行动帮扶贫困人口，加强扶贫工作。中国农村贫困人口的发展促进了社会和谐稳定和公平正义，也推动了经济和社会发展。2013年至2017年期间，中国已经帮助6600多万人摆脱贫困，生活得到切实改善的人口数量相当于法国人口总量。

local cultural heritage, pottery manufacturing, for example, was known to the outside world in Huamao Village, Guizhou Province, through road construction. The construction of a ceramic art museum facilitates the preservation and display of this cultural heritage and makes it possible to develop tourism. However, some villages are so remote and experience such difficult situations that the best solution remains the resettlement and the relocation of people. Wangfugou Village in Gansu Province has chosen this solution. These demonstration villages all over the country enable the most impoverished people to get rid of poverty completely. The resettlement of poor people has also helped sustain prosperity in Lizhai Village of Nanjiang county,[①] Sichuan Province, not far from Bazhong City, where the Fourth Front Red Army had been stationed before the Long March. It is often the ethnic group areas that have not yet shaken off poverty. Kizilto Village is among the Kyrgyz ethnic group communities living in Akto County in north-western Xinjiang. Of the 195 families, nearly 132 are below the poverty line. Thus, the plateau region of Akto is one of the most impoverished areas in the country. In this case, resettlement is once again the solution to difficult situations. The climate and agricultural conditions are bad in Wumapu Village of Lanping County. In November 2018, 92.89% of the families here lived below the poverty line, but they have been placed in the Demonstration Village of Tu'e Town in the past two years.

China's poverty alleviation work has made world-renowned progress. Poverty rates in rural areas have declined in recent decades, mainly due to China's impressive progress (*Agriculture for Development*, 2008). Since the mid-1980s, the Chinese government has promoted the development of deprived rural areas in an organized and planned manner on a large scale. It has successively formulated and implemented plans for poverty alleviation, including the National Plan to lift 80 million people out of poverty in seven years (1994-2000), the China Rural Poverty Alleviation Programme (2001-2010), and the China Rural Poverty Alleviation Programme (2011-2020), to help the poverty-stricken people and strengthen the poverty alleviation through the consensus and social activities. The development of the rural poor people in China has promoted social harmony and stability, equity and justice, thus stimulating economic and social development. Between 2013 and 2017, China has helped more than 66 million people get rid of poverty. The number of

① ZUO, Changsheng. (2018). The Evolution of China's Poverty Alleviation and Development Policy (2001-2015), Beijing, pp. 78.

减贫是整个人类社会的共同事业，中国农村贫困人口的发展是全球减贫事业的重要组成部分。中国已提前实现联合国千年发展目标贫困人口减半目标，为全球减贫事业做出了重大贡献。由习近平主席提出的这一中国式社会主义模式创造了一个经济奇迹，如今，中国正在分享这个奇迹，特别是为非洲提供这种成功模式的经验，为非洲国家制定发展政策提供了参考。

2001年，中国政府发表《中国农村扶贫开发的新进展》白皮书，随后定期发布其他报告，让我们对扶贫工作的进展有了更深入的了解。2012年中共十八大以来，政府推出一系列重要举措，启动农业扶贫"七年计划"和"十年计划"，加大农业扶贫力度。我们对此不做深入阐述，仅列举其中几项：《国家林业扶贫攻坚规划（2013—2020年）》《农业行业扶贫开发规划（2011—2020年）》《全国优势特色经济林发展布局规划（2013—2020年）》和将贫困地区生产的96种特产进行系统整合的《特色农产品区域布局规划（2013—2020年）》。这些政策似乎是闽东地区政策的延续，在每个村庄推广一种特产。

中国政府创新发展援助方式，实施精准扶贫、精准脱贫的基本战略。近年来，中国通过建立档案，明确贫困人口数量，分析贫困原因和发展需要，对贫困人口和贫困地区进行分类引导，并采取针对性措施。这套做法切实提升了脱贫攻坚的实际效果。中国通过落实有针对性的救助要求、设立有针对性的项目、分配有针对性的资金、对家庭采取有针对性的措施，确保贫困人口的生存权。

people whose lives have been actually improved is equivalent to the total population of France. [①]

Naturally, poverty reduction is a common cause for every human society, while the development of China's rural poor people is a crucial component of the global cause for poverty reduction. Nevertheless, ahead of schedule, China has achieved the goal of halving the poverty-stricken population defined in the United Nations Millennium Development Goals and has thus made a significant contribution to the global cause of poverty reduction. In the end, the Chinese-style socialist model proposed by President Xi Jinping has created an economic miracle. Today, China is sharing this miracle by providing this successful model for Africa and providing a reference for African countries to formulate development policies.

In 2001, the Chinese government also published the white paper entitled *Fighting Rural Poverty in China*, followed by the publication of other regular reports, offering us a better insight into the process of this plan. Since the 18th Congress convened in 2012, the government has launched a series of significant action guidelines, including the "seven-year plan" and the "ten-year plan" for poverty alleviation in agriculture, and stepped up efforts in agricultural poverty alleviation. Without aiming to be exhaustive in this survey, we recall in particular the national program to combat poverty through forestry (2013-2020), the program of development assistance in agriculture (2011-2020), the national plan on the development and distribution of competitive and specific economic forests (2013-2020), and the program on the regional distribution of agricultural specialties (2013-2020) methodically integrating 96 specialties produced in deprived areas. These policies seem to continue the eastern Fujian region's policies, promoting a local specialty in each village.

The Chinese government, innovating development aid methods, is now implementing the fundamental strategy of targeted assistance to the poor and the targeted eradication of poverty. In recent years, China has made a clear picture of the number of poor people by establishing an archive, analyzing the causes of poverty and the need for development to guide poor people and areas according to their categories, and implemented measures in a targeted manner. It improves the actual

① TAN, Weiping. (2018). China's Approach to Reduce Poverty: Taking Targeted Measures to Lift People out of Poverty, International Poverty Reduction Center in China(IPRCC), April 18, 2018, Addis Ababa.

脱贫致富
Out of Poverty

关于教育，我们论述得不多。中国教育部的一份报告指出，到 2019 年 11 月底，中等职业学校在减少贫困方面发挥了积极作用。在极端贫困地区，中国共有 347 所中等职业学校，在校生近 60 万人。该报告还称，2017 年，约有 14.2 万名中等职业学校毕业生找到了工作，就业率超过 90%。2017 年，共有 250 多万名学生获得奖学金和助学金，其中一半来自西部地区。习近平主席还指出，"让 14 亿中国人民享有更好更公平的教育"是"国家长远发展的基础"。这份成绩单令我们想到以顽强精神攻克每个难关的"铁杵磨针"精神。在《摆脱贫困》中有一章专门论述了教育问题，文中提到，1985 年全辖区内近 40.3% 的人是文盲。习近平主席早在 20 世纪 90 年代就大力鼓励增加和保障更多人口接受培训教育。

中国采取的各项扶贫措施终于取得了成效。自 1949 年成立以来，中国帮助 8 亿多人口摆脱贫困，对全球减贫的贡献率超过 70%。中国共产党还承诺到 2020 年彻底消除贫困，比联合国《2030 年可持续发展议程》中设定的期限提前了 10 年。中国的成绩甚至得到一向吝于赞美中国的美国赞赏。2020 年美国民主党总统候选人伯尼·桑德斯说："中国及其领导层在消除极端贫困方面取得的进展超过了人类文明历史上任何一个国家。"

这种经济活力正在基层显现。过去 40 年里，中国 GDP 以年均 9.5% 的速度增长。1978 年，中国国内生产总值仅占世界 GDP 的 1.8%，现在则正创造全世界 15% 的财富。此外，中国人均可支配收入从 1978 年的

effects of the fight against poverty. It ensures the right to live of the poor by materializing targeted assistance requirements, the establishment of targeted programs, the allocation of targeted funds, and the adoption of targeted measures to households.

We have only said some brief and quick words about education. A report by the Chinese Ministry of Education indicates that secondary vocational schools had played an active role in reducing poverty by the end of November 2019. There are 347 secondary vocational schools in areas of extreme poverty, with nearly 600,000 students enrolled. Furthermore, about 142,000 graduates from these schools have got employed in 2017, with an employment rate of over 90 percent. More than 2.5 million students from these schools received scholarships and grants in 2017. Half of them come from the country's western regions. President Xi Jinping also considered "better and fairer education for the 1.4 billion Chinese people"[1] as the "foundation of national development in the long run." This endeavor incidentally reminds us of the proverb, "An iron pestle can be ground down to a needle," in praise of this persevering spirit involved in the success of every task, and the reward after each long struggle. *Up and Out of Poverty* devotes a specific chapter to education. The article mentioned that in 1985, nearly 40.3% of the people in the jurisdiction were illiterate.[2] President Xi Jinping strongly encouraged the increase and guarantee of more people to receive training and education as early as the 1990s.

All these combined efforts are finally producing results. Since its founding in 1949, the People's Republic of China has helped lift more than 800 million people out of poverty, contributing more than 70 percent to global poverty reduction. However, the CPC has also promised to eradicate poverty thoroughly by 2020, ten years ahead of the United Nations' deadline in *The 2030 Agenda for Sustainable Development*. Even the United States, which has been stingy in its praise of China, has acknowledged this success: "China and its leaders have made more progress in eradicating extreme poverty than any other country in the history of civilizations," said Bernie Sanders, the Democratic nominee for president of the United States in 2020.

The impact of this economic vitality is being felt at the grassroots level. China's gross domestic product has grown by an average of 9.5 percent a year for the past 40 years. As a result, China, which accounted for 1.8 percent of the world GDP in

---

[1] XI, Jinping. (2014). Op. Cit., pp. 211-212.
[2] XI, Jinping. (2016). Op. Cit., pp. 207.

171 元（约合 21.86 欧元）跃升至现在的 26000 元（约合 3324 欧元），贫困人口减少了 94 个百分点。特别是在农村，农民各方面的生活质量都得到了改善。2017 年，全国农村人均可支配收入（按 1978 年可比价格）增至 2106.9 元，在 1978 年仅为 133.6 元，这意味着收入增长了 15 倍。在农业生产率增长的尾声，中国国家主席习近平强调一种新资源正在出现，即农村劳动力，这种资源既可能成为新的负担，也可能成为可利用的财富。中国鼓励有计划地将这些人口的一部分转移到第二和第三部门，这与圣保罗、开罗或加尔各答鼓励农村人口外流导致形成新的贫困群体的做法截然不同。

与此同时，中国家庭消费能力也显著提高。2017 年，农村人均消费（按 1978 年可比价格）达到 1719.8 元，是 1978 年的 14 倍。恩格尔系数（食品支出在收入中的比重）从 1978 年的 67.7% 下降到 2017 年的 31.2%，下降了 36.5%。中国强劲的经济增长为减贫做出重大贡献，但也扩大了收入差距，加剧了区域贫困。因此，中国采取了一系列措施来促进贫困地区的发展。其中一个细节值得注意：2001 年至 2010 年间，政府增加了对 15 万个贫困村庄的援助。因此，这些村庄的人均净收入年增长率比全国农村地区平均水平高 3%。贫困地区收入与农村平均收入差距缩小。贫困地区人均收入占全国农村人均收入的比重由 1985 年的 51.8% 提高到 2016 年的 68.4%。

金融（特别是小额信贷）也在支持中国国家扶贫计划。1482.5 万户贫困家庭获得生产发展金融扶持，累计贷款 5871.3 亿元，未偿还贷款 2346.8 亿元。贫困家庭贷款吸纳率从 2014 年的 2% 飙升至 49.5%。目前，在 832 个市级以上贫困地区，平均每个地区有 17 家企业，12.8 万个贫困村，每两个社区结成一个集体经济。另外，快递行业异军突起。中国电子商务的爆炸式发展是中国整体经济增长的一部分，这有助于减少收

1978, now produces 15 percent of its wealth. Moreover, China's average disposable income has jumped from 171 yuan (around 21.86 euros) in 1978 to 26,000 yuan (around 3,324 euros) today, reducing poverty by more than 94 percent. Especially in the countryside, the quality of life has improved in all areas. In 2017, the average per capita disposable income in rural areas (calculated at constant 1978 prices) was 2,106.9 yuan, compared with 133.6 yuan in 1978. This represents a 15-fold increase in income. At the end of the increase in agricultural productivity, President Xi Jinping highlights the emergence of a new resource, that of rural labor, which is likely to become either a new burden or a wealth to be exploited. Rather than encouraging the rural exodus and forming new layers of poor citizens, as in Sao Paulo, Cairo, or Calcutta, the controlled transfer of part of these populations to the secondary and tertiary sectors is encouraged. [1]

As a result, the consumption capacity of households has improved significantly. Also, in the rural areas, the average per capita consumption (calculated at constant price of 1978) reached 1,719.8 yuan in 2017, fourteen times that of 1978. The Engel coefficient (the share of income allocated to food expenditure) fell from 67.7 3% in 1978 to 31.2 3% in 2017, a decrease of 36.5 3%. This strong economic growth has contributed significantly to poverty reduction in the country, but it has also widened income disparities and aggravated regional poverty. Hence a series of measures have been taken to promote the development of these impoverished regions. One detail in particular: between 2001 and 2010, the government increased the aid granted to 150,000 poor villages. As a result, the annual growth of net per capita income in these villages was 3% higher than the average of rural areas. The gap between income in disadvantaged regions and the average income in rural areas has narrowed. The proportion of per capita income in impoverished regions in the country's per capita income in rural areas increased from 51.8% in 1985 to 68.4% in 2016.

Finance, particularly microfinance, is also supporting China's national poverty alleviation plan.[2] A total of 14.825 million poor households have received the financial support to develop their production, with 587.13 billion yuan in loans contracted and 234.68 billion yuan outstanding. The loan take-up rate for poor households has soared to 49.5%, up from 2% in 2014. At present, there are 832 poverty-stricken

---

[1] Ibid., pp. 198

[2] YANG, Bo, JIALALI, Paerhati & WEI, Xianhua. (2011). "Microfinance in China's Poor Area and Its Impact to Loan Type-Evidence from Xinjiang Uygur Autonomous Region", Fourth International Conference on Business

入不平等。2019 年，快递公司支持了 905 个地方农产品和地方特产推广项目。国家邮政局（NPO）数据显示，其中 23 个项目年投递次数超过 1000 万次，大型快递公司为贫困地区创造了 26.8 万个就业岗位，投递的产品价值 3.67 亿元（约合 5180 万美元）。今年前三季度，快递行业开发了 1100 多个同类项目，帮助在全国城镇地区销售地方农产品和地方特产 28.4 万吨（增长 69%），总交易额 38.8 亿元（增长 25.6%）。2019 年上半年，全国被划入"贫困"地区的农产品网络销售额达 1109.9 亿元，同比增长 29.5%。

一些特定的经济领域也参与中国减贫事业中，乡村旅游就是其中之一。一方面，随着中国人生活水平普遍提高，更多人选择到国内外旅游；另一方面，中国文化遗产和环境资产不断增加，在偏远农村地区，乡村旅游逐渐受到重视。中国发展乡村旅游作为消除贫困的有效手段，获得世界旅游组织的赞许。在中国的各个经济活动领域都可以找到这样的例子，文化部门也不例外。例如，2019 年 11 月初，第 20 届中国美食节在江西南昌举办，其中一个目的正是帮助贫困地区增加收入。CCA 主任说："餐饮服务业所需的大部分原材料和辅料都是初级农产品，在贫困地区大批量购买这类产品可以有效增加当地农民的收入。"

areas above the city level, with an average of 17 enterprises and 128,000 poverty-stricken villages in each area. Every two communities form a collective economy. Besides, the express delivery industry has suddenly emerged. The explosive development of e-commerce in China is part of China's overall economic growth, thus reducing the income inequality.[①] In particular, delivery companies supported 905 projects last year to promote the sales of local agricultural products and local specialties. 23 of these projects represent more than 10 million deliveries each year, according to figures from the National Post Office (NPO). Large delivery companies have provided more than 268,000 jobs in deprived areas. The products delivered are worth 367 million yuan (about US $51.8 million). During the first three quarters of this year, these companies developed more than 1,100 similar projects, helping to sell 284,000 tons of local agricultural products and local specialties (+69%) in the country's urban areas, with a total transaction volume of 3.88 billion yuan (an increase of 25.6%). Online sales of agricultural products in districts classified as "poor" at the national level reached 110.99 billion yuan in the first half of 2019, up 29.5% compared to last year.

Some specific economic sectors are also involved in China's poverty reduction. Rural tourism is one of them. On the one hand, as Chinese people's living standards generally improve, more people choose to travel at home and abroad. On the other hand, Chinese cultural heritage and environmental assets continue to increase. In remote rural areas, rural tourism has gradually been attached importance. The World Tourism Organization has welcomed the decision the Chinese authorities to promote rural tourism as an effective means of combating poverty. Examples such as these can be found in almost every field of Chinese economic activity. The cultural sector is not to be outdone. At the beginning of November 2019, for example, Nanchang, the capital of Jiangxi Province, hosted the 20th China Food Festival, intending to help poverty-stricken areas increase their income. "Most of the raw materials and accessories needed for the food service industry are primary agricultural products, and large-scale purchase of these products in poor areas can effectively increase the income of local farmers," stated the CCA director.

---

① CHEN, Yi & TSAO, Haitao. (2017). "A comparison of approaches of poverty alleviation through e-commerce", 3rd International Conference on Information Management (ICIM), Chengdu, pp. 78-82.

2019 年，位于中国西北部的新疆维吾尔自治区采取了一项具体而富有活力的行动。帕米尔高原某光伏发电项目产生的全部收益都将用于当地精准扶贫工作。该项目位于塔什库尔干塔吉克自治县，为两万千瓦光伏发电项目，已生产电量 4600 多万千瓦时。项目于 2018 年 5 月建成，是新疆首个也是唯一一个光伏扶贫电站。根据当地政府的数据，项目每年可以产生约 2000 万元（约合 283 万美元）利润，约占塔什库尔干预算收入的六分之一。一位名叫范磊的当地领导说："该项目不仅有助于扶贫工作，还可以促进农村地区振兴和典型工业发展。"塔什库尔干被称为新疆"离太阳最近的地方"，平均海拔超过 4000 米。由于自然条件恶劣，这里也是减贫工作最具挑战性的地区之一。

除了省政府或中央政府，私营部门也参与中国的扶贫事业中。自 2015 年以来，中国私营企业在国家的鼓励下投身扶贫事业。中国超过 8.8 万家私营企业共投入 139 亿元（约合 19.9 亿美元）扶贫资金。2019 年 10 月中旬，在北京召开的减贫与发展高层论坛公布了这些数据。截至 6 月底，新增工作岗位 66.15 万个，接受培训 94.1 万人。

继往开来

在《精神现象学》中，黑格尔提出了一个独特又令人不安的观点：先入为主的印象会扰乱常识，我们应谨慎看待身边最熟悉的事物。很多情况下，我们对习以为常的事物缺乏真正的了解。中国在电信、交通基础设施、出版、中等教育和大学教育等领域，以及在脱贫事业上，已经发生了无声的变革，取得了巨大进展。每一年，我们都能看到中国取得

For its part, Xinjiang Uygur Autonomous Region in northwest China, opted in 2019 for a concrete and energizing action for the region[1]. All the profits from a photovoltaic plant installed on the Pamir plateau have been used to reduce poverty. The 20,000-kilowatt plant in the Tajik Autonomous County of Taxkorgan produced more than 46 million kilowatt-hours. Constructed last May, it is the first and only photovoltaic power plant in Xinjiang dedicated to poverty reduction. The local government can generate annual profits of about 20 million yuan (around $2.83 million), about one-sixth of Taxkorgan's budget revenue. "The plant can help not only the poor but also promote the revitalization of rural areas and the development of typical industries," said Fan Lei, a senior district official. Dubbed "the district closest to the sun" in Xinjiang, Taxkorgan is located at an average altitude of more than 4,000 meters. Due to the harsh natural conditions, it is also one of the most challenging regions for poverty reduction.

Initiatives to combat poverty come from governments, whether provincial or central and from the private sector. Since 2015, private companies of China have been encouraged to participate in the national effort to fight poverty. More than 88,000 private enterprises in China have contributed more than 13.9 billion yuan (around US $1.99 billion) of investment to the fight against poverty. These figures were made public in mid-October 2019 in Beijing at a national action forum for targeted poverty reduction. By the end of June, they had provided 661,500 jobs, and 941,000 people had been trained.

Conclusion and opening

In the *Phenomenology of Spirit*, Hegel puts forward a unique and disturbing point of view that a priori offends common sense, inviting us to be prudent, concerning what is precisely most familiar to us.[2] Very often, what we think we know through habits is what we know least. China has undergone silent changes and made great progress in telecommunications, transportation infrastructure, publishing, secondary education and university education, and poverty alleviation. Every

[1] YANG, Yang & ZHANG, Aiping. (2016). "Precise Poverty Alleviation Problems and Countermeasures in Xinjiang Uygur Autonomous Region", 4th International Education, Economics, Social Science, Arts, Sports and Management
[2] HEGEL, Friedrich. (1807). *Phenomenology of Spirit*, Cambridge, 538 pp.

的成绩：中国在 2019 年 12 月公布的 PISA 成绩中重返第一；撒哈拉以南非洲基础设施和能源项目；维多利亚瀑布机场；正在讨论中的阿比让电信项目；2019 学年将有三所孔子学院在法国落成（波城、鲁昂、兰斯），在文化层面，法国成为中国的杰出合作伙伴（量化比较中仅次于美国）；中国在萨罗尼克湾地区，如在比雷埃夫斯投资。这个简短的总结不仅是一份普莱维尔式的清单，它还展示了一个勇于为自身提出规划、为其他国家做出表率的新中国，至于那些金融、社论和学术成果，不过是对这一点的印证，甚至只是附加说明。对于自身模式，中国更倾向于相互切磋，而不是强加，这种模式建立在一系列原则和哲理之上。中国也在不断地重新解读这些模式，以更好地利用。2013 年 7 月，即习近平主席在阿斯塔纳一所大学发表关于"一带一路"倡议的著名讲话之前两个月，一项关于孝顺父母、保护弱势群体的法案在中国推出。

　　欧洲权威的中国历史与管理专家艾蒂安·巴拉兹教授早在 1954 年就预言，中国即将在世界舞台崛起："到 21 世纪，中国世纪将取代俄美世纪。"未来将会证明他的预测是正确的。同样，库恩基金会主席罗伯特·库恩在接受新华社采访时也表示："未来的历史学家在撰写我们这个时代的编年史时，其中一个特写章节很可能就是中国的精准扶贫。"现在，中国与伙伴们分享的经验正在成为构建命运共同体全面方案与倡议的组成部分。新冠肺炎疫情再次证明，人类是一个共同体，是一个国际共同体，这是任何国家都无法反驳的。在后疫情时代，开放包容的全球化最终仍将是世界大势。"开放带来进步，封闭必然落后；经济形势越复杂，开放与合作就越重要，在经济、文化和学术领域，以及在共同抗击贫困方面，都是如此。"

year, we can see what China has achieved: China's return to the top spot in the PISA results announced in December 2019; infrastructure and energy projects in sub-Saharan Africa; Victoria Falls airport; the telecommunication projects in discussion with Abidjan; the inauguration of three new Confucius institutes in the prefectures of Pau, of Rouen, and the sub-prefecture of Reims in France during the 2019 academic year (At the cultural level, France has become an outstanding partner of China, second only to the United States in a quantitative comparison); and the investment in the Saronic Gulf region, such as Piraeus. This brief summary is not only a Prévert-style list, but it also shows a new China that dares to propose plans for itself and set an example for other countries. The financial, editorial, and academic achievements are just confirmation of this point or even only additional explanations. For its own model, China is more inclined to learn from each other rather than impose it. This model is based on a series of principles and philosophies, and China is continually reinterpreting them to make better use of them. A law on filial piety and the protection of vulnerable persons came into force in July 2013.[1] Two months later, President Xi Jinping visited the University of Astana, where he gave his famous speech on the Belt and Road Initiative.

Professor Etienne Balazs, one of the best European historians of Chinese History and Administration, predicted China's rise in the world as early as 1954: "Our Russian-American century will be succeeded by a 21st Chinese century". The future will tell if he was right. Similarly, in a recent interview with Xinhua Agency, Robert Kuhn, president of the Eponymous Foundation, said, "When historians of the future write the narrative of our times, one of the characteristics may well be the targeted reduction of poverty in China." This Chinese experience, shared with its partners, is today part of a more comprehensive proposal and initiative to enter into a world community with a shared future. COVID-19 proves that humanity is in this collective and international community once again and that no country can manage it alone. In the post-COVID-19 era, open and inclusive globalization will always represent the general trend of the world. "Openness leads to progress, and withdrawal leads to regression: The more complicated the economic situation is, the more important openness and cooperation are in economic, cultural, and academic matters, as well as in the joint fight against poverty."

---

[1] XI, Jinping. (2014). Op. Cit., pp. 315-319.

阿丽亚·阿尼皮娜
Aliya Anipina

阿尔达克·哈力吾拉
Ardak Kaliolla

中国扶贫改革

China's Anti-poverty Reforms

阿丽亚·阿尼皮娜,高级讲师,博士在读;任职于哈萨克斯坦阿里—法拉比哈萨克国立大学东方学系中文教研室。阿丽亚·阿尼皮娜一直从事一线教学工作,前后发表了25篇教科研方法论文章,编写了汉语语法、汉语语音教程教材四本,编纂出版了四本汉哈俄英词典。

阿尔达克·哈力吾拉,高级讲师,专业译者,硕士;任职于哈萨克斯坦阿里—法拉比哈萨克国立大学东方学系中文教研室。阿尔达克·哈力吾拉长期从事教学科研工作,发表了许多教科研方法论文章,参与编写《大众汉语(哈文版)》四部教材,为学习中文的学生和自学者编写了在线课程,并且翻译出版了大量汉语言教学资料、教科书和文学作品。主要翻译出版作品有"基础中文"教科书(共四册),《朱永新教育小语》等。

Aliya Anipina is a senior lecturer studying for her Ph.D. She is working in the Department of Sinology, Al-Farabi Kazakh National University, Kazakhstan. Aliya has been working in the front line of teaching and has published 25 methodological articles on textbook research, four textbooks on Chinese grammar and Chinese phonetics, and four Chinese-Kazakhstan-Russian-English dictionaries.

Ardak Kaliolla is a senior lecturer and a professional translator with a master's degree. She is working in the Department of Sinology, Al-Farabi Kazakh National University, Kazakhstan. She has published many methodological articles on textbook research, participated in the preparation of four textbooks of *Chinese for the General Public* (*Kazakh version*), developed online courses for students and self-learners of the Chinese language, and translated and published many Chinese-language teaching materials, textbooks, and Chinese literary works. Her principal translations and publications include four volumes of the textbook Basic Chinese and *Words of Zhu Yongxin on Education*.

在人类历史中，贫困是长期客观存在的社会现象，贫困现象是社会不平等的表现。不平等是指社会中不同群体占有的财富和资源数量不均。在一个社会中，富人占有更多财富和资源，导致形成了不同的社会层级。

每个国家都在抗击贫困。随着富人在社会中占有的份额不断增加，贫困问题变得更加严重，扶贫力度也需不断加大。这一点已在发达国家的经历中充分体现。

许多科学家已对贫困问题及国家在其中扮演的角色开展了研究。其中，查尔斯·布思和西伯姆·朗特里是最早对贫困问题进行实证研究的学者。亚当·斯密、托马斯·马尔萨斯和大卫·李嘉图等学者也曾对这一课题展开研究。托马斯·马尔萨斯认为，造成贫困的原因是人口过剩和粮食短缺。贫困是由人口过剩造成的，而穷人自身应对此负责。这一过程会受到疾病和战争的显著影响。

赫伯特·斯宾塞认为贫困是一种社会法则。他在《社会静力学》一书中指出，贫困和不平等是伴随社会生产增长而产生的。由于生产无法停止，贫困问题也无法得到彻底解决。斯宾塞称，贫困是一种个人问题。他还说，一些人可以解决自身问题而不招致麻烦，而另一些人也可以与贫困和平共处。他还认为，贫困的衡量标准是不存在的，乞讨是贫困最糟糕的形式。

贫困问题作为与经济发展相生相伴的一种现象，已在世界各国出现并持续存在。贫困不仅影响人民的生活水平，还会对社会和政治造成影响，导致犯罪增加。减贫已成为全世界的共同目标。

在许多国家，判断扶贫工作成功与否的标准主要是收入与消费。但富人也可能是文盲，因而无法做出关乎个人生活的重要决定。基于这一点，为了理解全世界的减贫实践，形成了以下几种观点。

- 以成功为标准
- 以基本需要为标准
- 以人的发展机会为标准
- 失去稳定收入是造成贫困的主要因素

In the history of humanity, the problem of poverty is an objective phenomenon in society. The phenomenon of poverty shows the inequality of society. Inequality is the amount of wealth and resources that belong to certain groups in society. The fact that they belong to the rich in society divides it into different levels of groups.

The fight against poverty takes place in any country. As the rich's share increases, poverty becomes more acute, and the struggle against it intensifies. It can be seen from the experience of well-developed countries.

Many scientists have studied the problem of poverty and the role a state plays in it. Among them are Charles Booth and Seebohm Rowntree, who were the first to research poverty empirically. Adam Smith, Thomas Malthus, David Ricardo studied poverty. According to Malthus, poverty is caused by overpopulation and food shortages. It means that poverty is due to overpopulation and the poor themselves are to blame. This process is regulated by effective phenomena such as disease and war.

Herbert Spencer says that poverty is one of the laws of society. In his book *Social Statics*, he writes that poverty and inequality arise in response to the growth of social production. Due to the impossibility of stopping production, this issue will not be fully resolved. H. Spencer says that poverty is each individual's personal problem. He also says that people can solve their problems without getting into trouble, while others can co-exist with poverty. Herbert Spencer also argues that it is impossible to determine the criteria for poverty. The worst form of poverty is mendicancy.

As a phenomenon that accompanies economic development, poverty has appeared and continues to exist in countries worldwide. Poverty affects not only people's living standards but also the social and political fibers of society, and in many cases, it leads to an increase in crime. Therefore, the task of reducing poverty is the goal of the whole world. In many countries, the fight against poverty is based on the concept of income or consumption. A person may be rich, but they may be illiterate and may not be able to make important decisions, which will affect their quality of life. With this in regard, to understand the problem of poverty in world practice, the following viewpoints have been formed:

- depending on success
- depending on basic needs
- depending on the opportunities for human development
- The main factor causing poverty is the loss of a stable income.

德国哲学家格奥尔格·黑格尔（1770—1831）提出国家的概念是基于内部目的而不是自然法。黑格尔认为贫困问题是一种主观决定，却忽视了对人形成助力的现代方法与资源。他在分析了英国的税收制度及针对贫困的特殊税收后得出这样的结论："人们有特殊的需求，是否努力工作并不重要，他们失去了靠自身劳动生活的权利，因此变得粗鲁。"

自邓小平时代以来，发展不平衡导致了许多问题。主要表现在：随着改革的深入，中国社会出现了富人和最贫困人群这两个阶层。据官方统计，中国最贫困人口占总人口的 3%，10% 的最贫困家庭的财产仅占中国财产总量的 1.4%，10% 的最富裕家庭财产占中国财产总量的 45%。

过去，贫困仅存在于农村地区。根据亚洲开发银行的数据，中国生活在最低生活标准以下的低收入者人数为 3700 万，占城市总人口的 8%。如今，城乡居民收入差距为 3.24:1。与此同时，中国的失业率也在上升。

目前，中国的贫困人口已从 9800 万减少到 1660 万。当今中国较 20 世纪 60 年代已发生了翻天覆地的变化。过去的几十年里，中国取得了巨大的进步。 2019 年，中国在庆祝新中国成立 70 周年之际重申了在 2020 年彻底消除贫困的目标。

中国自实施西部大开发战略以来，已投入大量资金用于西部省份的基础设施建设，农村社会事业也实现了跨越式发展。现在，中国全部的农村人口已纳入医疗保障体系，许多人能够领取基本养老金，最低工资实现了省级统筹。但中国也意识到，还需要继续抗击贫困，贫困是阻碍经济增长的关键因素。改革开放之前，由于经济落后和低经济增长率，中国的贫困率远远高于其他国家。现在，中国的贫困率已经下降。贫困地区积极贯彻国家扶贫政策，开展教育、文化、卫生及其他社会项目。中国在消除贫困这一方面已成为其他发展中国家的典范。 1949 年中华人民共和国成立前，中国是一个经济落后、大部分人口处于贫困中的国家。中华人民共和国成立后进行了全国土地改革，废除了延续了两千多

Georg Hegel (1770-1831), a German philosopher, developed the concept of the state based on the internal purpose, not on the principle of natural law. Hegel considered the problem of poverty in terms of subjective determination. He ignored modern methods and resources to help people. Analyzing the tax system in England, where there is a special tax on poverty, he concluded, "People have special needs. Where hard work does not matter, they lose the right to live by their own labor, and as a result, they become rude."

Since the Deng Xiaoping era, uneven development has caused many problems, mainly manifested: with the deepening of reforms, two classes have emerged in Chinese society: the rich and the poorest. According to official statistics, the latter makes up 3% of the population, 10% of the most impoverished families in China only own 1.4% of the entire property, while 10% of the wealthiest families own 45%.

In the past, poverty was limited to rural areas. According to Asian Development Bank, the number of low-income citizens living below the subsistence level is 37 million, accounting for 8% of the total urban population. Today, the income gap between the urban and the rural population is 3.24: 1. At the same time, unemployment is growing in the country.

Today, the number of Chinese living in poverty decreased from 98 million to 16.6 million. China has undergone tremendous changes since the 1960s and has made great strides over the past few decades. While celebrating the 70th anniversary of the founding of the People's Republic of China in 2019, China reiterated its goal of eradicating poverty by 2020.

Since it implemented the "Western Development" strategy, China has invested heavily in infrastructure development in the western provinces. The state has also made a big leap forward in the implementation of rural social programs. Now, 100% of China's rural population has access to health care, and many receive a basic pension. In China, the minimum wage is also being paid at the provincial level. The Chinese also recognize that the fight against poverty still exists, which is a key factor, and poverty is an obstacle to economic growth. Prior to the reform and opening up, China had a much higher poverty rate than other countries due to economic backwardness and low growth rates though it has dropped now. Education, culture, health, and other social projects are being developed in poor areas to implement the state policy to combat poverty. As a result, China has become a model for other developing countries in the fight against poverty. Before the founding of

年的封建土地所有制，农村的生产力大大提升。1953 年，中央政府在国家发展政策的基础上制订了"国家五年发展规划"。中国经济开始增长，城乡地区贫困人口开始减少。但 20 世纪 50 年代的公有制和集体经济与当时的生产力发展水平不相适应。因此，中国走上了优先发展重工业的道路。重工业是"大跃进"期间的重点，"大跃进"导致中国经济发展放缓。在长达 10 年的"文化大革命"期间，中国经济发展缓慢，并没有减少贫困。当时，中国人口迅速增长，经济基础设施岌岌可危。经济增长并没有使人民获益。研究指出，1966 年到 1977 年，贫困人口人均收入增长到 18 元，在 1979 年不足农村人口人均收入的一半。在此期间，村民平均年收入增长未能超过 15%，每天消耗 2100 卡路里。

1978 年，中国决定对外开放，当时中国农村贫困人口为 2.5 亿，贫困人口占总人口的 31%，但当时官方公布的贫困率非常低。于是，中国政府决定在农村开展扶贫工作。扶贫工作在三个方面展开：一是实现经济增长；二是适应抗击贫困的渐进措施；三是注重采取大量政府帮扶措施帮助农村地区困难群众。

20 世纪 70 年代末和 80 年代初，在推行家庭联产承包责任制的基础上，农村地区开始大力发展农业。粮食价格上涨 102%。中国不发达地区的贫困程度随之开始下降。

自 1990 年以来，中国政府实施了多项扶贫攻坚计划。在扶贫工作中，政府对贫困人口集中的地区给予不同程度的财政补贴，主要目的是在这些地区创造就业机会，从而促进经济增长，减少贫困。

进入 21 世纪后，中国政府调整了扶贫政策，将贫困人口也包括在内。首先，政府不再针对贫困地区，取而代之的是通过"无贫困村"项目对

the People's Republic of China in 1949, China's economy was backward, and most of its population was impoverished. After the founding of the People's Republic of China, it carried out national land reform to end the two-thousand-year feudal system, thus increasing rural areas' productivity. Based on the national development policy in 1953, the Chinese adopted a "Five-Year National Development Program." As a result, China's economy began to grow, and the number of poor people began to decline in rural and urban areas. However, the public ownership and collective economy in the 1950s did not match the level of productivity development at that time. Therefore, China gave priority to the development of the heavy industry. It became the focus of the "Great Leap Forward" period, which slowed down the Chinese economic growth. During the decade-long "Cultural Revolution," China's economic development was slow and did not reduce poverty. At that time, the population increased rapidly, and the economic infrastructure was precarious. Economic growth did not help the people. According to a study, from 1966 to 1977, the poor people's per capita income increased to 18 yuan, less than half of the rural population's per capita income in 1979. During this period, the villagers' average annual income growth did not exceed 15%, and they consumed 2,100 calories a day.

In 1978, China decided to open to the outside world. At that time, there were 250 million poor people in rural China, accounting for 31% of the total population. However, the official poverty rate at that time was very low. The Chinese government decided to carry out poverty alleviation work in rural areas and carried it out in three aspects. One was to achieve economic growth. The second was to adapt to gradual measures to fight poverty. The third was to take a lot of government assistance measures to help people in need in rural areas.

In the late 1970s and early 1980s, a strong focus on agriculture in rural areas began based on the reform of private land use. Grain prices increased by 102%. As a result, poverty began to decline in China's underdeveloped regions.

Since 1990, the Chinese government has been implementing various programs to combat poverty. In the fight against poverty, government agencies allocate financial subsidies at different levels to areas with high concentrations of the poor. The main goal is to create jobs in those areas. All this is to boost economic growth and reduce poverty.

In the new millennium, the Chinese government has made changes to the fight against poverty, taking into account the impoverished population. First, the

特定村庄进行帮扶。其次，通过扶贫项目投资对贫困地区农民工进行培训。近年来，中国还在农村推出了其他扶贫举措，例如取消农业税、降低农村儿童学费和提升农村儿童受教育机会。

农村医疗卫生工作进一步加强，社会救助制度使许多贫困地区的情况得到改善。通过 2005 年的调整，贫困人口减少到 2400 万。中国农村地区扶贫工作取得了显著效果。

在中国，城市贫困有其自身的衡量标准和成因。20 世纪 90 年代初，中国城市开始经济转型——中国政府推行企业改革，导致城市贫困加剧。城市家庭的主要经济支柱失去工作，家庭陷入贫困。全国各地大力开展扶贫工作。2013 年 1 月 18 日，时任国务院副总理刘延东重点强调了内蒙古、河北、江西、湖南等地区的扶贫工作。为了抗击贫困，中国为农村地区提供了更多受教育机会，国务院扶贫办主任刘永富表示，尽管经济增长放缓，但用于扶贫的资金不会减少。他认为，直接拨款只能取得短期效果，但教育投资对扶贫的作用是长期的，效果显著。2012 年，政府投入 2996 亿元扶贫资金。值得注意的是，全国主要大学加大招生力度，并提供用餐补助。

目前，中国的社会政策智库正面临一项艰巨的任务：如何缓解严重的不平等。导致这种状况的一个原因是收入与消费的"库兹涅茨效应"，这种效应发生在结构性变化期间，即劳动力从农业生产等低生产率部门向工业生产等高生产率部门转移期间。1955 年，哈佛大学经济学家西蒙·库兹涅茨提出了不平等与繁荣之间的 U 形关系。这意味着，在这方面，当劳动力离开土地，提升了自身生产力，开始挣更多钱时，不平等就会随之加剧。而当工业化结束时，受教育程度更高的公民将向国家提出再分配的要求，不平等现象将减少。

government does not target poor areas. Instead, specific villages will be assisted by the project "Villages without Poverty." Second, the government trains migrant workers in poor areas through investment in poverty alleviation projects. In recent years, China has also launched other poverty alleviation measures in rural areas, for example, the abolition of agricultural taxes, the reduction of rural children's tuition, and the improvement of rural children's educational opportunities.

The work of the rural medical system has also improved. The social assistance system has helped many poor areas. As a result of this restructuring in 2005, the number of poor people decreased to 24 million. The fight against poverty in rural areas has been successful.

In China, urban poverty has its own measurement standards and causes. In the beginning of the 1990s, Chinese cities underwent economic transformation. The Chinese government's reform in enterprises resulted in increased poverty in the city. The main breadearners in the family have lost their jobs , and Urban families have become poorer. The Chinese nation has struggled with this poverty. On January 18, 2013, the then Chinese Vice Premier Liu Yandong highlighted poverty alleviation in the regions of Inner Mongolia, Hebei, Jiangxi, Hunan and others. China has provided access to education in rural areas to fight poverty. Liu Yongfu, director of the State Service for Poverty Alleviation, said that despite the slowdown in economic growth, funding for poverty reduction would not decrease. According to him, the direct monetary impact can be only temporary, but the effect of education investment on poverty alleviation is long-term and has significant effects. In 2012, the government invested the funds of 299.6 billion yuan in poverty alleviation. It is worth noting that major universities across the country have increased their enrollment efforts and provided meal subsidies.

Today, China's social policy strategists face a difficult task. This is primarily due to high inequality. One of the reasons is the "Kuznets effect" of income and consumption, which occurs during structural changes when the labor force moves from a low-productivity sector in agricultural production to high-productivity industrial production. In 1955, Harvard economist Simon Kuznets marked the relationship between inequality and prosperity with the letter U. In this regard, inequality is exacerbated when the labor force leaves the land, becomes more productive, and earns more money. When industrialization is over, more educated citizens will demand the State for redistribution, and inequality will decrease again.

中国能否继续保持增长？"放缓论"的支持者认为中国的经济增长源于两点——廉价劳动力从农业部门转向生产部门，以及投资增长，但二者均几近枯竭。事实上，耶鲁大学的奥列格·钦维斯基认为，中国经济增长不会在不远的将来急剧放缓，私营企业生产率提高是促进经济增长的一个关键因素。在这方面，他借鉴了经济学家劳伦·勃兰特和朱晓东提出的"中国增长因素"，即"中国奇迹"的主要驱动力源于过去30年来私营非农业部门生产率的增长。1978—2007年，公共部门的生产率提高了1.52%，私营企业提高了4.5%。在此期间，私营企业创造了4.2亿个就业机会。如果中国向公共部门投入更多的财政资源，私营企业能否继续保持增长？2007年，一半资本投资流向公共部门，其中只有13%被花掉。在过去20年里，存款率从21%增长到40%。国内生产总值能够弥补对低生产率部门的效率低下的资源分配。耶鲁大学的斯蒂芬·罗奇在研究了中国的"十二五"规划后指出，中国的经济增长模式已经逐步转变，转为促进内需消费，这意味着中国的投资将会下降。

　　公共部门一直在接受稳定、低廉的融资流。许多中国人除了将存款存入国有银行之外，并无其他储蓄手段，他们通过这种方式获得较低的利息。这些资金绝大部分作为贷款流向公共部门。据中国创业投资有限公司首席财务官兼上海美国商会主席白德能称，中国90%的银行贷款流向国有企业，而国企创造的 GDP 仅占总量的50%，其余的10%银行贷款流向私营企业。政府向国有企业发放补贴，并签署对这些企业有利的资源协议，而向私营企业仅发放低额补贴，从而人为地制造壁垒。经济学家谢国忠指出，对国有企业固定资产的投资比私营企业高出20%～30%。与此同时，国有企业的临时成本比私营企业高50%。如果国有企业和私营企业在金融市场中能够获得相同的资金来源，中国经济将变得更有效率，并能够将利润分配给所有阶层。

Will China continue to grow? Proponents of the "slowdown theory" attribute China's growth to the near exhaustion of the two sources of growth, namely the transfer of cheap labor from the agricultural sector to production and the investment increase. In fact, according to Oleg Tsivinsky of Yale University, growth in China should not be expected to slow sharply in the near future. Productivity growth in the private sector is a key factor in economic growth. In this regard, he draws on the study of economists Loren Brandt and Zhu Xiaodong's "Growth Factor in China," where the main driving force of the "Chinese miracle" is the growth of productivity in the private non-agricultural sector over the past three decades. The 1978-2007 productivity in the public sector increased by 1.52% and by 4.5% in the private sector, which generated 420 million jobs during this period. Would the private sector growth continue to grow if China used the public sector's financial resources wisely? In 2007, the public sector accounted for half of the capital investment, of which only 13% was spent. The growth of deposits has increased from 21% to 40% over the last twenty years. GDP was able to compensate for inefficiently allocated resources to the low-productivity sector. Stephen Roach of Yale University, who studied China's 12th Five-Year Plan, said China's economic growth model has gradually changed to promote domestic consumption, which means China's investment will decline.

The public sector has been accepting stable and low-cost financing flows. Many Chinese have no other means of saving other than deposits in state-owned banks, and they earn lower interest rates in this way. Most of these funds flow to the public sector as loans. According to Robert Theleen, chief financial officer of ChinaVest, and the American Chamber of Commerce in Shanghai, 90% of bank loans go to state-owned companies, which produce only 50% of China's GDP, while only 10% of bank loans go to private companies. The government grants subsidies to state-owned enterprises and signs resource agreements that are beneficial to these enterprises, while granting only low subsidies to private enterprises, thus creating artificial barriers. According to economist Andy Xie, investments in fixed assets of state-owned companies are 20-30% higher than in the private sector. At the same time, the temporary costs of public sector companies are 50% higher than those of the private sector. If the financial market was informed that both types of companies would receive the same source of funding, the Chinese economy would be more efficient and would distribute the profits to all segments of the population.

经济学家针对如何抗击贫困提出了各种措施。北京师范大学收入分配研究院院长李实表示，财富再分配将"非常困难"，需要进行全面的、系统性的改革，个别的改革能够起到的效果微乎其微。在这方面，经济学家持不同意见。有人认为，应该增加社会保险的融资体系，如对医疗、住房、养老金和教育进行补贴。由于个人需要支付这些费用，才导致中国储蓄率如此高。向社会保障体系投入更多资金将鼓励中国人扩大消费支出，从而促进中国经济增长。

中国在建立社会保障体系方面已经取得很大进展。近年来，中国取消了针对农民的税费，并向所有农村居民发放养老金。政府进一步降低公立学校 16 岁以下学生的学费，并鼓励修建面向穷人的住房。与此同时，中国政府目前已实现医疗保险覆盖率 95% 的提升，而在 2000 年，医疗保险仅覆盖 15% 的人口。

经济学家指出，所有与税收、社会保障、公共支付有关的改革均属于二次分配。也就是说，改革涉及的二次再分配方法比结构性改革更有效，后者影响的是主要收入的分配。这些措施的主要目的是提高公共部门的经济效率，从而与私营企业竞争。同样，取消对资源、电和水的国家补贴也能起到作用，这些都有利于国家。在中国，减少不平等的主要有效途径是资本分配改革——减少或消除国有企业的融资优势。这样做不仅对私营企业有帮助，还能提供更多工作岗位，实现在整个经济体系中平均分配财富。当然，这些改革遭到了拥有权力的个体与组织的反对。目前，政府正在改善社会保障体系，从而减少这部分阻力，这样做既可以获得平民百姓的认可，也更易于实施。

中国政府已承诺，到 2020 年，帮助 200 个村庄的 6.8 万户低收入家庭脱贫。在中国最贫困的地区，人均年收入达到 1634 美元。在山西省，平均收入增长了 12%。政府和商人都在帮助穷人。

Many economists suggest a variety of measures to combat poverty. Li Shi, Dean of the China Institute of Inequality at Beijing Normal University and an economist, says the redistribution of wealth would be "very difficult" and would require comprehensive and systematic change. Individual reforms will have little effect. In this regard, economists' opinions differ. Some say that the system of financing social insurance should be increased, for example subsidies for health care, housing, pensions and education. China's high savings rate is due to the individual payment of expenses. Putting more money into the social security system will encourage Chinese people to expand consumer spending, thereby boosting China's economic growth.

The state has made great strides in creating a social protection system. In recent years, China has abolished taxes and duties on farmers and granted pensions to all rural residents. The government has further reduced tuition fees for students under the age of 16 in public schools and encouraged housing projects for the poor. At the same time, the Chinese government has increased the health insurance coverage by 95%, which only covered 15% of the total population in 2000.

According to economists, all reforms related to taxation, social security, and public payments are secondary distribution. In other words, the secondary redistribution method involved in reform is more effective than structural reform, which affects the distribution of primary income. The main purpose of these measures is to increase the economic efficiency of the public sector to compete with the private sector. Similarly, the removal of state subsidies for resources, electricity and water can also play a role, which will benefit the country. In China, the most effective way to reduce inequality is capital distribution reform, namely reducing or eliminating the financing advantages of state-owned enterprises. This would help private sector companies, employ more people, and distribute wealth equally throughout the economic system. Of course, the reforms are being opposed by powerful and influential individuals and organizations. At present, the government is improving the social security system to reduce this part of the resistance. This improvement will not only be recognized by the ordinary people, but also easier to implement.

Chinese authorities have promised to lift 68,000 low-income households from 200 villages out of poverty by 2020. In the most impoverished areas of China, the per capita annual income reaches US$ 1,634. In Shanxi Province, the average income increased by 12%. The government and businesses are helping the poor.

西藏自治区党委书记表示，2018 年有 18 万人脱贫，2019 年有 15 万人获得固定收入。2018 年，西藏开发扶贫项目 700 个，培训农牧民 3.6 万人，新雇用了 4.7 万人保护环境。

2018 年，内蒙古自治区政府投入 15 亿美元用于扶贫。全国贫困人口减少 23.5 万。当地政府计划建设高科技生产线，为失业者提供就业机会。

电商阿里巴巴公司也致力于扶贫。2018 年，阿里巴巴将中国 600 个贫困村庄变成"淘宝村"。此外，从 2015 年开始，在阿里巴巴发起的"万企帮万村"行动中，有 6 万家私营企业与该公司合作抗击贫困。

17 家林业公司与多个省份签署谅解备忘录，总金额达 2.5 亿美元。农民参与林业和园林绿化，解决了许多人的就业问题。参与林业和园林绿化的企业可以获得国家提供的补贴。

这些措施提高了中国贫困人口的收入，穷人数量开始减少。根据国家统计局的数据，2018 年，中国贫困人口平均收入增长了 6.5%。

根据国际货币基金组织的数据，2010 年，中国共产党在一次会议上宣布扶贫计划，当时的人均 GDP 是 4500 美元，5 年后达到 8200 美元，到 2018 年，人均 GDP 升至 9600 美元。

俄罗斯工业家和企业家联盟主席维塔利·曼克维奇称："中国的国内需求在增长，这意味着经济也在增长。此外，中国企业不再注重生产对进入国外市场至关重要的消费品，转而注重生产供国内使用的优质产品。随着中国人逐渐变得富裕，他们对优质产品的需求也在增加，因此中国企业越来越重视生产高质量的科技产品，以免失去不断增长的国内市场。消除贫困是'中国制造'计划的重要组成部分。这个项目对中国有着重要意义，因此，中国特别关注扶贫改革。"

According to the Secretary of the Party Committee of the Tibet Autonomous Region, 180 thousand people will be lifted out of poverty in 2018, 150 thousand people will receive a regular salary in 2019. By 2018, Tibet had developed 700 poverty alleviation projects, trained 36,000 farmers and herders, and employed 47,000 people to protect the environment.

The Inner Mongolia authorities will spend US\$ 1.5 billion on poverty alleviation in 2018. As a result, the number of poor people in the country decreased by 235 thousand. Local governments planned to create a high-tech production assembly line to provide jobs for the unemployed.

The online shopping service Alibaba is also helping to fight poverty. In 2018 it turned 600 poor Chinese villages into "Taobao villages." Besides, 60,000 private companies are working with the company in its poverty-alleviation initiative, which began in 2015 with the slogan "10,000 companies will help 10,000 villages."

Seventeen forestry companies signed memorandums of understanding with multiple provinces. The total amount is US\$ 250 million. The participation of farmers in forestry and landscaping has solved the employment problem of many people. Enterprises participating in forestry and landscaping can receive subsidies from the state.

These measures have increased the impoverished people's income in China, and the number of poor people has decreased. According to the National Bureau of Statistics, in 2018, the needy people's average income in China increased by 6.5%.

According to the data from the International Monetary Fund, the Communist Party of China announced a poverty alleviation plan at a regular meeting in 2010. The GDP at that time was US\$ 4,500 which reached US\$ 8,200 in five years. By 2018, the GDP rose to US\$ 9,600.

According to Vitaly Mankevich, president of the Russian-Asian Union of Industrialists and Entrepreneurs (RSPP), "Domestic demand is growing in China, which means that the economy is growing. Also, Chinese companies no longer focus on producing consumer products essential to entering foreign markets, but turn to producing high-quality products for domestic use. As the Chinese gradually become wealthy, their demand for high-quality products is also increasing. Therefore, Chinese companies pay more and more attention to high-quality technological products to avoid losing the growing domestic market. Thus, eliminating poverty is an important part of the 'Made in China' plan. This project is of great significance to China. Therefore, China pays special attention to poverty alleviation reforms."

2020 年 5 月 25 日，"两会"在北京召开，这是中国政治生活中的一件大事。"两会"总结了过去一年的工作，还提出了未来的目标和具体任务。"两会"指中国人民政治协商会议和全国人民代表大会，前者是中国最高的人民咨询委员会，于 5 月 21 日召开，而第十三届全国人民代表大会于 5 月 28 日闭幕。

会议开始后，与会者默哀一分钟，悼念因新冠肺炎疫情去世的同胞。"两会"讨论了各领域的问题。除了抗击新冠肺炎疫情，中国人民还在关注扶贫和未来的经济发展前景。《政府工作报告》指出，2020 年所有低收入农村居民将彻底摆脱贫困。中央和地方政府将削减预算支出。

到 2020 年，中国将摆脱贫困，14 亿人步入中等收入社会。中国主要官方媒体《人民日报》称，这意味着"中国将提前十年实现联合国可持续发展目标中的第一项目标"。

40 年来，7 亿中国人摆脱了贫困。这与中国从 1978 年开始实行的改革开放政策密切相关。过去几十年里，中国政府陆续推出一些旨在帮助低收入人群的项目。

中国还将自身的脱贫经验向其他国家推广。2019 年秋季联合国大会期间发布的《中国落实 2030 年可持续发展议程进展报告》介绍了中国参与的最不发达发展中国家的扶贫攻坚项目。中国通过在老挝、柬埔寨等发展中国家举办各类培训班和论坛、建设"扶贫示范村"等方式，与其他国家分享了本国的扶贫经验。

著名东方学家、汉学家尤里·塔夫罗夫斯基指出："中国已在贫困中挣扎了数十年。"习近平担任总书记后，中国政府加大扶贫力度，在习近平提出的中国梦中包括了到 2021 年（中国共产党建党 100 周年之际）彻底消除贫困的计划。

塔夫罗夫斯基曾在 2019 年预测，中国政府即将实现这一目标。然而，突如其来的新冠肺炎疫情为实现这个目标蒙上了阴影，但消除贫困的进程不会就此停滞。塔夫罗夫斯基说："我认为中国在 2020 年年底将宣布彻底消除贫困。中国将是全世界第一个实现这一目标的国家。"他还表示，

On May 25, 2020, a momentous event took place in China's political life. Two plenary sessions convened in Beijing to summarize the past work and set future goals and objectives. The two sessions refer to the Chinese People's Political Consultative Conference and the National People's Congress. The former is China's highest People's Consultative Committee, held on May 21, while the 13th National People's Congress closed on May 28.

The sessions began with a minute of silence to mourn the COVID-19 pandemic victims. Participants of the two sessions discussed issues in various fields. Besides fighting the pandemic, the Chinese people also pay attention to poverty alleviation and economic development prospects. The *Government Work Report* said that all low-income villagers would be lifted entirely out of poverty this year. Central and regional authorities will reduce budget expenditures.

By 2020, China will lift all its people out of poverty, and 1.4 billion people will enter a middle-income society. According to the *People's Daily*, China's leading official media, this means that "China will achieve the first goal of the United Nations Sustainable Development Goals ten years ahead of schedule."

Over the past 40 years, 700 million Chinese have been lifted out of poverty. It is closely related to the reform and opening up policy that China has implemented since 1978. In the past few decades, the Chinese government has successfully launched many projects to help low-income people.

China is spreading its experience in fighting poverty to other countries. In the *Report on China's Progress in Sustainable Development 2030* on the UN agenda, published in the fall of 2019, China participated in the poorest developing country's projects to fight poverty. China shares its experience by organizing various training programs and forums and building "poverty-alleviation model villages" in developing countries such as Laos and Cambodia.

Well-known orientalist and sinologist Yuri Tavrovsky points out, "China has been struggling in poverty for decades." After Xi Jinping became General Secretary, the Chinese government has increased poverty alleviation efforts. The "Chinese Dream" proposed by Xi Jinping includes the plan to eradicate poverty entirely by the year 2021 (the 100th anniversary of the founding of the Communist Party of China).

Tavrovsky predicts in 2019 that Beijing would soon achieve this goal. Of course, the COVID-19 pandemic has aggravated the situation, but it has not prevented China from achieving its goal to eradicate poverty. "I am confident that by the end of 2020, Beijing will announce that it will finally overcome poverty,"

其他国家应当学习中国的经验，目前在发达国家也仍然存在贫困和生活水平低下的问题。

塔夫罗夫斯基指出，1978 年，中国 95% 的人口生活在贫困之中。到 2012 年，仍有 9900 万贫困人口。到 2020 年，中国将摆脱贫困。

中国的贫困线是由各省自行确定的。塔夫罗夫斯基以新疆维吾尔自治区为例说明了当地贫困标准。该指标根据居民收入水平将人口分为四种颜色。绿色表示家庭年收入超过 5000 元（约 700 美元），这属于正常水平。其次是黄线，即家庭年收入在 4500 ～ 5000 元（630 ～ 700 美元），这通常意味着不足。然而，真正贫困的是被划入橙色和红色的家庭，其年收入分别为 4000 ～ 4500 元和 4000 元（约 560 美元）。

2020 年 5 月 23 日，习近平在参加全国政协十三届三次会议联组会时指出，"全国农民要走共同富裕的道路"，不能让任何人落在后面。他认为，农业的地位不应该降低，应当集中精力解决这一领域的问题。

至于新冠肺炎疫情后的中国经济形势，李克强总理在报告中指出，这是中国自 1994 年以来首次不设定国内生产总值增长的量化目标。新冠肺炎疫情对中国经济是一个重大打击，导致 2020 年一季度国内生产总值下跌 6.8%。李克强称国内生产总值下跌是为抗击疫情"必须承受也是值得付出的代价"。

习近平主席在 5 月 23 日的讲话中指出，应当"用全面、辩证、长远的眼光"分析经济形势，"努力在危机中育新机、于变局中开新局"。中国政府不再注重实现可量化的目标，转而制定更加灵活的目标。2020 年的主要任务是实现可持续就业、消除贫困和全面建成小康社会。但在全国人民代表大会上也提及了一些数字，其中包括创造超过 900 万个就业岗位，通货膨胀率不应超过 3.5%，失业率不应超过 6%。与此同时，中国的国家预算赤字为 1 万亿元（约合 1416 亿美元），占国内生产总值的 3.6%。

Tavrovsky said. "This is the first case in the world." According to the expert, other countries should learn from China's experience, as poverty and low living standards also exist in developed countries.

According to Tavrovsky, 95% of China's population lived in poverty in 1978. 99 million were still poor in 2012. But there should be no impoverishment left in 2020.

The poverty line in China is determined independently in each province. For example, Tavrovsky gave the indicators of the Xinjiang Uyghur Autonomous Region. It divides the whole population into four colors according to the level of income. Green means that the family's annual income is more than 5,000 yuan (about US$ 700), which is normal. The next is the yellow level, where the family's yearly income is 4,500-5,000 yuan (about US$ 630-700), which is usually not enough. However, the real poverty is the orange and red levels with an annual income of 4,000-4,500 yuan and 4,000 yuan (around US$ 560), respectively.

Xi Jinping said at a joint meeting of members of the National Committee of the Chinese People's Political Consultative Conference on May 23, 2020 that "Chinese peasants should follow the path of common prosperity" and that no one should be left behind. According to him, the status of agriculture should not be lowered, and all efforts should be focused on solving this sector's problems.

As for China's economic situation after the pandemic, Premier Li Keqiang pointed out in the report that this is the first time since 1994 that China has not set a quantitative target for GDP growth. The pandemic is a significant blow to the Chinese economy, causing GDP to fall by 6.8% in the first quarter of this year. Li Keqiang said that the GDP decline was a "necessary and worthwhile price" to fight the pandemic.

On May 23, President Xi Jinping said China's economic situation "should be analyzed from a comprehensive, dialectical, and long-term perspective" and "efforts should be made to achieve new opportunities and new achievements." The Chinese government has chosen to set flexible goals instead of achieving quantifiable goals. The main tasks for 2020 are to achieve sustainable employment, fight poverty, and create a society of moderate prosperity. However, at the National People's Congress, some figures were mentioned. Among them was creating more than 9 million jobs, keeping inflation below 3.5%, and the unemployment rate below 6%. At the same time, China's state budget deficit is 1 trillion yuan (about US$ 141.6 billion), which

政府的主要任务是帮助各地区提供就业岗位、维持生活水平并确保市场正常运转。这些目标的实现需要依靠预算间转移机制。此外，各地区 2020 年将发行总计 3.75 万亿元（约合 5259 亿美元）的专项债券，为扶助省级经济筹集更多资金。预算投资额将达到大约 6000 亿元（约合 841 亿美元）。

在税收负担方面，2020 年将减少 2.5 万亿元（3526 亿美元）税收。这包括降低或暂时取消增值税，降低养老金等基金的缴纳额，以及对中小微企业免征保险费。

2020 年 5 月 21 日，习近平在与代表会谈时强调要做好"六稳"工作、落实"六保"任务。"六稳"包括：稳就业、稳金融、稳外贸、稳外资、稳投资、稳预期工作。"六保"指：保居民就业、保基本民生、保市场主体、保粮食能源安全、保产业链供应链稳定、保基层运转。

中国政府对稳定和保障信念坚定，对经济形势充满信心。《政府工作报告》中提道："我们将稳中有进，为全面建成小康社会奠定坚实基础。"这就好比对运动员进行培训时，先让他们热身，接下来再执行更复杂的任务。

尤里·塔夫罗夫斯基解释道："之所以没有完全抛弃 GDP 的量化增长，主要出于两个原因。首先，要为可能暴发的第二波疫情做好应对准备。其次，中国出口的前景尚不明朗。目前还不知道出口额会达到什么程度。鉴于其他国家经济不稳定，疫情尚未控制住，中国出口能带来多大收益尚属未知。"

专家表示，中方对这个问题持积极态度。与此同时，塔夫罗夫斯基认为，抛弃具体的数字指标对中国领导层来讲是一个艰难的决定，由于实行了几十年的计划经济，中国领导人已习惯了参考量化的数字。

accounts for 3.6 percent of the GDP.

The authorities' main task is to help the regions provide employment, maintain living standards, and ensure the functioning of the market. It will be done through the mechanism of inter-budgetary transfers. Besides, the regions will issue most of the target bonds totaling 3.75 trillion yuan (about US$ 525.9 billion) this year to raise more funds to support the provincial economy. About 600 billion yuan (about US$ 84.1 billion) will be spent on budgeted investments.

The tax burden will be reduced by 2.5 trillion yuan (about US$ 352.6 billion) in 2020. It involves lowering rates of or temporarily removing VAT and contributions to pensions and other funds, exempting medium, small and micro enterprises from insurance payments.

Xi Jinping spoke with delegates on May 21, calling for stability and security on "Six Stabilities" and "Six Guarantees." The former means stabilizing employment, financial, foreign trade, foreign investment, domestic investment, and expectations. The latter means guaranteeing residents' employment, meeting the vital needs of the population, the principal markets, food and energy security, the stability of production and supply chains, and the continuous operation of grassroots governments.

Here, the Chinese government has a firm belief in stability and security and full confidence in the economic situation. The *Government Work Report* mentioned: "We will make steady progress and lay a solid foundation for building a well-off society in an all-round way." This is like training athletes to warm up first and then perform more complex tasks.

Yuri Tavrovsky explained, "The reason why the quantitative growth of GDP has not been wholly abandoned is for two primary reasons. First, China must prepare for the possible second wave of the pandemic. Second, the prospects of China's exports are still unclear. The export value is not yet known. Given the unstable economy of other countries and the fact that the pandemic has not been contained, it is still unknown how much benefit China's exports can bring."

According to the expert, China is very optimistic about this issue. At the same time, Tavrovsky believes that abandoning specific numerical indicators is difficult for the Chinese leadership, who have become accustomed to referencing quantitative numbers due to decades of a planned economy.

中华人民共和国成立伊始，人民仍然生活在极度贫困中。袁隆平从20世纪70年代开始研究杂交水稻种植，加上他在经营方面独具一格，杂交水稻研究取得了很大进展。得益于这位院士的贡献，中国的粮食问题已经得到解决。与此同时，中国的耕地面积占世界耕地面积的7%，却养活了世界20%的人口。多年来，中国一直是世界上最大的粮食生产国。由此，中国的贫困问题也得到了解决。过去70年来，中国的贫困人口已减少了8.5亿。

在庆祝中华人民共和国成立70周年招待会上，习近平自豪地宣布："千百年来困扰中华民族的绝对贫困问题即将历史性地画上句号。"他还说，这是"人类发展史上的伟大传奇"。

70年来，中国向170个国家和国际组织提供了4000亿元扶贫资金，派出60多万人道主义援助人员，援建了约5000个人道主义设施。在中国的努力下，1200万名专业人员在发展中国家完成了培训。这些数字充分说明了中国对自身使命的重视，以及中国作为世界大国的责任心。

中国发展模式和中国扶贫经验向世界呈现了全球减贫问题的"中国解决方案"。作为执政党，中国共产党把消除贫困作为社会经济发展的主要目标。中国共产党为实现这一目标制定了明确的时间表，并定期开展研究以灵活制定扶贫政策。

由于现有措施要求向低收入人群提供有针对性的援助，可持续发展的机会也随之增加。中国在消除贫困方面体现了中国特色。习近平主席指出，发展是消除贫困的主要动力。《习近平扶贫论述摘编》在发展中国家引起了广泛反响。许多非洲官员认为，这本书不仅是为中国人准备的，它也值得非洲等正在积极致力于消除贫困的地区借鉴。

联合国秘书长安东尼奥·古特雷斯表示，中国实施定点扶贫战略是消除贫困、实现联合国2030年可持续发展议程远大目标的唯一途径。

In the beginning of the People's Republic of China's founding, the Chinese people were still living in extreme poverty. Based on his research in the 1970s and his unique business approach, Yuan Longping has made great strides in growing hybrid rice. Thanks to the contribution of the academician, the problem of food in China has been solved. At the same time, seven percent of China's arable land could feed 20 percent of the world's population. For many years, China has been the world's largest food producer. As a result, China's poverty problem has also been resolved. Over the past 70 years, China's poor population has decreased by 850 million.

At a reception marking the 70th anniversary of People's Republic of China, Xi Jinping proudly said that poverty, which had existed in China for thousands of years, would be eradicated. According to him, the complete eradication of poverty in China will be a real miracle in human history.

Over the past 70 years, China has provided 400 billion yuan to 170 countries and international organizations to eradicate poverty, sent more than 600,000 people as humanitarian personnel, and built about 5,000 humanitarian facilities. Thanks to China's efforts, 12 million specialists have been trained in developing countries. These figures speak volumes about China's mission as a responsible world power.

The Chinese model and anti-poverty experience have presented the world with a "Chinese solution" to the global problem of poverty reduction. As the ruling party, the Chinese Communist Party considers poverty eradication to be the primary socio-economic development goal. The CPC has set a clear timetable for achieving this goal and conducts regular research to formulate a flexible poverty reduction policy.

As existing measures require targeted assistance to low-income groups, opportunities for sustainable development have also increased. China demontrates Chinese characteristics in poverty eradication. President Xi Jinping points out that development is the main driving force for poverty eradication. His book *Excerpts from Xi Jinping's Discourse on Poverty Alleviation* has aroused widespread repercussions in developing countries. Many African officials believe that this book is not only for the Chinese, but it is also worthy of reference for regions such as Africa that are actively working to eliminate poverty.

United Nations Secretary-General Antonio Guterres points out that China's targeted poverty alleviation strategy is the only way to eradicate poverty and achieve the United Nations 2030 Agenda for Sustainable Development's ambitious goals.

目前，全世界有 7 亿多人生活在贫困线以下。联合国《2030 年可持续发展议程》指出，消除贫困是全球发展的主要目标。中国是一个负责任的世界大国，在抗击贫困方面拥有成功经验，重视通过全球互惠互利和开放合作共同解决这一紧迫问题。中国将通过采取扩大进口、投资等措施帮助发展中国家增加可持续发展机会。

世界银行研究报告显示，"一带一路"倡议将帮助相关国家 760 万人摆脱极端贫困，目前全世界共有 3200 万人生活在极端贫困中。2015 年，中国设立南南合作援助基金。2019 年年底，中国在 30 多个国家开展了 200 多个救灾、医疗等领域的发展合作项目。在 2019 年 9 月举行的中非合作论坛峰会上，中方承诺与非洲国家开展合作，增强生产和发展能力，得到非洲领导人高度评价。

"中国杂交水稻之父"袁隆平院士说，种植杂交水稻，让人们过上幸福的生活，是他一直以来的心愿。袁隆平院士的梦想与中国的使命和责任不谋而合。今后，中国将继续同世界各国分享扶贫经验，积极协调扶贫机制，在共同发展中实现新的国际合作、减贫与共同繁荣。

Currently, more than 700 million people in the world live below the poverty line. The United Nations *2030 Agenda for Sustainable Development* states that poverty eradication is the main goal of global development. China is a responsible world power with successful experience in fighting poverty and attaches great importance to solving this urgent problem through global mutual benefit and open cooperation. China will help developing countries increase opportunities for sustainable development through measures such as expanding imports and investment.

The World Bank research report shows that the Belt and Road Initiative will help 7.6 million people in relevant countries escape extreme poverty. At present, 32 million people worldwide are living in extreme poverty. In 2015, China established the South-South Cooperation Assistance Fund. At the end of last year, China implemented more than 200 development and cooperation projects in disaster relief, medical, and other fields in more than 30 countries. At the summit of Forum on China-Africa Cooperation held in September last year, China promised to cooperate with African countries in stimulating production and development capabilities, which African leaders highly praised.

Academician Yuan Longping, "Father of Hybrid Rice" in China, said that his dream was to grow hybrid rice to feed people, thus making them to live happily. His dream coincides with China's mission and responsibility. In the future, China will continue to share poverty alleviation experiences with other countries globally, actively coordinate poverty alleviation mechanisms, and achieve new international cooperation. It will develop together with other countries by achieving further international cooperation in reducing poverty and the drive for shared prosperity.

诺伯特·莫利纳·梅迪纳
Norbert Molina Medina

中国，照亮贫困的新太阳

China, A New Sun that Shines upon the Poor

　　诺伯特·莫利纳·梅迪纳，委内瑞拉人，历史学家，2007 年毕业于委内瑞拉梅里达州洛斯安第斯大学（ULA），历史学硕士（ULA，2011 年），政治学博士学位候选人，洛斯安第斯大学人文科学与教育学部历史学院世界历史系非洲—亚洲地区研究（亚洲历史—中国历史）副教授。委内瑞拉中国研究会（AVECH）创始人兼秘书长。《中国笔记》（AVECH）和《中国文化笔记》（AVECH）编辑。中国—拉美多学科聚焦网络（REDCAEM，墨西哥）成员，"一带一路"学术出版联盟（BRAPA，北京—中华人民共和国）成员。

　　A Venezuelan historian, Norbert Molina Medina graduated from the University of Los Andes (ULA), Merida-Venezuela, 2007. He has a Masters degree in Venezuelan History (ULA, 2011) and is a candidate for a Doctorate in Political Studies (ULA). He is an Associate Professor in the Afro-Asian Area (History of Asia−History of China). A founder and Secretary-General of the Venezuelan Association for Chinese Studies (AVECH), an editor of Cuadernos de China (AVECH) and Cuadernos de Cultura China (AVECH), a member of the Red China & América Latina: Enfoques Multidiscip-linarios (REDCAEM, Mexico), and a member of the Belt and Road Academic Publishing Alliance (BRAPA, Beijing - People's Republic of China).

谋求发展的漫漫长路

1949 年 10 月 1 日，中华人民共和国成立。新中国主要领导人推动了旨在建立社会主义制度体系的一系列政治、经济和社会变革。当时，中国共产党作为负责应对这一巨大挑战的政治组织，其首要任务是在面临人口增长的同时改变经济、技术落后面貌和巩固国家统一。

中国开始寻找符合本国国情的发展道路。1953 年，中国开始实施其第一个五年计划，并且在粮食生产方面取得了重要进展；然而，在狂热的革命年代，五年计划被搁置。1976 年，周恩来总理和毛泽东主席相继逝世，中国共产党历经波折，最终邓小平成为中国第二代中央领导集体核心。这是一个非常关键的历史时刻，邓小平带领中国，继续坚持马克思列宁主义，并使之与中国实际相结合，发起根本性的社会与经济发展改革，实现了中国特色社会主义。自 1978 年中国改革开放以来，世界经历了一个深刻的经济转型过程。一项前所未有的社会实验正在如火如荼地进行，引起了全世界专家和学者的兴趣。中国经济在过去 40 年高速增长，印证了变革的复杂程度。得益于此，中国自 2010 年已成为世界第二大经济体（第一大出口国和第二大进口国，以及第二大外国直接投资来源）。

当前，中国有 14 亿人口。世界银行统计数据显示，尽管中国经济繁荣，但仍有 2500 万人尚未脱贫。自中国实施现代化发展战略以来，已有近 8 亿人脱贫。要想在未来 30 年实现中国梦，必须在中国共产党的指导和监督下不断调整自 1978 年以来形成的发展模式。

1978 年 12 月 18—22 日，党的十一届三中全会召开，全会的中心议题是讨论把全党的工作重点转移到社会主义现代化建设上来。这次会议具有重要意义，提出摒弃个人崇拜，并实现了中国社会过去 10 年间政

The long road towards development

The People's Republic of China was founded on October 1, 1949. Its top leaders promoted a series of political, economic, and social changes aimed at building a socialist system. At that time, the priority of the Communist Party of China (CPC), as the political institution responsible for carrying out such a huge challenge, was directed towards economic reconstruction, solving the technological backwardness, and consolidating national unity at the same time they were facing the threat of population growth.

China began to walk by itself in search of its own particular path. With the first five-year plan initiated in 1953, it achieved important advances in cereal production; however, the goals were cut short by the effervescence of the revolutionary struggle of those years. With the death of Zhou Enlai and Mao Zedong in 1976, some readjustments in the dynamics of the CPC brought Deng Xiaoping to power, which was a very crucial moment since he initiated a fundamental change of the conception of economic and social development, without moving away from Marxist-Leninist postulates, but through what he considered a reinterpretation of those constructs, implementing *socialism with Chinese characteristics*. With the Reform and Opening-up that began in 1978, the world has since witnessed a process of radical economic transformation. An unprecedented social experiment in full swing has aroused the interest of experts and scholars worldwide. The complexity of the changes they implemented can be explained by the high levels of growth in the last four decades, which have made China the second-largest economy in the world, beginning from 2010 (first exporter and second-largest importer, and largest source of foreign direct investment).

Nowadays, 1.4 billion people live in this Asian country. World Bank statistics show that despite China's economic prosperity, there are still 25 million people who have not been lifted out of poverty. Since China implemented its modernization development strategy, nearly 800 million people have been lifted out of poverty. To realize the "Chinese Dream" in the next 30 years, the development model that has been formed since 1978 must be continuously adjusted under the guidance, and supervision of the Communist Party of China.

The Third Plenary Session of the 11th Central Committee of the Communist Party of China, held from December 18 to 22, 1978, put "the change of the approach

183

治路线的拨乱反正。在此期间，最引人关注的是中国开始重返国际舞台。1971 年，中国恢复联合国合法席位。 1979 年，中国和美国正式建交，中国正信心满满地走对外开放之路。当时，中国决策者的目标是摆脱贫困和改变中国的落后面貌，并在自 19 世纪以来长期的战乱和危机之后恢复民族自豪感。

1977 年至 1979 年，中国政府提出了"四个现代化"，即农业现代化、工业现代化、科学技术现代化和国防现代化。这项计划并不是首次提出，周恩来总理早在 1975 年就宣布了这一计划。经历了几次失误之后，中国政府调整了这项计划，注重平衡粮食和其他农产品的生产，同时兼顾人口增长和工业活动。中国政府深知，发展出口导向型经济是至关重要的。为此，中国需要进行全面改革，以确保政治稳定，保证法制健全和个人安全、制度信心、基础设施建设和投资，提高生产率，提高人民收入和保证劳动力专业化分工等。简而言之，全面改革就是建立一种新的社会秩序，保证在短期内中国共产党政治计划的持久性和可行性。邓小平曾强调，实现真正政治独立的唯一途径是摆脱贫困。因此，中国在对内改革和对外开放的同时不能忽视脱贫，必须采用一切必要手段实现繁荣。

中国的现代化进程始于 20 世纪 80 年代初期，开展了一系列试验。1980 年，中国决定加入国际货币基金组织和世界银行等国际经济组织，并推行一种将外国投资与本国廉价劳动力和出口导向型生产相结合的策略。在此后几十年，中国需要完成几个阶段性任务： 1）以农业农村和经济特区为主要支柱，10 年内实现国内生产总值比 1980 年翻一番； 2）以城市、工业和集体财产为基本主体， 2000 年国内生产总值比 1980 年翻两番，这一任务实际上在 1996 年就已经完成； 3）2049 年中华人民共和国成立 100 周年时人均收入达到中等发达国家的水平，这也是实现中国梦的有利时机。

of the Party toward socialist construction and modernization" as a priority. This assembly was relevant as it proposed the abandonment of personal cult, as well as overcoming the politicization that had characterized the last decade of the Chinese society. The most important aspect about this process is that this Asian nation set out on the road back to the international stage. After the restoration of its seat in the United Nations in 1971 and the normalization of its relationship with the United States of America (USA) in 1979, the Chinese were gaining the confidence they needed for the economic reform and opening to the outside world. The goal of Chinese decision-makers was then to eradicate the poverty and backwardness and to recover national pride after a long period of disagreements and crises unleashed since the 19th century.

Four Modernization refer to the modernizations of agriculture, industry, science and technology, and national defense, was proposed between 1977 and 1979. It could be said that this was not an unprecedented proposal since Premier Zhou Enlai had already announced it in 1975. After the initial mistakes, readjustment was made to focus on the search for balance in the production of cereal crops and other agricultural items without neglecting population growth and industrial activities. China knew it was essential to orient its economy towards exports and, in order to make this possible, improvements were needed in all aspects: political stability, legal and personal security, institutional confidence, infrastructure, investment, greater productivity, increased salaries, specialized labor; in short, a new social order capable of guaranteeing in the short term the permanence and viability of the political project of the CPC. Deng had emphasized that the only way to achieve true political independence was to get out of poverty. Because of that, while implementing economic reform and opening-up to the outside world, China did not ignore the issue of poverty.

These modernizations began in the early 1980s through a series of successive experiments. In 1980, China decided to join some international economic organizations such as the International Monetary Fund (IMF) and the World Bank (WB). They promoted a strategy that merged foreign investment with cheap labor and export-oriented production. They were achieved in three steps during the coming decades: 1) doubling the 1980's GDP within a decade, with the main pillars being the agricultural economy in the countryside and the Special Economic Zones (SEZs); 2) quadrupling the 1980's GDP in 2000, which was actually achieved in

一方面，中国幅员辽阔（国土面积 960 万平方公里），政府必须对不同地区实行一定程度的分权治理。另一方面，科学技术的发展（充分利用所有的国外智力资源）、农村经济的转型和法律体系的升级变得尤为重要。目标是，在良好的投资环境、严格的社会规则、海外华人群体以及巨大的国内市场和廉价劳动力的支持下，根据国情制定正确的经济政策。这一试验的有利方面在于中国周边地区为其提供一个理想的环境。

一些城市（大部分是沿海城市）通过吸引投资促进经济发展，并成为经济特区：率先开放的中国城市为广东省南部的深圳、珠海和汕头以及福建省的厦门。通过设立经济特区，中国不仅吸引了外资，而且建立了各类公司并开展经济活动，吸引投资超过 120 亿美元。此外，中国还实行出口产品分散化、机会和优惠待遇的政策。1984 年 6 月，邓小平又提出，通过开放一些沿海城市，允许外资进入，作为社会主义经济发展的补充，有利于生产力的发展。中国实现了从计划经济向社会主义市场经济的转变，并且实现了前所未有的经济增长。

农业方面，国家控制的弹性化市场使得价格双轨制成为可能。农民完成国家规定的任务（以较低价格出售农作物），他们就可以以更高的利润出售剩余的农产品，此举能有效推动生产力的发展并调动农民的积极性。中国是一个以农村、农民和农业社会为基础的国家，这种制度使得中国众多农民的窘迫处境逐步得到改善。家庭联产承包责任制使作为生产和消费基本单位的家庭再次承担起决策者的责任并被赋予决策者权

1996, with cities, industry and collective property as its fundamental actors; and finally, 3) reaching the developed countries' standard of living by 2049, when the centenary of the foundation of the People's Republic of China will be celebrated, a propitious moment for the achievement of the Chinese Dream.

On the one hand, due to China's vast geographical area (9,600,000 km^2), it is essential for the authorities to grant certain levels of decentralization to the different regions. On the other hand, the development of science and technology (for which all intellectual resources from abroad should be used), the transformation of the rural economy, and the updating of the legal system were some of the aspects that became especially important. The objectives were aimed at providing a correct economic policy, in accordance with the country's circumstances and in the midst of a favorable environment for investments, with social discipline, with support from the Chinese community living abroad, with a huge internal market, and with ample cheap labor. The advantage of this experiment is that China's surrounding areas provide an ideal environment for it.

Ensuring investments to boost the new experience of economic development led some cities, most of them coastal, to become Special Economic Zones (SEZs): The first to open up were Shenzhen, Zhuhai, and Shantou in southern Guangdong Province; and Xiamen in Fujian province. With the SEZs, China not only received foreign capital but also witnessed the creation of various types of companies and economic activities, with more than twelve billion dollars in investment, along with a policy of decentralization of exports, opportunities, and preferential treatment. In June 1984, Deng Xiaoping asserted that opening some coastal cities and allowing the entry of capitalism would complement the promotion of the socialist economy, which would be favorable to the development of the productive forces. The transition from the planned economy to the socialist market economy has resulted in China's economic growth never seen before.

With agriculture, the easing of State control made it possible for a dual-price system to emerge. Once the farmers had achieved the amount set by the State (which was sold at lower prices), they could sell the surplus at much higher rates. This action could effectively promote the development of productivity and bring the farmers' initiatives into full play. Since China is a fundamentally rural, peasant, and agrarian society, the dual-price system allowed a gradual alleviation of millions of farmers' impoverished conditions. The household responsibility system gave the family,

力。中国农村地区深受计划经济、自然灾害和投资缺乏的影响，农村振兴计划将扭转这一局面。谷物和其他农产品产量的大幅增加，以及作物的均衡分布，使中国政府决策者对中国农村正在进行的变革更有信心。

另一个亟须解决的问题与外交相关，中国必须制定外交政策，以便同国际社会其他成员建立一个新的关系网。中国需要奉行更加灵活务实的外交政策，这不仅可以获得其他国家的承认，同时也有助于中国增强信心并确保扭转其过去几十年来的贫困、落后和依赖他国的国际形象。中国在 1955 年的万隆会议上提出的和平共处五项原则至今仍是中国外交政策的一部分。"和而不同"是中国的传统外交理念，中国承认不同国家文化的差异，把利益建立在互利共赢的合作机制之上。直到现在，中国一直设法解决边界问题，与 14 个邻国中的 12 个举行了友好对话，与超过 171 个国家建立了外交关系并互设大使馆，彼此之间保持对等的外交地位。而在半个世纪之前，中国还是世界上最贫穷和最孤立的国家之一。

虽然中国拥有这些经历并在努力提高人民生活水平，但这也带来了许多问题，比如城乡矛盾、区域发展不平衡、贪污腐败问题、人口增长及向主要城市迁移，以及工业活动对环境造成的负面影响。为如此庞大的人口群体提供粮食、教育、医疗卫生服务和就业并不是一件容易的事情。西方学术界和知识界一开始并不能很好地理解社会主义市场经济这种模式。他们将这种模式称为理论和实践上的矛盾和对经济的亵渎。然而，中国证明了这种模式的可行性和效率。将马克思主义经典理论与中国实践相结合成为解决问题的办法，其结果是近 8 亿中国人摆脱了贫困，中国经济对全球增长的贡献率接近 30%。在 21 世纪的第一个 10 年，尽管因为某些客观因素（国内消费更高导致经济结构不同，侧重于服务业和高科技、储蓄和出口）经历了一次经济增速放缓，中国的平均 GDP 仍然保持在 10%。

除了宏观经济数据、政治约束和经济规划中的不利因素，尽管中

which was a basic unit of production and consumption, the responsibilities and the power of decision-making once again. The revitalization of the countryside would reverse the reality of a sector that was widely affected by the planned economy, natural disasters, and the absence of investment policies. The substantial increase in the output of cereals and other agricultural products, as well as the balanced distribution of crops, gave Chinese government policymakers more confidence in the ongoing changes in rural China.

Another issue that needed to be resolved was related to the foreign policy. China had to formulate a foreign policy in order to establish a new network of relationships with other members of the international community. China needed to pursue a more flexible and pragmatic foreign policy, which not only could be recognized by other countries but also helped China to boost its confidence and ensure that it reversed its international image of poverty, backwardness, and dependence on other countries over the past few decades. The Five Principles of Peaceful Coexistence proposed at the Bandung Conference in 1955 has remained part of the Chinese diplomatic structure. Harmony without uniformity is a traditional Chinese principle that recognizes countries with different cultures, putting their national interest on mutually beneficial and win-win cooperation mechanisms. Until now, China has been trying to resolve its border issue. It has held friendly dialogues with 12 of its 14 neighboring countries and established diplomatic relations with more than 171 countries, setting up embassies on each other's territories and maintaining equal diplomatic status. But half a century ago, China was one of the world's most impoverished and most isolated countries.

Despite these experiences and China's process in bettering people's living standards, China has encountered many problems, such as urban-rural conflicts, uneven regional development, corruption, population growth and migration to major cities, and industrial activities' negative impact on the environment. Providing food, education, health, and jobs for such a large population has not been easy. The model, which they have called socialist market economy, was not well understood at the beginning by the academics and intellectual circles in the West. A model that they labeled as a theoretical and practical contradiction and an economic sacrilege. However, China demonstrated its feasibility and efficiency. It has become the solution to combine the Marxist classics with Chinese national conditions, which has got nearly 800 million Chinese out of poverty, with an economy that now contributes

国面临许多亟待解决的社会难题，但一直在自我适应和变革，并且逐渐减少了贫困和社会不平等现象。改革开放之后，香港和澳门分别于 1997 年和 1999 年回归中国。按照邓小平提出的"一国两制"政策，香港和澳门在回归之后成为中国的特别行政区。同样地，在政治层面上，中国共产党一直在强力反腐，同时在这个关键时刻也加强了国家的作用和功能。同样需要强调的是习近平主席的领导， 2017 年 10 月底举行的中国共产党第十九次全国代表大会通过，习近平新时代中国特色社会主义思想写入党章。在经济层面上，适度增长带来了更多挑战，例如中国正在努力改变其世界工厂的形象，更加注重可持续发展、提高科技含量、增强竞争力、减少资源浪费和污染。中国政府意识到需要更认真地研究新型公共投资并解决地方政府的债务问题和金融体系的重组。

中国选择的全面发展道路有一个非常危险的"敌人"：环境污染。中国共产党把环境污染作为一个极其紧迫的问题提上了议程。在这个意义上，我们可以负责任地说，中国为发展清洁技术一直在进行大量的投资，这些技术有助于减轻他们所倡导的发展模式所造成的生态破坏。2015 年 7 月至 8 月，我有机会第一次来访中国，目睹了中国的快速发展并对此进行了认真思考。我访问了北京、天津和西安。当时，我对北京的大气污染程度感到震惊，整座城市笼罩在一片灰蒙蒙的烟雾中，很难看到天空。然而，当我在 2017 年 8 月和 2018 年 7 月再次访问中国时，看到的是完全不同的景象，这表明中国政府和社会为扭转生态破坏做出了大量的努力。中国正在向注重质量和可持续性发展而非加速增长的经济模式转型。我们知道，未来几年中国还有许多问题需要解决，能否有效解决这些问题将决定中国梦能否实现。

nearly 30% of global growth. China's GDP still averaged 10% in the first decade of the 21st century despite the slowdown of economic growth because of several objective factors.

Despite macroeconomic data, political constraints, and unfavorable factors in economic planning, in addition to many social challenges, China has been adapting and transforming itself and gradually reduced poverty and social inequality. After the economic reform and opening up to the outside world, China resumed exercising its sovereignty over Hong Kong and Macao, in 1997 and 1999, respectively as Special Administrative Regions under Deng Xiaoping's "one country, two systems" policy. Likewise, on the political level, the CPC has been stepping up its anti-corruption campaigns, and at this critical moment, it has also strengthened the State's role and function. President Xi Jinping's leadership needs to be emphasized. His ideas were recently incorporated into the Party Constitution passed at the 19th National Congress of the Communist Party of China held at the end of October 2017. On the economic level, moderate growth has brought more challenges. For example, China is working hard to change its image as a world factory, paying more attention to sustainable development, increasing technological content, enhancing competitiveness, and reducing the waste of resources and pollution. The Chinese government realizes that it needs to study new types of public investment more seriously, resolve local government debt problems, and financial system restructuring.

The chosen path to China's full development has a very dangerous enemy: The environmental pollution, an issue that was recently added to the agenda of the CPC as a matter of extreme urgency. In that sense, and it is fair to acknowledge, China has been making great investments in the development of clean technologies that contribute to mitigate the ecological damage caused by the development model they have promoted. In 2015, between July and August, I had the opportunity to visit China for the first time and see first-hand part of the experiment that we are trying to reflect on. Beijing, Tianjin and Xi'an were the cities that covered my agenda. At that time, I was struck by the pollution levels in the capital, a metropolis where it was very difficult to see the sky in front of the prevailing smog curtain. However, I returned in August 2017 and July 2018 and the experience was totally different, which is a proof to the efforts of the Chinese government and the society to reverse the ecological damage. The country is in transition to an economic model that prefers quality and sustainability before quantity and accelerated growth. We know that there

中国脱贫行动

截至 1978 年，中国人口约为 9.62 亿，其中农村人口为 7.9 亿，占比 82.12%。实行必要的政策以使这一庞大人口群体的生活重回正轨是一项非常困难的任务，这需要将村落和小城镇共同纳入农村改革进程中。偏远的中西部地区一直是中国政府面临的最大挑战，那里是少数民族聚居地，是中国最贫困地区，少数民族人口占全国人口的 9%。确保该地区人民拥有基本的道路基础设施、灌溉系统、电力、电信以及教育和卫生机构，是政府消除贫困工作的一部分。自古以来，儒家思想在中国人心中根深蒂固，他们始终认为教育是摆脱贫困的有效方式。邓小平认为，如果不消除贫困，就不会实现真正的政治独立。创造新的就业机会、维持就业和扩大生产的目的是提高生活质量。

不可忽视的一点是，中国仅拥有世界上 7% 的耕地，但需要养活世界上近 20% 的人口。必须承认，家庭联产承包责任制是中国农业生产至少在 20 世纪 90 年代末之前继续保持增长的保证。当然，并不是所有旨在消除农村贫困的决策都取得了预期的成果，改革开放的过程跌宕起伏并且充满了各种矛盾。例如，由于人口的快速增长，农村和偏远贫困地区难以实现其发展目标。然而，确保为人口提供食物和控制通货膨胀是中国政府的主要目标。据统计，截至 1978 年，中国有 2.5 亿贫困人口，约占其农村人口的 31%。随着农村经济管理改革的初步实现，中国的贫困人口在 1985 年已经减半，尽管发展不平衡并且无法满足一部分农民的基本生活需求。

自 1986 年以来，中国政府还开展行动，为开辟特殊就业渠道提供或创造条件。中国的经济发展初见成效，但必须尽快解决人口向主要城市迁移的问题。据统计，自 1978 年以来，有超过 3 亿人离开了农村，为此，

are many pending issues to be addressed in the coming years, and the efficient response to them will depend on whether or not the Chinese Dream is achieved.

Some actions to reverse poverty in China

As of 1978, China's population was approximately 962 million, of which the rural population was 790 million, accounting for 82.12%. Implementing the necessary policies to get the lives of this enormous population group back on track is a challenging task, which requires the integration of villages and small towns into the rural reform process. The remote central and western regions have always been the biggest challenge facing the Chinese government. It is a place where ethnic groups live and is the most impoverished area in China. The population of ethnic groups accounts for 9% of the country's population. Providing them with basic road infrastructure, irrigation systems, electricity, telecommunications, education, and health institutions is part of the government's poverty eradication efforts. Since ancient times, Confucianism has been deeply rooted in the hearts of Chinese people. They have always believed that education is an effective way to get rid of poverty. Deng Xiaoping believed that if poverty is not eliminated, true political independence will not be achieved. The purpose of creating new employment opportunities, maintaining employment, and expanding production are to improve the quality of life.

It cannot be overlooked that China has only 7 percent of the world's arable land but has the huge responsibility for supporting nearly 20 percent of the world's population. However, it must be recognized that the household responsibility system guaranteed that agricultural production continued to grow at least until the end of the 1990s. Not all the decisions taken to eradicate poverty in the countryside had the expected results; the reform and opening-up experiment has been full of ups and downs and contradictions. For example, the accelerated population growth in the countryside and remote regions where very poor people live, has made it difficult to meet the objectives set in this area. However, food provision for the population and control of the galloping inflation were part of the primary goals. By 1978, it was estimated that 250 million people were in poverty in China, representing about 31% of the rural population. With the initial realization of the rural economic management reform, China's poor population was halved in 1985, despite the uneven development and the inability to meet the basic living needs of some farmers.

Since 1986, the Chinese government has also taken actions to facilitate the progress of special employment channels. China was beginning to show the positive results in its economic development. The phenomenon of migration to the main cities

中国在 2011 年实现了由农村化向城镇化的转变（城镇人口为 6.9079 亿，占总人口的 51.27%；农村人口为 6.5656 亿，占总人口的 48.73%），而同样规模的迁移在欧洲则经历了数百年的时间。

1996 年至 2000 年，中国实施了其第九个五年计划，引领中国在 20 世纪最后 5 年的发展，实现了人均国民生产总值比 1980 年翻两番。该计划提出了一个明确的目标：基本消除贫困现象，人民生活达到小康水平。基本原则是呼吁社会各界参与这场与贫困的战斗中来，努力确保经济发达地区将剩余资源用于改善落后地区的面貌，同时鼓励农民实践生态农业和可持续农业。中国对农村的投资和国家补贴促进了基础设施建设，并增加了获得改良种子、机械和其他农业生产资料的机会。

西部偏远地区自然条件艰苦、基础设施薄弱，帮助该地区发展是一件非常复杂的事情。但是，近年来，兴建大型水利项目、为生产活动提供土地和开发自然资源都为这些最贫困的地区带来了机遇。此外，公路、铁路和其他建设项目不仅将偏远地区和主要省道、国道连接起来，也为偏远地区的人们提供了就业机会。除了这些改进措施外，自 2007 年起，中国针对年平均收入低于国家法定标准的农村居民制定了农村社会保障制度，其主要目标是有效保障衣食住行和用水用电，换句话说，确保人们能够有尊严地生活。2009 年，国家推进了新型农村社会养老保险，截至 2011 年 7 月，覆盖了全国 60% 的农村地区。在中西部地区，中央财政 100% 承担了政府设立的养老金补贴，而在东部地区，这一比例为 50%。

2012 年 12 月，习近平总书记指出："消除贫困、改善民生、实现共同富裕是社会主义的本质要求。"他认为，中国还处于社会主义初级阶段，仍然有大量人口处于贫困之中，特别是在农村地区。习近平

had to be dealt with quickly. It is estimated that since 1978, more than 300 million people have left the countryside, a process that spent Europe hundreds of years. For this reason, China realized the transition from rural to urbanization in 2011 (690.79 million in the urban areas, 51.27% / 656.56 million in the rural areas, 48.73%).

Between 1996 and 2010, the 9th Five-Year Plan was implemented to guide China's development in the last five years of the 20th century, with a well-defined objective: to eliminate poverty fundamentally. It has quadrupled the per capita gross national product compared to that in 1980 to lead China to achieve moderate prosperity. A fundamental aspect of the proposal is to call upon the different sectors to join in this fight against poverty, ensuring that the economically advanced areas apply their surplus resources to improving the more backward ones, encouraging the peasants to practice ecological and sustainable agriculture. Investments in the countryside and State subsidies have enabled infrastructure construction and increased opportunities to acquire improved seeds, machinery, and everything needed for agricultural production.

The remote areas in western China have difficult natural conditions and weak infrastructure. Helping the development of the region is a very complicated matter. However, in recent years, large-scale water conservancy projects, land provision for production activities, and natural resources development have provided opportunities for these impoverished areas. Besides, roads, railways, and other construction projects have connected remote areas with major provincial and national highways and provided employment opportunities for people in remote areas. In addition to these improvement measures, China has since 2007 established a rural social security system for rural residents whose average annual income is below the national legal standard. The main goal is to effectively guarantee food, clothing, housing, transportation, water, and electricity, in other words, to ensure that people can live with dignity. In 2009, China promoted the new rural endowment social insurance, and as of July 2011, it covered 60% of the country's rural areas. In the central and western regions, the central government treasury is responsible for 100% of the pension subsidies established by the government, while in the eastern regions, the proportion is 50%.

In December 2012, President Xi Jinping stated that it was an essential requirement of socialism to eradicate poverty, improve living standards, and achieve shared prosperity. He argued that China was in an early stage of socialism, so

总书记强调，没有农村的小康，特别是没有贫困地区的小康，就没有全面建成小康社会，并督促党和政府加强在这方面的承诺与责任。为此，我们认真反思了政府和社会亟须克服的难题。当前，中国仍有数百万人的生活非常困难，他们的收入无法与城市居民的收入和福利相比，所得到的食物、医疗、教育、就业和基本服务机会仍然不完善，这不仅需要大量的财政和人力资源，还要确保其可行性、可持续性和持久性。

政府必须意识到，人口问题是现代化发展进程中的一个关键因素。计划生育控制了农村和城市的人口增长。邓小平强调，人口增长要与社会、经济、资源、环境相协调。自 1949 年中华人民共和国成立以来，先后开展了四次计划生育运动：1956—1958、1962—1966、1971—1978、1979—2015。最后一次计划生育运动，即独生子女政策，于1979 年开始实施，其主要内容是推迟结婚年龄，并且限制每个家庭只生一个孩子。当时的目标是，中国人口 1986 年 12 亿，到 21 世纪初增长至 13 亿（截至 2000 年，全国户籍人口为 12.65 亿）。由于实行计划生育，自 1979 年以来中国人少生了约 4 亿人。若不实行计划生育，预计将对国家的经济造成严重负面影响，导致更加严重的贫困现象。尽管独生子女政策实现了控制人口增长的目标，但人口老龄化和性别失衡等其他问题也相应出现，成为中国在未来几年需要解决的问题。从 2016 年开始，中国开始实施"全面二孩"政策。然而，社会发展模式和已经发生的社会变化决定我们在未来几十年仍将面临新的人口挑战。

中国已经率先实现联合国千年发展目标，将生活在极端贫困线以下的人口从 1990 年的 61% 减少到 2002 年的 30%，在全球范围内做出了重大贡献。然而，中国仍然需要兑现其承诺，即到 2020 年年底彻底消除农村地区的贫困。2015 年，中国农村贫困人口减少到约 5600 万，

many people were still in poverty, particularly in rural areas. President Xi Jinping emphasized that without a moderately prosperous society in rural areas, especially in poverty-stricken areas, there would be no comprehensive moderately prosperous society. He urged the Party and the government to strengthen their commitments and responsibilities in this regard. For this reason, we have seriously reflected on the problems that the government and society urgently need to solve. At present, millions of people in China still lead hard lives. Their income isn't comparable with the pay and welfare of urban residents. Their food, medical care, education, employment, and essential services are still incomplete, which requires a lot of financial and human resources. Still, it also needs to be viable, and sustainable over time, and durable.

The government must realize that the population problem is a key factor in the development of modernization. Family planning brought population growth in the countryside and cities under control. Deng Xiaoping affirmed that the population should grow in coordination with society, the economy, resources, and the environment. Since the founding of the People's Republic of China in 1949, China has launched four family planning campaigns in 1956-1958, 1962-1966, 1971-1978, and 1979-2015. The last one, known as the "one-child policy," came into effect in 1979, and its purpose was to delay the age of marriage and limit each family to having one child. At that time, the goal was that China's population would reach 1.2 billion in 1986 and grow to 1.3 billion by the beginning of the 21st century (as of 2000, the national registered population was 1.265 million). As a result of family planning, the Chinese have lost about 400 million births since 1979. With the implementation of family planning, it is expected to have a severe negative impact on the country's economy and lead to more severe poverty. Although the one-child policy has achieved the goal of controlling population growth, other problems such as population aging and gender imbalance have emerged correspondingly, which will become problems that China needs to solve in the coming years. From 2016 onwards, China has opened up the possibility for Chinese families to have two children. However, the development model and the social changes that have taken place will determine, in the coming decades, the behavior of the new demographic challenges that we have mentioned.

China has achieved the Millennium Development Goals (MDGs) by reducing the number of people who lived in extreme poverty from 61% in 1990 to 30% in 2002, thus becoming the first country to do so and making a significant contribution

贫困发生率下降到 5.7%。然而，新冠肺炎疫情和美国贸易战带来的意想不到的经济影响，可能会影响 2020 年消除贫困目标的实现。2016 年10 月，中国国务院发表了《中国的减贫行动与人权进步》白皮书。这份官方文件的重要性在于认为应在充分保障人权的基础上与贫困做斗争，强调了政策实施的中、短期目标：1)《国家八七扶贫攻坚计划》（1994—2000 年）；2)《中国农村扶贫开发纲要（2001—2010 年）》；3)《中国农村扶贫开发纲要（2011—2020 年）》。

《中国的减贫行动与人权进步》白皮书其他章节还规定了贫困人口的生存权和保护特殊群体（妇女、儿童、老年人、残疾人和 55 个确保享有优先权少数民族），提出了通过加强工程建设（水电项目、新道路）以及信息和电信基础设施建设来改善贫困地区环境。同时，扶贫需要中国政府和社会各界的参与和积极支持，不断创新，广泛动员群众，并总结扶贫过程中的成绩和遇到的问题。据统计，每年有近 100 万名残疾人在中国出生，他们也是受现行法律保护的中国公民，很大程度上代表着与贫困人口相关的弱势群体，国家和家庭有责任帮助他们。在 21 世纪的第一个 10 年，除了公共和慈善机构致力于照顾残疾儿童，中国政府还推动建立了帮助失聪、失明和有沟通障碍的儿童恢复健康的研究中心，以及 1500 多所特殊教育学校。

中国最重要的社会变化之一是妇女社会地位的提升。在过去的传统旧式家庭中，妇女被剥夺了很多权利并依附于男性。1992 年颁布的《中华人民共和国妇女权益保障法》是自 1950 年《中华人民共和国婚姻法》（已废止）开始实行的一系列改革成果之一。这些法律与经济和社会转型热潮中形成的新法规都是对妇女这个重要群体及其社会地位的保护，

to this issue worldwide. But China still has a commitment to fulfill: to eradicate total poverty in rural areas by the end of 2020. By 2015, rural poverty had decreased to almost 56 million people with an incidence rate decreasing to 5.7%. However, the unanticipated economic effects of the COVID-19 pandemic and the U.S. trade war are likely to affect the 2020 target's accomplishment. In October 2016 the State Council of China issued a whitepaper *China's Progress in Poverty Reduction and Human Rights*, taking actions to alleviate poverty and make progress in human rights. The importance of this official document lies in the fact that it considers the fight and eradication of this scourge to be essential for the full enjoyment of human rights. And its highlight of the policies to be implemented in the medium and short term with these objectives: 1) the Seven-year Plan to lift 80 million people out of poverty (1994–2000); 2) the Program for the Elimination of Poverty through Development in Rural Areas (2001–2010); and 3) the Program for the Elimination of Poverty through Development in Rural Areas (2011–2020).

Other chapters of the white paper also stipulate the poor's right to survive and the protection of special groups, ensuring that priority is given to women, children, the elderly, the disabled, and the 55 ethnic minorities. They propose the construction of information and telecommunications infrastructure to improve the environment in impoverished areas. At the same time, poverty alleviation requires the participation and active support of the Chinese government and all sectors of society, continuous innovation, extensive mobilization of the public, and a summary of the achievements and problems encountered in the poverty alleviation process. It is estimated that nearly 1,000,000 disabled people are born in China annually. The State and the family have a responsibility to support them. They are part of the Chinese people protected by current legislation and represent a vulnerable social group mainly associated with the impoverished sectors. In the first decade of the 21st century, the Chinese government has promoted research centers to habilitate deaf, blind, communication-impaired children, besides the effort to establish public and charitable institutions dedicated to the care of disabled children and over 1,500 special education schools.

One of the most significant social changes China has experienced is the improvement of women's social status. They were deprived of rights and subordinate to men in the traditional old family in the past. To continue the reforms that had started with the *Marriage Law* in 1950, China promulgated the *Law on the*

女性和男性一样在政治、文化和教育问题上拥有同等的权利，可以更多地参与国家事务、经济和社会活动。当代妇女很快适应了现代社会的新模式，她们理应获得体面的工作和就业福利，享有人身和财产权利。妇女在过去几个世纪所遭受的创伤痕迹仍然存在，但在日益城市化的社会中，妇女的社会面貌和社会行为都发生了变化。当前，中国妇女有权利上大学、参加工作和参政议政。但愿中国现代化进程不会导致基本的传统家庭价值观消失。这些都与扶贫计划密切相关。中国妇女有了更多参与社会活动的机会、权利和义务，妇女能顶半边天，她们已经摆脱了过去的禁锢和压迫，成为一支活跃的社会力量。

中国决定精准收集贫困人口数据。《中国的减贫行动与人权进步》白皮书显示，截止到 2015 年，中国有极端贫困地区 14 个，贫困地区 832 个，贫困村庄 128000 个，总共约 5600 万贫困人口。这些贫困人口生活条件非常艰苦，并且没有自我发展的能力，很难摆脱当前的困境。出于这个原因，自 2016 年以来，中国设定的目标为每年帮助 1000 万人口脱贫，并确保不忽视那些本可以脱贫但由于自然灾害、疾病以及购房、医疗和教育等原因返贫的人群。据统计， 2017 年有 1289 万人脱贫，贫困率从 2016 年的 4.5% 降至 3.1%。

中国共产党第十八届中央委员会第五次全体会议于 2015 年 10 月 29 日审议通过了第十三个五年规划。"十三五"时期，中国要发展成为工业现代化国家，国内生产总值年均增长速度保持在 6.5% 以上，转变生产方式，实现更高质量和效率。在技术和环境领域，围绕绿色经济框架，政府鼓励在传统乡镇工业中使用互联网技术积极推动农业现代化，减少污染，保护环境。考虑到城镇人口的增长，该计划还提出，在 5 年内新增 5000 万个城镇就业岗位。到 2020 年，城镇人口占总人口比例将达到 60%。也就是说，在估计的 14.2 亿总人口中，约有 8.5 亿人为城镇人口。中国城镇化的迅速发展是中央政府和地方政府密切关注的一个问题，确保为其提供基础服务、就业机会、社会保障、教育和娱乐设施等，不允许产生贫困和不安定等因素，否则将意味着国家面临更严峻的社会问题。

Protection of Women's Rights and Interests promulgated in 1992. These laws, coupled with the recent legal regulations emerging in the heat of the economic and social transformation, have allowed this critical sector of China to legally enjoy the social position and rights that men have in political, cultural, and educational matters. Contemporary women have also adapted to new patterns that came along with modernity. They deserve decent work and employment benefits, as well as personal and property rights. The marks of trauma suffered by women in the past few centuries still exist. Still, in an increasingly urbanized society, women's social outlook and social behavior have changed. Chinese women today go to university, work, participate in politics, propose solutions to problems. Hopefully, modernization does not make fundamental ancestral values associated with the family disappear. These are all aspects closely linked to poverty alleviation. With greater participation and opportunities, rights, and duties, women in China have emerged from stagnation and subjugation to become an active part of today's society.

China has decided to identify accurately those inhabitants who are still in poverty. According to the white paper, China had 14 impoverished areas, 832 poverty-stricken areas, and 128,000 poverty-stricken villages, totaling approximately 56 million in poverty as of 2015. These poor people have challenging living conditions and cannot develop themselves. It is difficult to get rid of the current predicament. For this reason, China has since 2016 set the goal of getting 10 million people out of poverty every year. It also makes sure not to ignore those who could be out of poverty but have returned to poverty due to natural disasters, diseases, housing purchases, medical care, and education. According to statistics, 12.89 million people were lifted out of poverty in 2017, and the poverty rate dropped from 4.5% in 2016 to 3.1%.

The Fifth Plenary Session of the 18th Central Committee of the Communist Party of China reviewed and approved the 13th Five-Year Plan on October 29, 2015. During the "13th Five-Year Plan" period, China will develop into an industrially modernized country, maintain an average annual growth rate of GDP above 6.5%, transform production methods, and achieve higher quality and efficiency. In the field of technology and environment, around the framework of a green economy, the government encourages Internet technology in traditional township industries to actively promote agricultural modernization, reduce pollution, and protect the environment. The plan, which considers the growth of the urban population, also proposes adding 50 million urban jobs within five years. By 2020, the urban

我的中国行

2012 年 6 月，我开始在委内瑞拉梅里达州的洛斯安第斯大学（ULA）担任中国历史学教授。从那时起，我的研究目标就是了解这个亚洲国家，并密切观察始于 20 世纪 70 年代末的现代化进程给这个国家带来的变化。三年后，也就是 2015 年 7 月至 8 月期间，我第一次受邀参加了北京国际汉语研修学院（BICC）为委内瑞拉官员举办的中国历史文化研讨会。

在历时一个多月的中国之旅中，我访问了北京、天津和西安（陕西省）三个城市。来自委内瑞拉政府机构的 30 名官员参加了这次重要的文化交流研讨会，我是其中唯一的学者。在这三个城市举办的各种交流活动是研讨会的一部分。我们对这些城市发达的基础设施和居民生活质量赞叹不已。半个世纪前，中国还处于赤贫状态，但现在其现代化建设已经取得重大进展。如今，中国不仅现代化程度很高，还是一个国际化国家，当你漫步在主要城市的街道上时，能看到很多外国人，他们定居在此，求学、做生意。中国是一个正在崛起的大国。

西方人很难理解中国人是如何在短短 40 年内就实现了经济结构转型和高水平发展，包括如何从农业社会转变为一个城市化社会，同时还帮助近 8 亿人口脱贫（世界银行数据）。

population will account for 60% of the total population. In other words, of the estimated total population of 1.42 billion, approximately 850 million are urban residents. The rapid development of urbanization in China is an issue that the central government and local governments pay close attention to, ensuring that they are provided with basic services, employment opportunities, social security, education, and entertainment facilities. Factors such as poverty and instability are not allowed. Otherwise, it will mean that the country will face more severe social problems.

My experience in China

I started to be a professor of Chinese history at the Universidad de Los Andes (ULA), Merida-Venezuela, in June 2012. From that moment on, my objective was to get to know this Asian country and observe closely the changes made by the modernization that began in the late 1970s. Three years later, namely July-August 2015, I was invited for the first time to participate in a seminar on the history and culture of China, organized by the Beijing International Chinese College (BICC) for Venezuelan officials.

Beijing, Tianjin, and Xi'an (Shaanxi Province) were the three cities I visited during my journey, which lasted over a month. Thirty officials from Venezuelan government institutions participated in this important cultural exchange seminar, and I was the only academic in that group. Various exchange activities were part of the trip in the three cities. It was impossible not to be amazed at the advances in infrastructure and quality of life of the inhabitants of those cities we visited. Modernity has come to stay in a country that half a century ago was in absolute poverty. Nowadays, China is not only a modern country but also a cosmopolitan one. When you walk on the streets of major cities, you can see many foreigners who settle here, study, and do business. China is a rising power.

It is difficult for Westerners to understand how the Chinese have achieved economic structural transformation and high-level development in just 40 years, including how to transform from an agricultural society to an urbanized society, and at the same time help nearly 800 million people out of poverty (according to the WB).

这不仅是一个经济数字和统计学方面的问题，而且关乎 20 世纪末和 21 世纪初中国人的心态转变。国家建设需要全体中国人的参与，因此，集体主义力量是一个不可忽视的重要因素。在中国，脱贫也许是经济规划者和政治领导人最关心的问题，他们知道，只有在财富分配和集体富裕方面实现最大限度的参与和机会平等，才能实现小康社会。

2015 年访问中国时，我们能够近距离观察到将农村社区和少数民族融合的小型生产活动。我们访问了西安市户县东韩村，在那里目睹了社会主义新农村的风采。村里的农业生产活动、用于旅游贸易的小机械产品和手工艺品的生产制造为该地区贫困人口带来资源和收益。9 月 2 日，委内瑞拉玻利瓦尔共和国社会发展和革命代表团副团长与中华人民共和国国务院扶贫办在北京联合签署了《2015—2017 年工作计划》，旨在促进两国消除贫困。我们不知道上述法律文件的具体内容，但中国的经验可以在这方面帮助我们，这一点对我们来说尤为重要。

在历史古城西安，我们参观了秦俑工艺厂和回民街。在回民街我们看到了各种手工艺品、美食、纺织品和鞋子，这些小型经济活动联合在一起，会对旅游业产生积极影响。目前，旅游业是中国非常重要的一项经济收入来源。上述生产活动的从业人员来自基础设施、交通、水、电、互联网和卫生条件最差的农村地区、城市贫困地区和一些少数民族地区。每天都有许多国内外游客在此游览，呈现出一派欣欣向荣的景象。

我在北京麦子店社区的所见所闻证明了中国政府正在致力于减少贫困。在该社区，我目睹了弱势群体的生活状况，小型日用消费品的生产状况及相关商业活动。在中国的经历，我发现中国的社会矛盾和贫困问题还未完全得到解决。中国若要实现其目标，还有复杂、艰难的任务需要完成。但从经济环境、法律和公共安全、技术和后勤保障、环境污染和生态治理方面所取得的进展来看，中国将继续采取有力措施，打赢脱贫攻坚战。

This is not only a question of economic figures and statistics but also a change in the mentality of the Chinese at the end of the 20th century and the beginning of the 21st century. National construction requires the participation of all Chinese people. Therefore, the power of collectivism is a crucial factor that cannot be ignored. Poverty alleviation in China is perhaps the most significant concern for economic planners and the political leaders. They know that only by achieving the most significant degree of participation and equality of opportunity in the distribution of wealth and collective prosperity can a moderately prosperous society be realized.

During the 2015 visit to China, we observed up close small-scale production activities that integrate rural communities and ethnic groups. We visited Donghan Village, Hu County, Xi'an City, where we witnessed the New Socialist Countryside. The village's agricultural production activities and the small mechanical products and handicrafts produced for the tourism trade bring resources and benefits to the poor people. By the way, on September 2, the Sectoral Vice Presidency for Social Development and Revolution of the Missions of the Bolivarian Republic of Venezuela and the Office of the State Council for the Mitigation of Poverty and Development of the People's Republic of China signed the *2015-2017 Work Program* in Beijing, to promote the eradication of poverty between both countries. We do not know the specific content of the above-mentioned legal documents, but China's experience can help us in this regard, which is particularly important to us.

Similarly, in the ancient city of Xi'an, we visited the factory of the Terracotta Warriors. We toured the Muslim Quarters, where we saw how small-scale economic activities are combined: crafts, gastronomy, textiles, and shoes, with a very positive impact on tourism, which is currently an important source of economic income in China. As mentioned above, the production employees come from rural areas, poverty-stricken urban areas, and some ethnic groups' areas with the worst infrastructure, transportation, water, electricity, Internet, and sanitation. Many domestic and foreign tourists visit here every day, presenting a thriving scene.

What I have seen and heard in the Maizidian community in Beijing is another proof that the Chinese government is committed to reducing poverty. I witnessed disadvantaged groups' living conditions in this community, small daily consumer goods production, and related commercial activities. All the mentioned experience does not mean that China has entirely solved its social problems and poverty. On the contrary, as we have pointed out before, there remains a very complex and

中国还需要解决不平等问题，扭转地区间的发展不平衡、财富分配不均，消除腐败和浪费现象，坚持高质量、可持续的经济发展路线。正如我所说的，生态问题是中国共产党优先解决的问题之一，到目前为止已取得良好进展。中国非常重视替代能源研究和应用，并在这方面投入了大量资金。大城市公共交通系统和电动汽车的发展不仅减少了对化石燃料的消耗和依赖，而且对环境也产生了直接的影响。中国政府惩治和关停环境违法企业体现了保护环境的决心。

在农村，推广可持续生态农业是农民培训的其中一项内容，这促进了绿色农业经济的发展。中国目前的经济指标虽然令人满意，但与发达国家相比还有很大差距，因此，中国始终认为自己是一个发展中国家。"中国梦"的核心目标可概括为"两个一百年"，也就是：到2021年中国共产党成立100周年时，确保实现全面建成小康社会的宏伟目标，实现国内生产总值和城乡居民人均收入比2010年翻一番；2049年中华人民共和国成立100周年时，将国家建设成为富强、民主、文明、和谐的社会主义现代化强国。

此外，我还曾两次到访中国。2017年8月，我受邀参加2017年中外文学出版翻译研修班（SFLTP）。2018年7月，我参加了一个由中国政府发起名为"通往未来的桥梁"的活动，这次活动针对来自中国、拉丁美洲和加勒比海地区的青年领导者，旨在加强相互了解、加深友谊和深化不同领域之间的双边合作。2018年到访中国的时候，我在北京和四川成都参观了生产面向国内消费市场和出口渠道的产品的公司及微型企业。在成都，我们还参观了四川大学省级创新创业中心，以及"你我他"（一个致力于社区文化发展的非政府组织）。在上海，我们参观了张江高科技园区，了解了中国当前正在发展的部分先进科学技术。

challenging task to achieve the goals proposed. However, the economic environment, the legal and personal security, the technological and logistic resources, and the progress made against environmental pollution and ecological damage give the impression that the country will continue to take decisive steps and win the fight against poverty.

Similarly, China still needs to solve the problems of inequalities, the imbalances between regions, the unequal distribution of wealth, corruption and waste, and insist on high-quality, and sustainable economic development. As I have said, the ecological issue is one of the priorities handled by the CPC, and positive progress has been made so far. China has attached great importance to research and implementation of alternative energies and invested a lot. Public transport systems and electric vehicles in large cities have reduced consumption and dependence on fossil fuels and directly impacted the environment. Sanctions have been imposed against and closed those who do not comply with the established legal regulations, showing the determination of Chinese government to protect the environment.

In the countryside, the promotion of sustainable agriculture, with ecological methods, is part of the peasants' training to facilitate a green agricultural economy. China considers itself a developing country because the current economic indicators, although they are satisfactory, still fall short of those already developed. However, there are two centenary goals to be achieved. By the 100th anniversary of the founding of the Communist Party of China in 2021, China will have achieved the grand goal of building a moderately prosperous society in all respects, with its GDP and per capita income of urban and rural residents doubling those of 2010. When the People's Repulic of China celebrates the 100th anniversary of its founding in 2049, it will have become a prosperous, democratic, civilized, and harmonious modern socialist country.

I had two more opportunities to go back to China. In August 2017, I was invited to participate in the 2017 Sino-Foreign Literature Translation & Publishing Workshop (SFLTP). In July 2018, I attended a program named Puente al Futuro, organized for young leaders from China, Latin America, and the Caribbean, an initiative created by the Chinese government to strengthen mutual understanding and friendship, to deepen bilateral cooperation in different fields. During my visit to China in 2018, I observed dynamic companies and micro-enterprises dedicated to producing various products for domestic consumption and exports, both in Beijing and Chengdu,

我想强调的是我们不仅看到了农民、年轻学生和工人的日常工作是什么样子，而且目睹了社会各界，包括高校、非政府组织、农村及城市的工人都在响应政府号召，为帮助减少贫困贡献自己的力量。

2015 年第一次访问中国后，我抱着极大的兴趣继续研究其当代历史进程。为此，我提议在洛斯安第斯大学（ULA，委内瑞拉梅里达州）历史人文与教育学院开展一个免费的研讨会，研讨会主题为"中国：改革开放和全球化"。自 2016 年起，我就在洛斯安第斯大学政治学（法律与政治科学学院）和经济学（经济与社会科学学院）的研究生课程中开设了主题为"中国的现代化进程：理解中国改革开放的关键"的研讨课程。课程的研究目的是：1）了解中国改革开放前的政治、经济和社会状况；2）评估冷战背景下的国际形势和中国在寻求国际认可过程中所扮演的角色；3）分析中国经历的社会和经济转型；4）分析现代化进程中的政治、经济、社会和生态成果。在这些研究目的下，我们试图让学生了解 1978 年以前中国的状况，形成这种状况的因素，以及为什么中国有必要在过去 40 年进行经济和社会转型。

从上述研究来看，中国主要的社会矛盾得到了解决，消除贫困成为最令人关注的问题。这并非巧合，1978 年，中国还是一个非常贫困的国家。起初，一些西方学者认为，根据其他发达国家的经验，社会主义市场经济是不可能成功的。但事实证明，中国在很短的时期内就实现了惊人的经济增长水平，而且在扶贫方面有了显著效果。研究中国各历史阶段的发展是许多当代中国和外国学者以及汉学家的使命，他们需要分析中国的发展优势和劣势，尝试解释这些近代史上罕见的发展模式，并构建一个在全球层面上研究中国问题的独特的社会工程实验室。

Sichuan. In the latter city, we visited the Provincial Center of Innovation and Entrepreneurship University of Sichuan and the Ni-Wo-Ta (I-You-She), an NGO dedicated to developing community culture. Finally, in Shanghai, we went to the Zhangjiang Hi-Tech Park and witnessed part of the technological advances that China is making nowadays. What I want to emphasize is that in each of these experiences, we saw not only the workdays of peasants, young students, and workers but also how the various university sectors, NGOs, rural and urban workers are committed to the call made by the authorities to contribute and help alleviate poverty.

After that first contact with China in 2015, I returned with the motivation to continue studying its new historical process. For that purpose, I proposed setting up a free seminar for the School of History of the Faculty of Humanities and Education of the University of Los Andes (ULA), in Mérida, Venezuela, which we call *China: Reform, Opening up and Globalization*. Likewise, since 2016 I have started the seminar *The Process of Modernization in China: Keys to Understanding its Reform and Opening up*, in the postgraduate courses of Political Science (Faculty of Legal and Political Sciences) and Economics (Faculty of Economic and Social Sciences) of the ULA. The objectives of this seminar were: 1) understanding the political, economic, and social situation in China before the transformation made by reform and opening-up; 2) evaluating the international situation in the context of the Cold War and the role of China in its search for international recognition; 3) analyzing the economic and social transformation experienced by China; and 4) determining the political, economic, social and ecological consequences of modernization. With these objectives, we try to inform our students about the state of China before 1978, the factors that determined that situation, and why the economic and social transformation of the last four decades was necessary.

According to these research objectives, the main social problems of China have been addressed, with poverty alleviation receiving the most attention. And this is no coincidence, since by 1978, China had still been a very poor country. At first, some Western scholars believed that based on the experience of other developed countries, it was impossible for a socialist market economy to succeed. But facts have proved that China has achieved an astonishing level of economic growth in a short period of time, and remarkable results in poverty alleviation. It is the mission of many contemporary Chinese and foreign scholars and sinologists to study the development of China in various historical stages. They need to analyze the advantages and

如今，新的威胁正笼罩着这个亚洲国家。一方面是美国对华贸易逆差而挑起的贸易战；另一方面是2019年年底和2020年暴发的新冠肺炎疫情。这两个因素肯定会影响经济发展目标的实现。

当前，实现减贫目标并不容易，特别是在必须保持就业水平、食品和药品供应链、投入，并保持总体生产平衡的情况下。此外，中国出口预计会下滑，这对整个经济会产生不利影响。据中国官方报告统计，由于新冠肺炎疫情，2020年第一季度国内生产总值下降了6.8%，国际货币基金组织（IMF）等国际机构也警告称，世界经济将萎缩3%。但这些国际机构也指出，中国将成为为数不多的几个仍然有能力维持经济增长的国家，大约能增长1.2%。同时，亚洲开发银行（ADB）的年度报告称，亚洲经济将停滞在2.2%的水平，同时预测中国的经济增长率将高于国际货币基金组织预估的2.3%。

考虑到这一背景，完全渡过新冠肺炎疫情危机之后，中国有可能会重新制定其解决贫困和不平等问题的指导方针。我们只能静观事态发展，以便分析世界，特别是中国的形势。几个月后，我们就能知道疫情造成的真实后果。无论如何，中国决不会放弃扶贫攻坚计划。国际关系、经济和历史学者以及汉学家们预测，21世纪将是中国的世纪。一些与中国有密切贸易关系的西方国家会极力阻挠中国的崛起，并在政治层面上对中国进行围追堵截，但似乎并不能改变中国崛起的事实。世界秩序正转向其他经济、科技和文化势力中心。我们希望新千年始终维持和平与稳定，人人享有繁荣和平等的机会。

disadvantages of China's development, seek to explain these rare development models in modern history, and build a unique social engineering laboratory to study China on a global level.

Today, new threats are looming over this Asian country. On the one hand, the trade war was provoked by the U.S. trade deficit with China; on the other hand, the new COVID-19 outbreak in late 2019 and 2020. These two factors will affect the realization of economic development goals.

Achieving poverty alleviation goals is not an easy task at this moment, especially when it is imperative to maintain employment levels, food and medicine supply chains, inputs, and keep the entire production dynamic. Besides, China's exports are expected to decline, which will bring negative effects on the whole economy. The Chinese authorities have reported a 6.8% fall in its GDP in the first quarter of 2020 due to the COVID-19. Agencies such as the IMF have warned that the world economy will shrink by 3%, but they also noted that China would be one of the few economies with the capacity to grow this year, with an estimated increase of 1.2%. By contrast, the Asian Development Bank's (ADB) annual report said that Asia would stagnate at 2.2% while forecasting China's growth rate will be above 2.3% estimated by IMF.

Considering this background, once the COVID-19 crisis is over, China will likely redefine the guidelines for its fight against poverty and inequality. We can only wait to see how things will develop to analyze the world's events at large and China's in particular. In a few months, we will know the consequences of the pandemic. In any case, China will never give up on its plan to eradicate poverty. Scholars of international relations, economics and historians, and sinologists predict that the 21st century will be the century of China. Some Western countries with close trade relations with China will try their best to obstruct China's rise and pursue and intercept China at the political level, but it seems that they cannot stop China's rise. The world order is shifting to other centers of economic, technological, and cultural power. We hope that peace and stability will always be maintained in the new millennium, and everyone will enjoy prosperity and equal opportunities.

金胜一

Kim Seung Il

中国扶贫之我见

Poverty Alleviation in China as I See It

金胜一，韩国东亚大学教授，长期致力于翻译中国当代作家作品和研究中国近代文学，对在韩国推广传播中国文化做出了积极贡献。

Kim Seung Il is a professor at Dong-A University, South Korea, who has worked for a long time translating contemporary Chinese works and doing research on recent modern Chinese literature, and has made great contributions towards promoting Chinese culture in South Korea.

何为贫困

关于贫困的成因，有两种观点。一种是从贫困人口自身找问题，还有一种是从社会结构不平等的角度进行阐释。

前者指的是因为个人的懒惰、自控力和发展动能不足，不愿意努力生活而导致的贫困；又或者是因为残障、疾病和年老等问题，在社会上难以获得成功而导致的贫困。

后者指的是社会结构导致的贫困。在这种情况下，总有一些人无论工作如何努力，都无法摆脱贫困。其原因在于阶级、性别和种族社会之间的不平等不利于他们脱贫。换句话说，贫困阶层是社会结构的受害者。

以上两种观点，各自都具有一定的合理性，但同时也都存在明显的局限性。个人原因论忽略了与个人努力或能力无关的诸多因素，例如，某些地区经济欠发达、就业机会不公平、职业之间收入有差距等。而社会结构原因论则忽视了个体因素对收入的影响，例如，个体在人脉关系、个人努力和个人意志上的差异等。因此，要正确看待贫困成因，就必须在这两个视角之间取得平衡。

当今时代，贫困问题正在从绝对贫困扩大到相对贫困。但是，这并不意味着绝对贫困威胁人类生存的短缺问题已经完全消失。时至今日，仍有许多人还在为食物、饮用水等生活必需品以及最低水平的医疗服务担忧。当然，全球范围内，绝对贫困人口一直在迅速减少，但日益增长的不平等问题也逐渐成为引发新型社会矛盾的诱因。

贫困通常分为以下四类。一是"绝对贫困"，即收入在贫困线以下的生活状态。二是"政策性贫困"，即未能达到特定社会的最低生活保障标准。三是"相对贫困"，即与所属社会的其他成员相比，个人拥有相对较少的资源。四是"主观贫困"，即个人认为自己没有拥有足够的资源。

What is poverty?

There are two views as to causes of poverty: One looks into problems in the poor, and the other tries to explain from the angle of inequality in a social structure.

The former refers to either poverty caused by laziness or a lack of self-control and motivation or poverty attributed to disability, disease, old age, and other problems that make it difficult for people to achieve success in society.

The latter refers to poverty caused by a social structure where there are always many people who, however hard they work, cannot get out of poverty. And the cause is inequalities between classes, genders, and races, which keep poor people from shaking off poverty. In other words, the poor class is the victim of the social structure.

The two views described above are, to some extent, reasonable, but obviously, they both have their limitations. The theory of personal causes ignores many factors that have nothing to do with individual effort or ability, such as underdeveloped economies in certain areas, unfair employment opportunities, and income gaps between occupations. The theory of social structure ignores the influence of individual factors on income, for example, the differences in personal relationships, personal efforts, and personal will. Therefore, to correctly view poverty causes, it is necessary to strike a balance between these two perspectives.

In today's world, the problem of poverty is expanding from absolute poverty to relative poverty. However, this doesn't mean that absolute poverty or scarcity that threatens human survival has already completely disappeared. There are still many people thus far who are worried about how to access the necessities of life like food and drinking water as well as minimal health care services. The number of people living in absolute poverty has admittedly been decreasing across the globe, but the problem of increasing inequality has gradually become a cause of new social contradictions.

There are generally four types of poverty: "Absolute poverty," a state of living on an income below the poverty line; "policy-related poverty," failure to reach the subsistence standard of a particular society; "relative poverty," personal possession of a smaller quantity of resources compared with other members of the same society; and "subjective poverty," an individual's perception of inadequate resources that he/she owns.

具体而言，首先，所谓的绝对贫困是指"未能达到维持生理功能所需的最低食物需求量"。1901年，英国学者西勃海姆·朗特里把绝对贫困定义为，"仅能够维持其生理功能最低需要的收入水平"。由此，我们也能理解，"绝对"贫困线是极低水平的贫困线。相对贫困是指"不足以达到社会平均水平的生活状态"。一个社会，如果收入水平越高，那么，贫困线也就越高，进而，还可以反映出经济社会的变化。所以，除相对贫困概念以外，我们还应重视相对差距的问题。与上述客观贫困线不同，"主观贫困"侧重于"贫困（认识）的主观性"。换言之，即使是收入水平相当的家庭，由于需求和选择的差异，在消费上也会感到满足或不尽如人意，这就是贫困现象的"多元性"。

　　可以看出，贫困概念的关注点从先前的较高贫困线阶段在往多维方向转变。这当然得益于从绝对贫困到相对贫困，再到多维贫困概念的累积和发展。同时，也意味着贫困概念从收入贫困角度往强调综合生活水平的方向变化。

　　就扶贫问题，专家们大致提出了四种解决方案。但是，这些方案也都存在着缺陷。

　　第一，是最低工资制度。对非熟练或没有经验的工人来说，实行最低工资制度后，大部分人的收入都会高于市场平均工资水平。但是，这样一来，企业的劳动力成本就会水涨船高，对劳动力的需求也会随之减少。所以，结果就是最低工资制度导致部分劳动者的失业率增加。也就是说，获得就业岗位的劳动者可以享受到高薪待遇，但是那些有意就职于低薪工作岗位的劳动者连最低工资标准的工作都找不到。

　　第二，是政府对贫困人口的收入补助。这一政策会削弱就业意愿，也会引发未婚妈妈人数剧增等问题。

　　第三，是负所得税政策。即对高收入者征税，对低收入者给予减免所得税的制度。这一政策的优点是不会减弱劳动积极性。但是，对于因失业、疾病或残障等问题而无法就业的人群来说毫无帮助。

So-called absolute poverty refers, above all, to the "inability to meet the lowest demand for food needed to maintain physiological functions." In 1901, English researcher B. S. Rowntree defined absolute poverty as "an individual's level of income that only can sustain his/her minimum needs of physiological functions." So we may also understand an "absolute" poverty line as a poverty line of a very low level. Relative poverty means "a state of living short of the average level of a society." For a society, the higher its income level, the higher its poverty line, which also reflects economic and social changes. Therefore, we should also pay attention to the problem of relative gaps, in addition to the concept of relative poverty. Unlike the objective poverty line described above, "subjective poverty" stresses "subjectivity of poverty (perception)." In other words, even families at roughly the same level of income may, due to their different needs and choices, feel satisfied or unsatisfied in terms of consumption. This is the "multidimensionality" of poverty.

The focus of the concept of poverty is observably changing from relatively high poverty lines to multiple dimensions of poverty. Of course, this benefits from the progressive change in concept from absolute poverty to relative poverty and then to multidimensional poverty. This also means that the concept of addressing poverty is changing from the angle of increasing income to emphasizing improving comprehensive living standards.

To alleviate poverty, experts have proposed four solutions, which nevertheless are all somewhat flawed.

First, a minimum wage system. With a minimum wage system in place, most non-skilled or inexperienced workers would have an income higher than the average level on the labor market. But enterprises' labor costs would increase, and their demand for labor decreases accordingly. And the result would be a rise in the unemployment rate among some workers. In other words, while working people are well paid, some of those willing to work in low-paid jobs could not even find jobs that pay the minimum wage.

Second, the subsidy from governments to poor people. Such a policy would weaken people's willingness to work and give rise to such problems as a drastic increase in unmarried mothers' number.

Third, an income tax policy, which taxes high-income people but exempts low-income people from income tax or reduces their tax. While this policy has the advantage of not dampening people's enthusiasm for work, it is utterly of no help to

第四，是实物补助政策。即通过直接向贫困人口提供生活必需的财物或服务，来提高其生活水平。这一政策虽然能阻止贫困人口酗酒或吸毒，但在提高其生活水平方面收效甚微。

综上所述，即使是再好的扶贫方案，仅靠借助物质补助等人为的扶持政策是无法解决贫困问题的。

中国扶贫政策的世界历史意义

1978 年起，中国共产党开始施行改革开放政策。由此，国民收入大幅提高，生活环境方面也有了诸多改善。但与此同时，贫富差距也增加了，许多社会问题随之而来。为此，习近平总书记提出"全面建成小康社会"的奋斗目标，并推进了一系列扶贫政策。这些政策一定程度上解决了真贫问题，我们可以从习总书记的讲话中感受到这一点。例如，习总书记经常提到的"真扶贫，扶真贫""精准扶贫，精准脱贫""全面建成小康社会，一个不能少，共同富裕的路上，一个不能掉队"等。

习总书记也经常讲："小康不小康，关键看老乡。"这句话，最能体现他"以人民为中心的发展思想"，也是习近平新时代中国特色社会主义思想的重要内容和特征。

1978 年年底，中国农村贫困人口达 7.7 亿，农村贫困发生率高达97.5%。改革开放以来，中国贫困人口大幅减少。2013 年至 2018 年间，中国农村贫困人口累计减少 8000 多万，贫困发生率由 10.2% 下降至1.7%。

那么，在 20 世纪 70 年代尚还吃不饱、穿不暖的中国，是如何在扶贫贡献方面做到世界第一的？其中有几个原因。

the jobless and the people who are unable to get employed due to illness or disability.

Fourth, a material assistance policy, namely, directly providing poor people with essential goods or services to improve their living standards. Though discouraging poor people from alcohol or drug abuse, such a policy has little effect in improving their living standards.

Therefore, a poverty alleviation solution, however good it is, cannot solve the problem of poverty if it relies simply on such a policy as material assistance.

What does China's poverty alleviation policy mean to the world and history?

The Communist Party of China (CPC) initiated the reform and opening-up policy centered around the actual economy in 1978. Since then, Chinese people's income has increased drastically, alongside considerable improvements in living conditions. Simultaneously, China has seen a widening gap between the rich and the poor, as well as many social problems. To address these issues, President Xi Jinping has put forward the goal of "building a moderately prosperous society in an all-round way" and has pushed ahead with a series of poverty alleviation policies. To some extent, these policies have addressed genuine poverty, which we may sense from President Xi's speeches. For example, President Xi often mentions, among others, "Poverty alleviation should reach those who truly need it and deliver genuine outcomes," "alleviate and eradicate poverty in a targeted manner," "establish a moderately prosperous society to be enjoyed by each and every one" and "on the march toward common prosperity, no one shall be left behind."

He often says, "Rural people's living standards are the measure of success in our drive toward moderate prosperity in China." This statement best demonstrates his "people-centered development thinking" and is an important component and feature of his thought on socialism with Chinese characteristics for a new era.

By the end of 1978, rural China had a poor population of 770 million, with a staggering poverty rate of 97.5%. China's poor population has drastically dropped since the start of China's reform and opening-up. Between 2013 and 2018, China's rural poor population decreased by more than 80 million, with a poverty rate going down from 10.2% to 1.7%.

第一，他们有着突出的制度优势。习总书记强调："坚持党的领导，发挥社会主义制度可以集中力量办大事的优势，这是我们的最大政治优势。"为此，党的十八大以来，中国政府积极推进贫困治理，形成了专项扶贫、行业扶贫、社会扶贫"三位一体"的扶贫格局。而这正是得益于中国有任何一个国家都不具备的全国性组织体制。

第二，是推行了符合区域实情的政策。"推进扶贫开发、推动经济社会发展，首先要有一个好思路、好路子。要坚持从实际出发，因地制宜，厘清思路、完善规划、找准突破口。"从习总书记的讲话中，我们就可以看到精准扶贫的目标和方向。这一点，从联合国开发计划署驻华代表戴文德的发言中也可以确认："从政策必须符合区域实情的角度来说，中国堪称其他发展中国家脱贫的典范。"

第三，是凝聚起全社会的最大合力。正如习总书记所说："脱贫致富不仅仅是贫困地区的事，也是全社会的事。"中国动员了全社会力量，广泛参与扶贫事业中。

第四，是扶贫政策背后有一批堪称"精锐"大军的领导干部。70年来，广大的共产党干部不忘初心，精心绣出了脱贫的"幸福之花"。

70年来，从救济式扶贫到开发式扶贫，中国再次确立了正确的扶贫脱贫基本方略，开辟了一条中国特色扶贫之路，为世界扶贫机构贡献了中国的智慧，人类脱贫由此揭开了新的篇章。因此，预计到2020年年底，中国绝对贫困问题即将历史性地得到解决。

How, then, has China, whose people had less than enough food and clothing in the 1970s, come first in the world in terms of contribution to poverty alleviation? There are several reasons, as shown below.

First, China has an institutional advantage that cannot be copied elsewhere. President Xi stresses, "Upholding the Party's leadership and leveraging the institutional advantage of concentrating resources to get things done is our supreme political advantage." Since the 18th CPC National Congress, the Chinese government has stepped up poverty governance and formed a "trinity" pattern of poverty alleviation through specific programs, industrial development, and involvement of diverse social sectors. This is attributable to China's unique national organizational system.

Second, China practices policies in light of regional conditions. "Advancing poverty alleviation and development and promoting economic and social development require, above all, good ideas and approaches. We must start from reality, take action in light of local conditions, have clear thinking, improve plans, and find the right points to make breakthroughs." From this statement made by President Xi, we can see the goal and direction of targeted poverty alleviation. This point was echoed by what Devanand Ramiah, the Deputy Country Director for UNDP China, said in a speech, "From the angle that a policy must agree with actual situations of a place it targets, China can be said to be an exemplar of poverty alleviation for other developing countries."

Third, China musters the biggest possible force of a society. Just as President Xi puts it, "Poverty alleviation is not simply business of poor areas; it is business of the whole society." China mobilizes the entire society for its drive to eradicate poverty.

Fourth, behind poverty alleviation policies is an "elite" legion of leading officials. Over the past 70 years, the CPC officials have remained true to the founding mission of the Party and embroidered carefully "a flower of happiness" in the course of poverty alleviation.

In the meanwhile, from assistance-based poverty alleviation to development-oriented poverty alleviation, China once again established a correct basic strategy for poverty alleviation and opened up a poverty alleviation path with Chinese characteristics, contributing China's wisdom to poverty alleviation all over the world and turning a new page for mankind's poverty eradication. Therefore, China is expected out of poverty by the end of 2020, thus historically solving the problem of

"小康不小康，关键看老乡"，中国农村贫困人口的脱贫就是这样实现的。

"扶贫工程"是当代中国最大的民生工程，也是中国最大的"利民、惠民、富民工程"。

1992年12月22日，联合国设立了"国际消除贫困日"，旨在消除贫困和饥饿，唤起世界各国的关注。而后，在2015年10月举行的第70届联合国大会上，通过了《2030年可持续发展议程》和"联合国可持续发展目标"。这是所有成员国必须实现的总目标，也是人类历史上联合国所有成员国首次全部达成一致的议题。联合国可持续发展目标作为未来十五年（2016—2030）各国发展工作指导性体系，包括贫困、教育、妇女和儿童权益、治理等17个目标，169个细分目标和241个量化指标。其中，贫困问题是首要议题。由此看来，贫困问题是全球性问题中的核心问题。

脱贫问题上，最先受到联合国关注的国家就是中国。正是得益于为建成小康社会而做的努力，中国才能突破人均国内生产总值1万美元的大关，也才能实现非城市区贫困率的显著下降。而这就是联合国关注中国脱贫问题的动机。由此，中国的扶贫政策在世界史上留下了伟大一页。

"新村运动"，韩国的扶贫之道

管子曾说："仓廪实而知礼节，衣食足而知荣辱。"这句话很好地说明了物质丰富对个人的重要性。但是，对物质富裕的追求不能成为人的唯一目标，更不能成为终极目标，这是当今社会的共识。为此，最好的方法就是要提高道德文明修养。孟子说："百亩之田，勿夺其时，数口之家可以无饥矣；谨庠序之教，申之以孝悌之义，颁白者不负戴于道

absolute poverty in the country.

"Rural people's living standards are the measure of success in our drive toward moderate prosperity in China." It is by this standard that China is lifting rural poor people out of poverty.

The "poverty alleviation project" is contemporary China's biggest project aimed to improve people's well-being, and its biggest "project that benefits and enriches people."

On December 22, 1992, the United Nations made the resolution to found the "International Day for the Eradication of Poverty" to arouse the world's attention to eradicating poverty and hunger. At the 70th Session of its General Assembly in October 2015, the *2030 Agenda for Sustainable Development* and the Sustainable Development Goals (SDGs) were adopted. These goals are the ones that all UN member states must achieve, a consensus that all UN member states reached for the first time in human history. As a guidance system for development in the countries in the next 15 years (2016-2030), the SDGs include 17 goals on poverty, education, women's and children's rights and interests, and governance; 169 targets; and 241 quantitative indicators. Among these goals, the top priority is given to poverty alleviation. Therefore, the problem of poverty is at the center of global issues.

On poverty alleviation, China is the first country to have caught the attention of the UN. Due to its effort to build a moderately prosperous society, China has surpassed the per capita domestic gross product of US$ 10,000 and significantly decreased poverty rates in its non-urban areas. And this is the very reason why the UN has paid attention to poverty alleviation in China. Therefore, China's poverty alleviation policy has made a glorious page in world history.

"Saemaeul Undong Spirit", way of poverty alleviation in China going forward

Guanzi said, "People observe etiquette and know honor and shame only after they are well-fed and clothed." It is a perfect illustration of the importance of material wealth to individuals. But the pursuit of material wealth can be seen as neither the sole purpose nor ultimate goal of people, which is a consensus of society today. The best way, therefore, is to increase people's ethical and cultural standards. Mencius said, "Let there not be taken away the time that is proper for the cultivation

路矣。"他还强调，要教学生德、善、廉耻、信任、自律和人伦。当然，这些也都写进了社会主义核心价值观之中，但更重要的是如何去实践这些理念。这一点，我认为中国可以参考韩国1970年开始推广的"新村运动"。

"新村运动"通常被认为是一次谋求经济自立的实践运动。但是从效果上来说，比起这一点，它更加强调精神层面，即对以往扭曲的生活习惯及精神状态的改变。正是得益于"新村运动"对精神层面的改变，才能让道德、守法和协同意识根植于韩国人的精神世界中。也正因为如此，在抗击新冠肺炎疫情的过程中，韩国因其在社会秩序、道德良俗、医疗设备、公共事务等方面的表现，广受好评。

如习总书记所说，"治国有常，而利民为本"，千言万语抵不过付诸实践。就实践来说，比起强制的教育，更需要自悟的自觉教育。自觉教育的方法可以参考韩国的新村运动，而且从中国政府历来的政策实施过程来看，这一点也是完全可以实现的。

KDI国际政策研究生院的爱德华·里德教授，曾从如下五个方面肯定了韩国的新村运动所取得的成果。

（1）积极的政治和社会环境，为农村发展做出了贡献；

（2）对农民的新看法，为政府与农民关系带来了积极影响；

（3）新农村干部培训课程，培养了新村运动的接班人；

（4）强调农村女性的作用（带动储蓄和投资，分享特殊知识）；

（5）从传统的共同体合作模式转变为可持续发展的新型合作经营。

of the farm with its hundred *mu*, and the family of several mouths that is supported by it shall not suffer from hunger. Let careful attention be paid to education in schools, inculcating in it especially the filial and fraternal duties, and grey-haired men will not be seen upon the roads, carrying burdens on their backs or their heads." He also stressed the necessity of educating students on morality, benevolence, honor and shame, trust, self-discipline, and ethics. These indeed have been incorporated into the core socialist values. But more important is how to fulfill these values. In this regard, I think that China may learn from the Saemaeul Undong, or the New Village Movement, which South Korea launched in the 1970s.

The Saemaeul Undong is generally seen as a practical campaign that attempted to seek economic independence. In effect, it placed more emphasis on the spiritual aspect, that is, changing the distorted living habits and spiritual states. It is the Saemaeul Undong's change of the spiritual aspect that has made moral, law-abiding, and cooperative awareness take root in the spiritual world of the South Korean people. It is also because of this that South Korea has been widely praised for its outstanding performance in fighting the COVID-19 in respect of social order, ethics, medical equipment, and public affairs.

Just as President Xi says, "Governance should deliver benefits to the people." To put it differently, no words speak louder than actions. Practice requires more education for self-awakening rather than compulsory education. China may draw on the Saemaeul Undong with regard to the methods for conscious education. And judging by the Chinese government's implementation of policies in the past, this can be achieved entirely.

Edward Reed, a professor at the KDI School of Public Policy and Management, once praised the outcomes of the Saemaeul Undong in five aspects:

（1）Positive political and social environments, which contributed to rural development;

（2）New views on peasants, which produced positive effects on the relations between the government and peasants;

（3）Training of officials, which supplied successors to the Saemaeul Undong;

（4）Emphasis on the roles of rural women (in encouraging savings and investment and sharing special knowledge);

（5）A shift from traditional community cooperation to new-type sustainable cooperative management.

"新村运动"是从农村开始的，其最初目的也只是提高农户收入。但是，在农村广泛开展、收效显著的同时，也逐渐深入城市、公司和工厂中，最终发展成了以"勤勉、自助、协同"为基本精神的意识改革运动。通过这一政府主导的国民近代化运动，国家经济得以自立，市民意识大大增强，向发达国家行列迈进的意志也深植于韩国国民心中。可以说，新村运动是对韩国国民和社会的双重改革。

　　其中最重要的一点是，这场运动让韩国国民有了自信，有了"我们也能做到"的自信。自信带来的结果，就是脱离贫困，过上有品格、有文化的生活。进而，由个人到邻里，大家互相关爱，互相帮助，共同建设宜居社区。并且它让国民领悟到，不能只放眼于当下一代人，建设美丽家乡的目标应放在更长远的未来和子孙后代身上。

　　就这样，在开展新村运动的过程中，全韩国人民都有了"懂了方法就去做、努力做、自助做、全村邻里一起做"的精神和情怀。

　　新村运动取得成功有以下四个原因。

　　第一是基于严格而公正的赏罚分明原则。新村运动是以村为单位，全国农民依靠自己的力量开展事业。而政府的作用旨在营造氛围，引导农民积极参与村庄的现代化建设中。对成绩优秀的村庄给予重点扶持，对表现不佳的村庄则停止支援，政府层面实行了严格而公正的赏罚分明制度。

　　第二是引入了"综合发展"的概念。从新村运动的推进方式来看，"一揽子计划"或"综合发展"概念都得到了有条不紊的实施。

　　第三是带动了民主主义的发展。新村运动不是一两人就能完成的工作，而是全村人全部参与推进的事业。

　　第四是培养了真正的爱国之心。农民在挥洒汗水、建设宜居社区的同时，也从劳动中收获了成就感。这些成就感也让他们在为国家做贡献的过程中明白了人生的真正意义，明白为国劳动的人是真正的爱国者。

The Saemaeul Undong started from rural South Korea and was meant at first only to increase the peasants' income. But, with the movement widely carried out in rural areas with remarkable effects, it gradually spread to cities, companies, and factors, ultimately morphing into an awareness reform movement accentuating "diligence, self-help, and collaboration." Through this government-led nationwide modernization movement, the South Korean economy became self-sustaining, with a greatly boosted civic awareness and a deep-rooted national will to move into developed countries' ranks. It is fair to say that the Saemaeul Undong was a double reform of the South Korean people and society.

The most important thing about the South Korean movement is that it kindled the people's confidence that "we can do it, too." With such confidence, the people try to get out of poverty and live a quality life. And from individuals to neighborhoods, everybody cared about and helped one another and worked together to build livable communities. Moreover, the movement made the South Korean people aware that instead of keeping an eye on merely the present generation, they must take a farsighted approach to build beautiful communities.

In this way, in the course of carrying out the movement, all South Korean people came to have an awareness of "taking action with learned methods, working hard, and helping and collaborating with one another."

There were four reasons for the success of the Saemaeul Undong. First, there were strict and just rules for reward and punishment. The movement took villages as units, with peasants pursuing projects by relying on their own strength. The government worked to raise morale and guide peasants to participate in the modernization of villages actively. According to a strict and just reward and punishment system enforced by the government, significant support was given to well-performing villages, and assistance was suspended for bad-performing ones.

Second, an "integrated development" concept was introduced. From how the Saemaeul Undong was advanced, the concept of "package program" or "integrated development" was implemented in an orderly manner.

Third, democracy was promoted. The Saemaeul Undong was not a job that one or two persons could do, but a cause that all the villages worked together to advance.

Fourth, true patriotism was fostered. While laboring to build livable communities, the peasants also gained a sense of achievement, which made them understand the true meaning of life and made them see that people working for the

当时的韩国与中国现在的大环境几乎如出一辙。有国家领导人政治意志实践，有可以保障这一实践目标得以实现的集权制政治生态，以及全体公务员的积极参与，这些都与中国极其相似。

结论

虽然可以说中国已经进入小康社会，但高收入群体与低收入群体间的生活水平差距也更加明显。

就缩小贫富差距和缓解绝对贫困方面，经济学家和社会学家已有很多讨论。但这些理论，多是以资本主义社会为基础，与当下中国的国情不符。这是因为，在资本主义社会的情况下，收入是按照个人能力进行分配，不能由政府主导。因此，只能依靠市场经济。落后国家及发展中国家，虽然可以进行由政府主导的改革，但是进入中等发达国家行列以后，政府控制力变弱，只能倚仗经济刺激政策。

但中国正在走一条中国特色社会主义道路。比起资本主义国家，中国在消除和缓解贫困方面非常有优势。因为中国可以由政府主导脱贫，进而开展精神运动，让国民通过合作共生，创造财富、改善生活。

最后，希望中国通过努力成为世界脱贫的模范国家，也希望中国能发展为领导世界的真正大国。

country were true patriots.

South Korea then was in roughly the same situation as China today: the political will of the state leader, a centralization system that guaranteed the achievement of the goal, and active participation of all public servants.

Conclusion

Though it is fair to say that China has already built itself into a moderately prosperous society, gaps in living standards between high-income people and low-income people have become more noticeable.

While there has been much debate among economists and sociologists about narrowing the rich-poor gap and mitigating absolute poverty, existing theories are mostly grounded in capitalist societies. They disagree with China's national situation because, in capitalist societies, income is distributed according to personal ability rather than government guidance. Therefore, only a market economy can be relied on. Underdeveloped and developing countries, which can carry out government-led reforms, though, after joining the ranks of developed countries, will face weakened government control and rely only on economic stimulation.

But China is advancing on a socialist path with Chinese characteristics. Compared with capitalist countries, China has performed quite outstandingly in terms of eradicating and mitigating poverty because China can promote government-led poverty alleviation, and move on to carry out an awareness movement, making its people create wealth and improve their lives through collaboration.

Finally, I hope that China can genuinely build a moderately prosperous society through awareness reform and become an exemplar of poverty alleviation for the world. And I also hope to see China will grow into a true world-leading power.

图书在版编目（CIP）数据

海外专家谈中国扶贫：汉、英 /（荷）斯蒂芬·彼
得曼等著；图书编委会译 . -- 北京：光明日报出版社，
2021.12

　　ISBN 978-7-5194-6379-3

　　Ⅰ.①海… Ⅱ.①斯… ②斯… Ⅲ.①扶贫 – 研究 –
中国 – 汉、英 Ⅳ.① F126

中国版本图书馆 CIP 数据核字（2021）第 238129 号

海外专家谈中国扶贫

HAIWAI ZHUANJIA TAN ZHONGGUO FUPIN

著　者：（荷）斯蒂芬·彼得曼等　　　译　者：图书编委会

责任编辑：章小可　　　　　　　　封面设计：横竖设计
特约编辑：赵燮烽　　　　　　　　责任印制：曹　净
责任校对：慧　眼

出版发行：光明日报出版社
地　　址：北京市西城区永安路 106 号，100050
电　　话：010-63169890（咨询），010-63131930（邮购）
传　　真：010-63131930
网　　址：http://book.gmw.cn
E – mail：gmrbcbs@gmw.cn
法律顾问：北京市兰台律师事务所龚柳方律师

印　　刷：北京华联印刷有限公司
装　　订：北京华联印刷有限公司
本书如有破损、缺页、装订错误，请与本社联系调换，电话：010-63131930

开　　本：165mm×230mm　　　　印　　张：15.25
字　　数：200 千字
版　　次：2021 年 12 月第 1 版
印　　次：2021 年 12 月第 1 次印刷
书　　号：ISBN 978-7-5194-6379-3

定　　价：78.00 元